BOOT-STRAP YOUR LIFE

BOOT-
STRAP
YOUR
LIFE

BOOT-STRAP YOUR LIFE

HOW TO TURN £500 INTO £350,000,000

OLIVER COOKSON

PIATKUS

PIATKUS

First published in Great Britain in 2021 by Piatkus
This paperback edition published in 2024 by Piatkus

1 3 5 7 9 10 8 6 4 2

Copyright © Oliver Cookson 2021

The moral right of the author has been asserted.

All rights reserved.
No part of this publication may be reproduced, stored in a retrieval system, or transmitted, in any form, or by any means, without the prior permission in writing of the publisher, nor be otherwise circulated in any form of binding or cover other than that in which it is published and without a similar condition including this condition being imposed on the subsequent purchaser.

A CIP catalogue record for this book
is available from the British Library.

ISBN: 978-0-34942-920-5

Typeset in Bembo by Hewer Text UK Ltd, Edinburgh
Printed and bound in Great Britain by Clays Ltd, Elcograf S.p.A.

Papers used by Piatkus are from well-managed forests and other responsible sources.

Piatkus
An imprint of
Little, Brown Book Group
Carmelite House
50 Victoria Embankment
London EC4Y 0DZ

An Hachette UK Company
www.hachette.co.uk

www.littlebrown.co.uk

CONTENTS

Foreword	vii
Introduction	xvii
1. 'My future'	1
2. Make the most of your inner resources	9
3. Some seriously wrong turns and a pivotal moment	19
4. Work hard to play hard	30
5. A developer in the making	42
6. Understanding the working environment	52
7. My eureka moment	62
8. A product in the making	70
9. Bootstrapped – debt-free within a week	77
10. 'Sixteen-hour days'	96
11. No-bull marketing	110
12. Innovative thinking – discovering new ideas that work	136
13. Strategy: be like water	156
14. Striving for continuous improvement	168
15. Building a first-class team	189
16. Chess and the art of leadership	209

17. Runaway growth	230
18. Going for gold – preparing for the sale	241
19. Crossing the finishing line – the sale	254
About the author	265
Acknowledgements	267
Index	269

FOREWORD

When Oliver sent me a copy of his book, I thought about the title and did not really understand what 'bootstrapping' meant, so I looked it up in the dictionary and realised that, not only was Oliver an extremely successful bootstrapper, but also that it describes exactly what I have been for the whole fifty years of my business career. Bootstrapping is to get into or out of a situation using your own existing resources, with the emphasis on 'your own'. I increasingly saw the similarities between Oliver and me: we were both working class boys who did not take the academic route, although I was lucky enough to have a Michelin tyre company apprenticeship and gain a HNC in mechanical engineering. Neither of us are pretentious; both of us are very down to earth. Oliver is extremely charitable and extremely successful and, like myself, has an enormous amount of wisdom to share with the world, and that is exactly what this book is all about. It is to inspire a new breed of entrepreneurs, who can benefit from his experiences and the hard-earned lessons he learned en route to his phenomenal success.

We have not known each other for a long time; in fact, only for five years. Oliver moved to Monaco and wanted to meet people and get involved with sport. His bank introduced him to my partner, Modesta, who was previously a top, world-class cyclist and an Olympian, both as a social contact but also for Modesta to train him as a cyclist, which at that time was one of her business ventures. As a result, Oliver became a friend of the family and he joined us on our boat for a holiday. It was clear to me from the outset that Oliver is a singularly determined individual, but until the manuscript for the book you hold in your hands landed on my desk, I didn't quite realise the similarities in our paths to get to where we are today.

Entrepreneurship is vital for the growth of any economy. To be a successful entrepreneur requires a set of attributes and talents: ambition, drive, passion, resilience, commercial intellect and leadership. It is essential for anybody going into business to understand how much of each of these attributes they possess. You never get anywhere without ambition, but if you do have a huge ambition, you really better have an abundance of the other five attributes, especially drive and resilience. To grow something of real scale you will need leadership and commercial intellect. Of all the attributes, resilience might be considered to be the most important. When everything is collapsing around you, to be able to dig deep, work long hours, and for your health, both mental and physical, to fully hold up is vital.

Oliver and I both have an intimate knowledge of fitness and nutrition, but whereas Oliver turned that passion into a business idea that was to become a market leader, I never turned any of my many interests into any business benefit. I only ever looked for what I considered to be an exciting and scalable opportunity. In fact, I would go as far as to say that following your passion for your hobby or interest through into business could often be a big mistake, because it might not be a significant opportunity if you are analytical about it. Of course, in Oliver's case, nothing could be further from the truth, since the amazing creation of his business and its subsequent sale created a personal wealth in excess of £350 million.

As I write this, Covid is causing more businesses than ever to bootstrap. They have to do everything in their power to survive, with limited income, and to innovate in ways they would previously have never dreamed of doing. Unfortunately, the pandemic has divided society even further. Many businesses that had a great online presence have profiteered massively, as a result of the enforced revolution to online trading. Those more traditional businesses have had and are still engaged in a real battle for survival.

Businesspeople will have learned a huge amount about bootstrapping in recent years. The ability to survive and prosper from your own wit, ingenuity and graft is vital at some point in the life of most businesspeople, but, in my case, it was vital almost every week of my business life as I was thrown into a succession of crises on an almost continual basis. Every crisis I tried to turn into an opportunity that would ultimately benefit the business. Of course, you cannot always achieve that, but the goal is still to 'bust a gut' trying.

One of the biggest challenges in any expanding business is cashflow, and it is here that your mettle can be really tested. As you grow the business it becomes ever more cash hungry, and trying to find ways of satisfying the appetite of the money-munching monster you are creating can be one of the greatest tests you can face. Many businesspeople end up diluting their own shareholding significantly as an undesirable, though in some cases, essential consequence.

Being at the very top of an organisation, no matter how small or large, can be extremely lonely. When the business's prosperity, or even survival, rests solely on your shoulders, the pressures can be immense. It might even be that whatever team you have disagrees with you, and that makes it lonelier still. I found myself in that position many, many times. I had no mentor and every one of my key managers disagreed with me, and yet, in an act of full-blown dictatorship, I insisted on my namesake Frank

Sinatra, and 'did it my way'. I can think of many occasions when doing it my way transformed the business, and none where it did any real damage. As an example, a complete transformation took place the day I cycled from our head office to one of my Birmingham shops, a distance of forty-five miles.

I arrived at 8.30 a.m. It was closed. I waited with my bike and watched people walking past on their way to work, clocking the footfall in my head. At 9.30, I saw a guy in a suit – the manager – walking towards the shop.

'Morning,' I said. 'Why don't you open at 8 a.m.? I've seen lots of people walking past. They could be potential customers.'

He did a double-take. No doubt his heart sank when he realised it was me, John Caudwell, boss of the whole company, with his bike outside his shop.

'There's no trade,' he said. 'They are all on their way to work. It's not worth it.'

I said nothing. I fully understand I may be very intimidating, and it makes me chuckle now to think of the poor guy being faced with me, unannounced in my cycling gear, on a cold but sunny Monday morning. All I was concerned about then was getting answers, observing my business on the ground and finding out information. We went into the shop. The interrogation continued.

'How many mobile phones have you sold this month?' I asked.

'None,' he answered, trying not to look uncomfortable. 'I'm the manager. I manage the team. I don't sell.'

I was genuinely confused. 'How can you manage a team if you're not selling? How are you going to understand any issues with customers, questions about tariffs? How on earth can you get any feedback, or know what to get your staff to focus on, if you are not selling yourself?' To me, this was basic common sense. He looked blank. The veritable rabbit caught in the headlights.

'You need to be one of the best sales people in the shop,' I continued, genuinely horrified by what I was hearing. 'You need to lead by example. Give the staff targets, show them how it's done. These shops are here to sell mobile phones, not to manage staff.' The poor guy was flushed in the face, but he gamely stood his ground and shook his head.

'But what about all the emails I have to answer from head office?' he stuttered, opening up his computer and showing me yards and yards of emails clogging up his inbox. 'There's four hours' worth of emails to answer here. I have to go through all of them and answer the relevant ones. That's what I do all day, unless there's a problem in the shop.'

I stared at the computer, looking at the massive amount of names in the distribution box of each email. There were names of people from head office, area managers, regional managers, directors. Most of the emails were completely irrelevant to the manager of the Birmingham office who hadn't had time to sell a single phone since he was given the job.

'Thanks very much,' I said. I shook his hand and left. He looked like he needed a stiff drink to get over the shock of that fifteen-minute meeting. But I'd had a bigger shock. And I had a revolutionary solution.

I cycled back to the head office in Newcastle-under-Lyme and, as I pounded the pedals on the forty-mile journey, what had happened was turning over in my head. I arrived in the office and immediately gathered my directors. 'Right,' I said. 'From tomorrow I'm banning all-company emails. No one is to send emails from this office.'

They looked at me in horror. Possibly some of them believed I was still stuck in my 'feigned madness' routine from the previous year, but I was deadly serious.

'Emails are the cancer of business,' I announced. 'You're all sending out hundreds of huge group distribution emails. Most of them are completely irrelevant. I have managers who should be selling, but they're spending every hour answering 'yes' and 'no' emails to head office, and people here are spending yet more hours sending yet more emails backwards and forwards. Wasted time is wasted money and wasted opportunity. This has to stop.'

There was immediate uproar, with everyone telling me that the business would be plunged into chaos and confusion. I eventually agreed to set up a night shift, where one bulletin would go out every night for managers, area managers and regional managers to read the following day.

All of the directors were shaking their heads in disbelief as they left my office that day. I knew that even my very top team was dead against me. Evidently they thought I was on a kamikaze mission. But I knew that I was right. I had absolute faith in my decision. I had looked at those emails, and approximately one in one hundred had any relevance whatsoever to the recipient. Think of the time wasted. We were in the telecommunications business – if there was a serious problem, just pick up the phone and call. Or, even better, go and check out the high street shops. At the same time, I put in targets for every shop manager, area manager, regional manager and sales director in the business to sell phones.

This in itself made a huge difference, but there were half a dozen other equally dramatic key actions that transformed the business over a short space of time.

Within a year, our profits had risen by £100 million. I later worked out that the email Bermuda Triangle had been costing about £20 million a year. Since they had been banned, sales were going through the roof, managers were given better targets and incentives to open shops earlier if they believed it would increase trade. Now the Phones 4u brand was shining like a real jewel.

Bootstrapping often flies in the face of convention. It is a talent that a full-blown entrepreneur has to do things differently and sometimes rather contentiously, in order to achieve a great result. We need this mindset in abundance over the next few years for post-Brexit Britain to reach its full potential and to show the world why we are Great Britain. Whatever your own personal goals are and whether or not you have the luxury of a mentor to turn to, there is always something to be learned from the success of others. Start with what you have inside you – your ambition, drive, passion, resilience, commercial intellect and leadership – even, and perhaps especially, if your resources are limited. You have this book in your hands, and that's a good place to start.

John Caudwell

'Give a man a fish, and you feed him for a day; teach a man to fish, and you feed him for a lifetime'

INTRODUCTION

You may be wondering why someone who managed to take an idea and a £500 overdraft and turn it into a third of a billion pounds has decided to write a book. It's certainly not for money, and I am anything but famous. Even if you are one of the millions of people who use the sports nutrition brand I founded, you probably will not have heard of me until now.

There are a few reasons I decided to share my journey with you. First of all, my account is a genuine rags-to-riches story, so if you haven't found your way yet, perhaps this book will help you to figure it out.

In some ways, I am now at the beginning of a new journey. Business has always felt like a high-stakes game to me, and some would say that's why I have been successful. Let me be clear though. I take business extremely seriously, but you don't get to win in business by being afraid of taking calculated risks. We give it our best shot, and a lot of enjoyment comes from being focused on making the right decisions.

When it's only a game, it's easier to maintain a healthy perspective about winning and losing. In life, the consequences of our actions can have a long-term impact, so fear of getting it wrong can make us so risk-averse that we don't seize the opportunities that are meant for us. You have to take chances to succeed, and if it goes wrong, you take it in your stride and move past it.

Selling my business ended a huge chapter of my life, one that had forced me to learn many lessons 'on the job'. Since then, I have enjoyed exploring new avenues and playing new hands. Writing this book has allowed me to reflect on how I have got to where I am today and the lessons I have learnt along the way. I am proud of what I have achieved, but my life is far from over, and self-reflection is a powerful tool for enabling personal growth. By looking back at my journey from a different perspective, I am gaining fresh insights that I had not consciously recognised the first time round, and I am happy to share these with you.

You will often hear people say that life is the best teacher. While I acknowledge that we learn a lot through experience, I believe we are our own greatest teachers. That means seeking out the most fruitful experiences to deliver the most valuable lessons for the path we have chosen to take. It is a little like preparing a specific reading list to match a degree course rather than going into a library and picking up books at random. When you live a purposeful life, nothing happens by accident.

We are all born with the tools to succeed, but you have to learn how to make them work to your advantage, playing to your strengths and your competitors' weaknesses, and this is something I will be covering later in the book. Learning stems from being curious, resourceful and tenacious.

'Learn to trust your instincts' has become a bit of a cliché, especially in business books, but I always say if something's a cliché, it's a cliché for a reason. By the same premise, the law of averages also became a 'law' for a reason. Remember, a well-trodden path is often the right path, and there is nothing wrong with that, but you must stand out from the competition and seek continuous improvement if you want your business to grow. Just make sure you use your instincts, as well as metrics or research where possible, before you deviate from the beaten track in search of something original in your quest to be unique.

If you take anything away from this book, it should be that your gut feelings are there to help you. That's not to say that if the thought of something makes you feel a little anxious, you should back away from it. That's fear. Most of our fears are based on things that we imagine will happen but rarely do, which is why one of my favourite mottos is 'Fear is a liar', a phrase I picked up from one of my oldest and greatest friends, Carl Boon.

There is a difference between being afraid of stepping into a new environment and having a hard-to-ignore gut feeling that something isn't right. I have always been poor at maths, and I strongly believe I may have dyslexia as well as dyscalculia, but that doesn't mean I don't recognise when an idea is clearly profitable. I can use a calculator to work out the specific figures, and it's not as though I haven't got a solid accountant to help me with the number crunching.

Our instincts and intuition work together to keep us out of danger. Somehow our mind absorbs the whole situation and assesses whether that path is going to benefit us or do us harm, and it is usually correct. Unfortunately, there is no calculator for working out how a situation will play out, so if you get it wrong, you learn the hard way – through experience – but, typically, these are the lessons you are most likely to remember.

I am sure there are other reasons for wanting to put pen to paper that I am not consciously aware of, so you could say I am being encouraged to write this book by instinct and intuition. It feels like the right thing to do and the right time to do it. Again, I know it sounds clichéd, but that is what's happened. The book has almost come about by itself – naturally.

One question that people ask, and which I have often considered, is whether entrepreneurs are born or made, and given the story you are about to read, I believe it is worth considering.

Entrepreneurship has fascinated social scientists for decades. Typing the word 'entrepreneur' into any search engine will quickly reveal countless articles and white papers on whether these creative, money-making individuals are born or shaped. Loads of research has been carried out to get to the bottom of the subject, new studies are cropping up all the time, and the discussion will probably continue for decades to come.

Are there particular traits that entrepreneurs tend to share? Research suggests there are. They tend to be open-minded, curious and tenacious. I can certainly relate to these characteristics as I recognise them within myself. Entrepreneurs are good at understanding what people want and developing commercially viable solutions to problems, and this is how we evolve as a society. Problems arise, people solve them, and everyone benefits.

Entrepreneurs have the vision to see beyond the status quo and identify opportunities to provide new products and services or to improve on what is already available. They instinctively know what others are going to want and need in the future. Sometimes that is because they have asked themselves simple what-if questions – *What if I could make this myself, and how would I improve it?* However, there are plenty of would-be entrepreneurs who share these innate tendencies yet never become entrepreneurs or even attempt to start a business. Why is that?

I don't believe I was born to be an entrepreneur, but I am confident I would have succeeded with any kind of online consumer business even though most businesses fail. That's not meant to sound cocky in any way either. The method that I used – which evolved as I figured out how to make the best use of my natural abilities, developed skills and experience – would have worked whether I was selling white goods, fashion items or any other product that could be sold online. My circumstances drove me to find a way of succeeding on my own terms. But for those who are determined to make it, I believe the entrepreneurial mindset is something that can be cultivated.

Being from a working-class family and a broken home meant we didn't have disposable income. I was given all the love I could have wished for, but we simply couldn't afford all the latest things, and holidays were a rarity. There was very little stability, and as I was an only child until I was around sixteen years of age, I spent a lot of time alone.

The odds were stacked against me from a young age, and the education system didn't provide me with any means for shifting things in my favour. I left school with just one GCSE, which I scraped. It was a 'D' in science – a subject that has always fascinated me.

I learnt many things at school, but I have never been academically strong, preferring a much more hands-on approach to learning. You could say I got my education by other means. For a start, I was so determined to make some money for myself that I found ways to do it while I was still at school. Well, studying the French Revolution was never going to help me buy the things I wanted, and even if I was the next great historian waiting to happen – I wasn't – those history lessons weren't going to bring rewards as quickly as I wanted them. At least, that's how I saw it at the time.

As I have grown older, I have gained more of an appreciation of history, and now it interests me a lot. In recent years, I have come to recognise that many of the things we take for granted in the Western world are only possible because of the discoveries made by our ancestors. And I am extremely grateful for the fact that with the twist of a tap, I have access to fresh, clean water. Far too many people around the globe still don't. I have learnt to appreciate the small things and not to assume everyone else can enjoy the same privilege.

If I could speak to my ancestors directly, I am sure I would find their stories fascinating. But life runs in cycles. We sow seeds, watch them grow, reap what we have sown, and then we restart the cycle by planting again. Just as we are benefitting from the hard work and discoveries of our ancestors, it is time for us to give back in whatever way we can and leave a rich legacy for the generations to come. We are the ancestors of tomorrow's people. I want them to benefit from what I have learnt, and if I can do that, my time on this planet will have been even more worthwhile. I have prospered, so I want to help the next generation of entrepreneurs to prosper, and that is another reason why I feel compelled to write this book.

While I was growing up, getting stuck into the business of using my own initiative to generate cash taught me valuable lessons. I discovered my passions at quite a young age and threw myself into them, often losing all sense of time for long periods as I became immersed in my own projects. That was energy well spent. The stuff I learnt while in the zone later proved to be essential for building what would become the number-one sports nutrition brand in the world.

When I look back, especially to the early days, I still feel that I created my own destiny through hard work, determination and a strong sense of purpose. That is not to say I never received any support or guidance from others. The most important people in my life were those who knew me long before I started my sports nutrition brand. They were the ones I hung around with when I was mostly partying and wasting time instead of focusing on the future, and I don't regret a single moment of any of that – they were some of the best times of my life. They were the most important people to me then, and they still are today. In fact, I'd say 80 per cent of my closest friends are those whom I've known for at least twenty years – some for as long as thirty-five years or more. They are like family to me, and there will always be a very special place in my heart for them. You know who you are!

Having converted a £500 overdraft into £350 million, most would consider me a relatively successful entrepreneur, but my friends assure me I am the same Oliver they've known for decades. I want to share a warts-and-all account of my childhood, the key events that shaped me, insights into how I tick, and how I built a world-class brand from scratch. You can decide whether I am a natural-born entrepreneur, or my environment made me this way.

Whichever conclusion you draw, I hope my account helps you with your journey, not only in the business sense but in everyday life. My business was bootstrapped, but so was my life. We are all far more resourceful than we think. If you want to learn how to make the most of your resources and embark on the most rewarding journey you could ever experience, this book is for you.

It's time to bootstrap your life.

CHAPTER ONE

'MY FUTURE'

'I hope one day I become a great businessman, with control over many people. I like the idea of being my own boss. I also like the idea of creating jobs for others. I would make a good boss and would look after the staff well.'

These are the words of an eight-year-old schoolboy, sharing his thoughts in a letter for a teacher. They weren't penned by Steve Jobs, Alan Sugar or any other well-known rags-to-riches entrepreneur you will have heard of. I wrote those words when I was at primary school. Does that mean I am a natural-born entrepreneur?

How many eight-year-olds do you know who would come out with a phrase such as 'creating jobs for others'? Not many, in my opinion. I'd argue it's not natural for a child of such a young age to be thinking that way – especially an ordinary, working-class lad from inner-city Manchester. And that's not to suggest there is anything wrong with having those aspirations; it's just not what we expect from children.

Typically, children are expected to be concerned with themselves and their own happiness, and we nurture them to be thoughtful, considerate and kind to others. They are still finding their feet and exploring the world. They have an open-minded perspective on life, but this is often hammered out of them by the time they become adults. Anything is possible to a child. Of course, even eight-year-old children can be bossy, and some will admit to wanting to control other people. You can see that in any playground anywhere in the world. But creating jobs for others? That's a different matter.

For a child to talk about creating jobs suggests one who has absorbed the world around them, seeing how it all works and sussing what makes society tick. Those words could easily have come out of the mouth of a politician today. Pick your party, visit their website and you will probably find some would-be prime minister or president talking about creating jobs for the future. I believe a child who wants to create jobs for others is made, not born. The difference is not the circumstances we are born into but how we respond to them.

HUMBLE BEGINNINGS

The circumstances I was born into were not great. I was born in Withington Community Hospital, in inner-city Manchester, on 17 February 1979. My parents were living in a bedsit in Stretford, just outside Manchester city centre. Stretford was one of the city's more deprived areas at that time, but it might have improved since then. Dad was a used car dealer. He used to buy cars from BCA car auctions in Belle Vue, Manchester, and sell them from home. Mum worked as a secretary in the city centre.

We moved to Bury, in North Manchester, around six months after I was born. I didn't go to nursery and was an only child, so at a time when I should have been mixing with other children, I only had adults for company. Another move to a place called Heald Green, when I was around four years old, meant more upheaval. A feeling of isolation, instability and a boatload of dreams sum up the first few years of my life quite accurately.

I would not describe my early life as miserable. It is hard to say whether it is how I am wired, or a case of needs must, but I was well suited to my situation. Like any other young child, I wanted things – toys, sweets, experiences and other treats – and as I evolved, so did my desires, and I became interested in gaming, consoles and technology.

By my middle to late teens, I'd been introduced to motocross by my cousin Lee, whom I really looked up to. I used to love spending time with Lee and my other cousins – his three younger sisters – and it was only a matter of time before I really got into the motocross. But nothing comes for free, and my passion for scrambling under Barton Bridge in Trafford, and other off-road locations, soon became another reason to succeed and make money. No sooner had I warmed the seat of one bike, I'd be looking to buy a better one.

When I reflect on my earliest memories, it is only now that I can see clearly and understand why my eight-year-old self would aspire to become a great businessman, employing people, and why he would like the idea of being his own boss. I was a product of my environment – one that could crush me or that I could learn to adapt to and thrive within.

We had to move again, after my parents split up, when I was around nine years old. Mum and I went to live in Stockport, in a block of flats in the middle of a council estate. My family was broken, and I had lost easy access to all my friends again. Clearly there was no point depending on friendships as a source of happiness, and life was proving to be anything but settled.

DEVELOP A MINDSET FOR SUCCESS

Certain traits were already coming to the fore, and they were working for me. I guess you could say a mindset was being formed, and I believe it was one that would help me to succeed in business later in life. From an emotional perspective, I had learnt not to count on having other children as friends and that it was better to be strong, independent and confident in my own space, with or without anybody else's support.

Only children have a few options. Either they are desperate to be with other children, in which case they learn how to make friends quickly, or they find peace on their own terms whether there are other children to play with or not. It is not unusual to find only children doing everything they can to gain friends, including splashing the cash. Being the only child in the house sometimes means their parents dote on them and ensure they have whatever material items they want. That wasn't the case for me. I found happiness by immersing myself into whatever I was doing.

Being surrounded by adults all the time can influence a child in other ways. Just as a pet dog might think it's human, a child who spends too much time with adults can become more serious-minded. I am willing to accept that might have been the case with me.

An emotionally independent mindset is extremely useful for anyone, regardless of whether they are aspiring to be entrepreneurs or not. It empowers you to be able to focus on achieving goals rather than spending mental energy on emotional needs. I am not saying there's anything wrong with you if you care about having a partner and loads of friends. Humans are a highly sociable species, but if you can learn how to become emotionally self-sufficient, you will have fewer distractions.

I must stress the difference between being emotionally independent and being cold-hearted. Success in business has allowed me to give more to the people I love than I could have imagined when I was working in a typical nine-to-five job in my early twenties. And it's not just about money either. Now, I can focus my attention on the things that matter, such as spending quality time with the people who count, experiencing things I could only dream of before, and helping the less fortunate through charitable acts.

Being emotionally independent meant I could spend long periods in solitude, which is something that I still enjoy. I was always well suited to spending time alone because of my natural tendency towards self-sufficiency, a trait that permeates almost every aspect of my life. I'm a firm believer in the 'if you want to get something done, do it yourself' philosophy!

You need to be determined if you want to be self-sufficient. You can't run for help at the first sign of a problem. Don't forget, life had taught me that I couldn't count on anyone else. If I encountered an obstacle, I had to figure it out for myself. Once I'd entered my teens, I discovered that between the hours of 9 p.m. and 1 a.m. I was able to hyperfocus and enter a zone where the three main aspects of my mindset – self-sufficiency, focus and determination – came together most powerfully. I felt I could do anything if it interested me and I put my mind to it. This is the kind of approach that many elite performance coaches try to instil in their clients, but I believe many people can figure it out for themselves as long as they recognise the conditions that enable them to operate better. Some people are early birds, but I was never a member of the '5 a.m. club'. You have to find what works for you.

Another feature of being self-sufficient is not having to rely on others to offer reassurance or validation. In a way, long before I owned any real business, I was my own boss. I was bootstrapping my life, relying on myself for company, entertainment and education. And I had my own vision for how my future was going to turn out. It wasn't included in the letter I wrote as an eight-year-old, but I used to tell myself and others that I would be a millionaire before reaching the age of thirty – not in an arrogant way, but just as part of one of those conversations about how things might turn out in the future. It wasn't a case of me trying to convince myself with my own inner voice. It was a conviction. I just knew. Of course, other people told me it wasn't going to happen, but it did. In fact, on reflection, it happened on paper by the time I was around twenty-six, but I distinctly remember writing myself a dividend cheque for one million pounds when I was around twenty-eight. I had probably banked at least that amount before then, in smaller tranches, but actually writing 'One million pounds' on a cheque was a profound moment.

There are many books, and people, that discuss the power of visualisation, the 'Law of Attraction' and similar concepts, so I am not going to add to that. Action, and a strong plan, are what get results. You need to know where you are going, and it is your determination to get there that will motivate you to find solutions to the toughest challenges.

I have always been naturally curious. Had I not been, I think it is unlikely my life would have unfolded in the way that it has. Curiosity is a key part of my story. Had I not been curious about how my then go-to whey protein product was made, how would any of this have happened? This is something I will be delving into in much more detail in a later chapter, but, for now, I will say this much: you look at what is, and you imagine what could be. You have to ask questions:

- 'Is there a better way of doing this?'
- 'Is there a quicker way of doing this?'
- 'Is there a less expensive way of doing this?'
- 'What can I do to make this better?'

Questioning doesn't just open the door to improvement. It presents you with more possibilities when you need the solution to a problem. The less imaginative you are, the fewer options you will have. Curiosity broadens your mind. It broadened mine without any doubt.

I believe you learn to become more intuitive when you spend a lot of time alone, especially as a child. Whenever I met a new child, I had to decide whether they were friend or foe, trustworthy or disloyal, good people to be around or troublesome. All children have to do that, but I think that sense might have been heightened in my case as I was an only child. I've always chosen my friends and associates carefully, and I believe I am an excellent judge of character. I trust my gut.

Intuition is a kind of magic that combines various other skills. It involves internalising the world, extrapolating various possibilities and identifying the most likely outcomes, and assessing their impact. The result of that equation is a feeling of knowing – *this direction will bear fruit, proceed with care, avoid at all costs*, etc.

Entrepreneurs take calculated risks. They are decisive. Deciding to take a risk, whether it is a calculated one or not, takes courage. Nothing is certain. It could go wrong. I am very grateful to Carl Boon for sharing his 'Fear is a liar' principle with me. This became one of my mantras, because a lot of the time, the things we worry about don't happen. They are figments of the imagination – what-ifs gone wrong. It is good to keep a handle on what can go wrong but only so you can better prepare for every outcome. 'Fail to plan, plan to fail' is another much-used phrase in business books, but no plan is complete unless you have considered the worst possible scenario. That is usually my starting point when building a plan, and I build out the rest from there.

Risk is a fact of life for everyone, but in business often the stakes are especially high because if we mess up, it can impact on the people we employ. The difference is that we have the chance to take control of our destiny. Given the choice between being in a full-time job, where I could be laid off at any time through no fault of my own, or running my own business, I'd take the latter every day of the week. The risk-to-reward benefit is a no-brainer. If I am going to have to take risk, I want the rewards to be worth it.

When you are self-employed or you are running a business that employs others, the risk is in your face – including the possibility of losing a lot of money and still having to pay your staff. It is your dream, your vision, your time, your money and your hard work. Sometimes it doesn't pay off. You learn how to move on when it doesn't. That's where resilience comes into play.

Over the next few chapters, I am going to talk in more detail about my formative years and how I started to gravitate towards becoming a businessman. As I do so, I will highlight how some of the traits I have talked about came in handy. I want to show how bootstrapping doesn't just apply to growing a business. Every person is unique, with their own set of traits and talents. If you can learn how to make the most of your strengths and dampen the impact of your weaknesses, your dreams can become reality.

CHAPTER TWO

MAKE THE MOST OF YOUR INNER RESOURCES

You have to make the most of what life gives you and learn how to turn weaknesses into strengths. I realised very early on that school was not working for me in the way it was for others. Although I have never been formally diagnosed with a learning disability, I strongly suspect that I suffer from some form of dyslexia, especially where mathematics is concerned.

Dyslexia sometimes goes hand in hand with a condition called dyscalculia, otherwise known as 'number blindness'. Being afflicted with dyscalculia bears no relationship whatsoever to a person's age or their ability in other areas. No matter how smart someone is in every other respect, if they have this condition, they will struggle with figures. That's me all over – arithmetic can baffle me.

Even now, many teachers are unaware of conditions such as dyscalculia, and children with dyslexia often fall under the radar as well. Don't forget that I was educated in the eighties and nineties, when teachers had less experience or knowledge of these conditions, so they could have been forgiven for thinking I wasn't interested, wasn't very intelligent or both. Perhaps they were as confused about me as I am with mathematics!

This end-of-year report from The Kingsway comprehensive school in 1996 sums up my memories of school quite accurately:

Oliver is a pleasant and reliable student who is usually willing to offer help in the form periods and he is well liked by his peer group. Whilst he is ready for a chat at any time he does not always show the same approach in actual lessons.

He is full of energy and enthusiasm, but needs to have it channelled in the right directions. He requires more self discipline to succeed in unfamiliar situations. In Expressive Arts he has matured greatly, but still requires to do more about his control. He is a very practical person who has little time for the paperwork aspect of life.

He is able to co-operate with others top [sic] get things done, and no doubt has benefitted from his work experiences both in school and out of school as a catering assistant at Manchester City Football Club. He plays five-a-side football out of school and this is his main sporting activity.

In school P.E. he has shown determination to succeed and in the practical areas of Art and Design he has made steady progress through his approach to the subject and his resourcefulness. He has also demonstrated ability in Electronics on his short course and has a flair for computer [sic] and I.T.

I have no doubt he will be successful in life wherever [sic] he does due to his personality and lively approach to anything he attempts.

My form teacher managed to capture quite a few of the key features that helped me to succeed later while highlighting some of the challenges I was up against. They acknowledged that I was neither an unhappy nor disruptive student and was able to fit in well with others. One of the things I find most notable about the report is the reference to my determination to succeed and resourcefulness. These traits have served me well.

Paperwork was not my thing and still isn't to a certain degree. I have always been a more hands-on person, so that is where I focus my energy. This explains how I only managed to obtain a U-grade for my GCSE in IT despite being able to demonstrate 'ability in Electronics' and 'a flair for computer [sic] and I.T.'

All things considered, my teacher's assessment of me was pretty fair, and while the school failed to identify any kind of learning issue such as dyslexia, they had little doubt that I'd succeed in whatever activity I focused on.

LEARN TO READ THE ENVIRONMENT

While I might not have stood out as a star pupil on paper, I made up for it in other ways. School can be a difficult environment for any child who does not learn to adapt and fit in with other students quickly. Children can be cruel and insensitive, and anything that makes a child stand out can leave them open to being marginalised or attacked. Things could have turned out differently for someone like me who couldn't always add up that well and lacked confidence. Sometimes, my shyness made me feel a little awkward when I was around people, whereas I always felt comfortable in my own space, so I tended to be a bit of a loner during my earlier years in secondary school. I used to be known by my full name, Oliver Nobahar-Cookson, when I was at school, which made me a target for would-be bullies. But regardless of how much I found having to go to school boring and tedious, I always knew how to get on with everyone else.

I developed an instinct for the social dynamics of whatever environment I was in. You don't need a degree in psychology to recognise how people around you are feeling, but I appreciate that some people are better at this than others. It is only in hindsight that I can see the importance of my school years in shaping my view of friendships, people and social skills. That period of my life provided me with a strong foundation to build on in terms of understanding myself and others – a strength that set me in good stead for working with and leading people later in life.

Primary school taught me the basics in terms of being able to read and write, and I was able to fit in with others even though I was quite shy. I guess I lacked confidence as I was not used to being with other children at home. The most significant event from my early childhood was the break-up of my parents' relationship, without a shadow of a doubt. While it didn't mean me having to move schools, we had to move to a new address about three miles away, so I couldn't just pop round to my friends' houses any more after school.

At the end of each school day, I used to stay with childminders until my mum could pick me up after work. They were lovely people, and they had a couple of children of their own – Michelle, who is a year younger than me, and Jeff (Junior), who sadly passed away in an accident a number of years ago. Rest in peace, Jeff. I still bump into Michelle now and again, and she is a lovely woman.

I got on well with Michelle and Jeff and their parents, but not being able to play with my mates in my year was frustrating. While my friends were spending time together after school, sharing experiences, learning and growing together, I was out on a limb. It was only a matter of time before my relationship with them became weaker, and that knocked my confidence even more.

Things hadn't changed much by the time I went to secondary school. On my first day, I remember being very upset because I didn't know how to do my tie. The school caretaker noticed how distressed I was, came to the rescue and showed me what to do. This incident demonstrates just how vulnerable I was as a boy.

A NEW FRIEND AND A NEW OLIVER

During what we used to call 'Fourth Year', or 'Year 10' in today's terms, I went on work experience at an IT training company in Stockport. That's where I met Carl Boon, who was everything I wasn't at the time – oozing with confidence, one of the cocks of the school[*] and the cool kid who everyone else wanted to be like and who all the girls fancied. His charisma was contagious.

Carl and I got on great from the get-go. Some have said I was led astray a little and my friendship with Carl marked the period of my life when I started to go off the rails. But truthfully, it was being around someone as free-spirited and confident as Carl that encouraged me to be myself and to find my own way, and I made my own mistakes from there. He was the catalyst I needed to come out of my shell and grow. It was the beginning of a new process of learning my strengths and weaknesses in social situations and finding out who I was. I wouldn't change anything about those years for the world. Carl and I really could write a book about our early years alone.

Those days on work experience with Carl were the best days of my school life, and they were also pretty wild. I can't remember how it happened, but somehow or other, we ended up coming across a bottle of amyl nitrite and overindulging in sniffing that during work experience. God knows how many brain cells we killed, but the laughs we had made it seem worthwhile to my mind back then. The most profound change that came about from my friendship with Carl was my new-found confidence, which had an enormous impact on all aspects of my life in and out of school.

---

[*] 'Cock of the school' is predominantly a Northern term for the boy who all the other boys look up to. They might be the best fighters or just the most popular, but they are viewed as leaders.

Following my stint in work experience, I returned to school as a new person, and I was much more willing to engage, take chances and join in with my peers than I had ever been before. A more confident, daring and adventurous Oliver was coming to the fore, and he was determined to take his place in the group. This led to some unintended consequences.

The worst day of school came when I was suspended for attempting to steal three hot dogs, which I hid up my sleeve and in my inside pocket, from the school canteen. Not the best move I've ever made. I can only put it down to the peer pressure I felt at the time. Retrospectively, I think that while all adolescents feel pressure to do things that are not very smart, something about my mindset enabled me to take things a step further. I have always been more of a doer than a talker. If something is worth doing, it's worth doing right now. Fortunately, as I matured, I made much wiser decisions – but not before I made plenty of other mistakes along the way.

A very dear friend of mine, Natalka, was chatting to me recently about the good old days when we were teens. She said she remembers that I was usually planning some stunt or other – often something mischievous – and when I said I was going to do something, I would always follow through. Although I had no idea of it at the time, my determination to see things through to the end was clearly making an impression on my friend, who remains one of my closest mates today. If I've achieved anything by being so open with you, I have demonstrated how accurate my teacher's assessment was when they said I needed to channel my energy and enthusiasm in the right directions. The self-discipline was probably there, to be honest, but I was applying it to the wrong things. There was a lack of focus on what I should have been doing. I was young, and I didn't always think about the consequences. The young Oliver would decide on a goal and set his heart on scoring it, and that's what Natalka and others clearly noticed.

While my approach to life might have lacked direction as a teen, and I often focused on the wrong things, there was one passion of mine that paid real dividends. When I was around seven years old and Mum and Dad were still together, we lived next door to the Gill family, which included a boy called David. He was around five years older than me, but I think we were both similar people in the sense that he was also a very self-contained, self-sufficient person.

David had suffered from ill health from birth. Physically, he was disadvantaged, but mentally, he held a trump card. David was an extremely smart individual with a natural talent for computers and computer programming. He enjoyed showing me the ropes and sharing his knowledge and experience with me, and I lapped it up. I have since found out that he went on to become one of the top computer programmers in the country, specialising in gaming.

Unfortunately, after my parents split up when I was nine and I had to move away, I didn't see as much of David. I'd spend around two or three hours with him on a weekend when I visited Dad, but it wasn't enough, and we drifted apart. All my memories of David are very fond ones.

DISCOVERING MY ENTREPRENEURIAL SPIRIT

Another consequence of Mum and Dad's split was the financial impact it had on my mum. Money was tight, but I still wanted things, especially as I was emerging from puberty. Learning about computers from David had added fuel to my passion for computer games, but with the money situation, I couldn't afford to buy anything fancy. I'd buy a second-hand, low-spec Windows-based PC and use the skills I had learnt from David (and had discovered for myself by trial and error) to upcycle it – buy a new processor, add memory, install an improved graphics card, etc. This was a far less expensive and more interesting way of acquiring a superb computer that would give me the performance I wanted.

It was never my intention to flip PCs for money, but that's how the situation evolved. My friends at school got to know that I was handy with computers, so it was only a matter of time before I started helping people out. I didn't always charge my mates for repairs, but I had realised the opportunity to make money. Even then, my initial motivation had been to make enough money to buy the latest, off-the-shelf, brand-new, highest-spec computer. I signed up for a free account with *Loot*, which was effectively like Gumtree but in a printed format that came out every week as a free-ads newspaper.

Things went better than I expected. It was so easy. One sale turned into ten sales, which turned into a hundred. I was buying several second-hand computers at once, doing whatever I could to improve them, re-advertising them on *Loot* and making a healthy profit with every sale. Business was booming until...

Loot pulled the plug on my activities. They weren't happy with the fact that was I running a business on a free account, so I was banned from the platform, and I couldn't register as a business account as I was only around fourteen. I did set up alternate accounts, but there were only so many phone numbers I could use at that age. I'd learnt a valuable lesson: if you can take a product and add value, you can make money.

PART OF THE IN-CROWD

During my later school years, I got into the habit of smoking. I wasn't a real smoker though. It was something I did to be part of the crowd, so I would only smoke five or so a day, if that many. I never felt addicted to the nicotine. It's a terrible habit, and I am not encouraging anyone to smoke, but when you see smokers in any situation, it is easy to spot the sense of solidarity between them. Whether you remember the days when smokers would gather in a 'smoke room' at work or you observe them standing under an outdoor smoking shelter, you can see how the common urge binds them together. That bond is no stronger than at school where adolescents have the added excitement of knowing they are doing something that's a bit rebellious. Things were no different when I was at school. Everyone used to go to the bottom of the playing field at breaks for a 'cig'.

Back in the day, most of us smoked cigarettes that included a 'special' filter marking, so we'd refer to someone saving a little on their cigarette as 'double spesh'. But given that none of us were old enough to buy them, those of us who looked older than sixteen, as I did, would be asked to go into the shop to buy for everyone else. My dad's Persian, so by the time I was fifteen I was growing a healthy amount of facial hair and already looked like a young man. I can still hear what they used to say as though it were yesterday: 'Oli, get us a pack of cigs, will ya, mate?'

Cigarettes have always been expensive, especially for schoolkids who mostly rely on their parents for any money they have, so most of us couldn't afford to buy them. Those of us who did might only be able to buy a packet of ten, and these would soon run out if the others needed us to hand them out. I recognised an opportunity to help others out while making sure I had enough cigarettes left for me.

You could only buy cigarettes from the shop as packets of ten or twenty. That was fine for adults but too pricey for most of my friends. I spotted a new minimum viable product – the single cigarette. When one of my mates wanted a smoke, what they really wanted was one cigarette. That was all they needed to feel a part of the group, and if everyone had another smoke later, they could buy another single one then. By selling cigarettes instead of giving them away, all of us could afford to smoke and I got mine for free. The fact that my status in the group became elevated – because people saw me as the one who always had the solution – was an added bonus.

Now, you may be thinking that buying and selling computers and being the one-stop cigarette solution at school demonstrated some entrepreneurial spirit. Maybe there was a little of that going on, but, at the time, I was just solving problems – funding my hunger for gaming and making sure I could be useful to my friends.

There was one venture I got involved in that grew so big, I was serving customers throughout the UK. But by the time I was twenty-one, it had all come crashing down, and I was in the national newspapers for all the wrong reasons.

CHAPTER THREE

SOME SERIOUSLY WRONG TURNS AND A PIVOTAL MOMENT

By the end of my teens, I had already demonstrated some entrepreneurial flair, buying and selling computers and even flogging single cigarettes to my mates during school breaks. It wasn't as though I was even trying to be an entrepreneur at that time. Situations would arise, and the opportunities to make money would present themselves as I tried to solve whatever problem was in front of me. It was all fairly innocent if you overlook the fact that I wasn't supposed to be buying cigarettes as a fourteen-year-old and was using a free, personal-use *Loot* account to sell upcycled PCs. All that was about to change.

By my middle to late teens, I looked like one of the cool kids, partly thanks to my close association with Carl Boon and one of my oldest friends, Gary Baggaley, who I have known since I was five – we used to walk to the bus stop on the way to school every morning – and this created the right conditions for me to come out of my shell. But despite my passion for motocross and my love for the Hacienda and the rest of the Manchester dance scene, I was still a computer geek at heart – just not the extremely shy, scared-to-make-eye-contact, socially inept stereotype that most people tend to think of.

David, the older boy I lived next to when Mum and Dad were still together, had taught me a lot about computers, and I'd lapped it up because high-powered computers opened the door to something else I was really excited about: gaming.

THE IRC

These days, our children can chat to each other online while they are competing or collaborating in high-tech, 3D, virtual reality games. The latest cheats and walkthroughs can be discovered through YouTube videos, talking to other gamers in online forums and social media groups. However, things were very different in the late nineties. This was the pre-social media age. All those platforms we now take for granted – Facebook, Twitter, Instagram and the messaging apps such as WhatsApp and Telegram – didn't exist. I am talking about a time when even MySpace wasn't around! But you have to consider the origins of the internet.

A long time before ordinary people were using the World Wide Web to talk about what they'd eaten that day, post philosophical quotes or talk about which party everyone else should vote for in elections, scientists, researchers and even government intelligence operatives were using the internet to exchange information. So were all the computer geeks. Like me!

I used to spend many an hour communicating with likeminded computer and gaming enthusiasts using a protocol called Internet Relay Chat (IRC) on a network called EFnet, which has been around since 1988. It is still in use today, although usage has dropped significantly because of all the new ways to communicate online. IRC facilitates real-time text messaging between internet-connected computers. Although you can engage in private discussions with other users, it is mainly used to host chat rooms or 'channels' where people can come together to talk about specific topics and learn from each other.

There were rooms about hacking, gaming cheats, hardware, programs – you name it. Everyday people didn't know anything about it or how to access it – not like today where people type a word or phrase into a search engine and then get shown whatever the algorithm sees fit to reveal.

I was mainly on IRC to talk about gaming, developing and hacking, and within a relatively short time and as a popular user, I gained the status of 'operator' within the rooms that I frequented. An operator was the equivalent of what you'd call a moderator or page admin. Having operator status gave me a little more kudos within IRC channels, and it meant people were more likely to share information with me because I was moderating what went on in the rooms. One of the things I had an interest in was hacking, but that was mostly related to my love of gaming. However, entering the realms of IRC was a bit like opening Pandora's box in that you never knew what you might discover – a little like going into a supermarket today where you only intend to buy a pint of milk but come out with a sun lamp, a tent for six people and a solar-powered desktop.

I came across a neat exploit that allowed me to send a desktop pop-up notification to any IP address in the world. It exploited a 'bug' in Windows 98. I was more driven by the desire to develop an idea and make it happen than to take people's money, and what I did was never intended to be malicious, but it was annoying. I guess you could call it adware. A read-only pop-up would appear on some unsuspecting person's computer screen, telling them that they had an issue and giving them instructions on how to solve it. Although it was annoying, it was totally harmless to their computers and their data.

For anyone who is tempted to judge me in a certain light, please bear in mind that I am telling my story from the beginning. It was more than twenty years ago at a time when I was certainly no saint, and the man writing this book is not the same kid who was fascinated with hacking and coding. The fact is that even then something inside me told me it was wrong, so I packed it in quickly and moved on. It was a project that had got out of hand. The reason I have included it in this book is because it is part of my story and it demonstrates a certain aptitude for finding things out and recognising how to turn knowledge into opportunity. I also want to show that while I could have gone down that route, the route of making money by any means possible, I chose not to.

GREY IMPORTS

Another area I discovered in the IRC network was grey imports. For the uninitiated, 'grey imports' is the term used for hardware, films, games and similar intellectual property that is imported into a country where it has not been officially released. In my case, I discovered a source in Hong Kong that was selling the legendary Super Nintendo Entertainment System (SNES), which had been released over there but not in the UK. That led to the formation of Paradox Supplies, where people in the UK could buy the hottest console, almost straight out of the factory.

Was it legal? Well, excuse the pun, but it's a grey area, and I am not a lawyer, so I am not going to delve deeper into the legalities. The way I saw it, I was providing a valuable service to people who were just like me and loved gaming. Would I buy the product? You bet I would, so I didn't feel I was doing anything wrong. But there was another product offered by Paradox Supplies. It was one that I had seen advertised by someone else.

Another company I found through IRC, called Bung Enterprises and also based in Hong Kong, was selling backup devices for Nintendo 64 games. They'd developed a machine called the Doctor V64, which had its own internal memory and allowed gamers to back up the cartridge they were playing onto this. This meant they could take time out, play other games, and then come back to the game they'd been playing simply by reinserting the backup cartridge. This was all good and perfectly innocent, except for one small problem.

The problem, of course, was that there was another way of looking at this backup device. With just a moderate amount of technical know-how, it was possible to doctor the Doctor V64 to enable copying of the raw game cartridge for the purpose of distribution. People were able to duplicate Nintendo's copyrighted material without having to pay them for the privilege. Again, if anybody had asked me about the product, I was selling it as a backup device, and that's how it was advertised. I wasn't tampering with it. I was selling a gaming backup unit. It was another grey area. And if somebody wanted to misuse the backup device to create an illegal copy of a Nintendo game, who was I to judge? That was none of my business. Nintendo did take legal action to try to stop the sale and distribution of the Doctor V64, but this action was aimed at Bung and not the small resellers such as Paradox.

Many of those who were buying the illegitimate copies were probably doing so because they weren't able to afford the official versions. I am not going to pretend to be some kind of Robin Hood character – I was running a business and so were many of the people who bought the machine from me – and I don't condone illegal copywriting, but if I was helping people to access a better gaming experience they otherwise couldn't afford, there were definitely worse things I could've been doing.

Whatever you might be thinking about my buying and selling activities, something far more significant was going on behind the scenes. Products don't sell themselves. Unlike the PCs, which I had sold through a printed medium, I was selling grey imports and Doctor V64s via a website. Even though I was barely eighteen years old at the time, I was already a highly skilled developer, so I was able to build an e-commerce website for Paradox Supplies from scratch using just a text editor like Notepad.

CROSSING THE LINE

Up until this point, nothing I had done was going to get me into any real trouble. I had been engaging in activities that hovered in that grey area that exists between legal and illegal. But the next opportunity I identified meant stepping over the invisible line into territory that was most definitely illegal.

It was the late nineties and cable television was becoming increasingly popular, giving British people access to more channels than ever before. But it was expensive. Typically, it would cost around £7 a month for a basic package, which wouldn't give you much more than Sky One and a few other extras. A premium package would cost almost £35 a month, and even then, customers might have to pay around £11 a time on top for certain extras such as pay-per-view boxing events.

Thanks to the IRC, I'd got to know a guy who'd figured out how to unscramble the analogue signal that the most popular cable TV provider was using to transmit its channels. I asked him if he could send me a sample to look at, and he did. He was a super geek, and he had figured out how to produce a circuit board that could unscramble the television signal, but it needed more work to become a commercially viable product. Together, we refined it until we ended up with a black plastic box, which was fitted with input and output slots, so it could sit between the cable television signal and the cable box. With a little work, we'd produced an easy-to-use descrambling interface, and it only took around ten minutes to get it working once out of the box.

It was great. All you needed was the basic cable package, which gave you access to the signal, and then you could connect the descrambler, or 'cable cube', as we called it, and you got every channel and every pay-per-view event for free. The cable cube gave you access to everything. I asked my contact to send me another, which I then gave to a friend, and it worked just as well for them. There was a business opportunity here, but I was going to have to operate with complete anonymity. To this day, I don't know what my contact's real name is. We all used fake names and various methods to hide our IP addresses on IRC.

I set up another website on one of the free hosting platforms that were available at the time. That was a hassle-free way of establishing an online shop without having to register my name anywhere. The website address was something along the lines of freewebserve.com/cablecubesuk, so it wasn't flash, but it did the job.

The website solved one part of the problem. I could send cable cubes to paying customers anonymously. The second part of the equation – how to get paid – was just as easy. Customers were asked to pay by cash, and this had to be sent to a PO Box address, which protected my identity. Easy. The system worked like clockwork, and the 'business' grew very quickly. I set up a referral scheme so people who wanted to cash in on the enterprise could flog the cubes to their friends, and they'd get a slice of the cake as well. Everything was done by mail, apart from the odd phone call that would be conducted on a dedicated pay-as-you-go phone so nothing could be traced back to me.

It was 1999, I was around twenty years old, and since I was making more money than I had been able to before, thanks to the cable cubes, I wanted to live a little. I'd always wanted to travel, and now I had the chance. Gary Baggaley and I used to share a dream of a once-in-a-lifetime trip to somewhere a million miles from the cold, wet, miserable streets of Manchester, where we could enjoy the sun and live a completely carefree life.

We finally made the decision to go for it and apply for a tourist visa for somewhere on the other side of the world. We were going to pick fruit in Australia! That's another chapter all by itself. It's what happened back home while I was in Australia that I want to share with you now. As the cable cube enterprise had become busier, I needed an extra pair of hands to keep up with the orders, so I invited a really good friend of mine to join me. The cable cube market was huge. I later found out that somewhere between 750,000 and one million homes were using a cable cube at that time. Cable cubes were big business.

FORCED TO FACE THE FACT . . . AND THE MUSIC!

If I was going to escape to Australia, it was only natural that my friend should take the reins and handle the cable cube business while I was away. He knew the business as well as I did, and I would trust him with my life, so he took over the operation, and I went to follow my dream. For almost nine months, everything continued to go well. The cable cube enterprise was ticking over nicely, and I was sunning it in Australia with my mate Gary.

When I left the UK, there was never an official handover to my friend. It just happened. He knew how the business worked, and there was a clear understanding between us about how the operation was supposed to run. One of my unwritten rules – and I mean that literally – was that I would never meet anyone in connection with cable cubes. I never met the supplier – we didn't even know each other's name – and I never met the customers. Anonymity was the key. However, rules make perfect sense until something unusual comes along to make you reconsider. That thing came along while I was away.

My friend was approached, via the website, by a couple of people who claimed they could shift a huge quantity of cubes for us. They wanted to buy in bulk. You can see the attraction. Why spend so much time packing individual units when you can make a massive profit on one order? That would turn anyone's head. But there was one condition – and it was risky. If they were going to be trusting us with such a large order, they wanted to make a test purchase first, and they wanted to know who they were dealing with, eye to eye. They demanded a face-to-face meeting.

It presented him with a dilemma. It's easy for you or me, or anyone, to say we would refuse the meeting, that it was too risky, that anonymity had to be maintained. But sometimes, if the reward is great enough, the risk can seem worth taking, and these people wanted to place a huge order. My friend went with his instinct and agreed to the meeting. They agreed a time and a place, and it was game on.

When the time came to meet the prospects, everything seemed to be running smoothly. My friend arrived at the agreed meeting place, the atmosphere was relaxed and friendly, they shook hands, and everyone was full of smiles and pleasantries. After all, they were planning to collaborate, and great things were going to happen. Except that once he had produced a sample and the conversation had turned to quantities and costs, his new contacts pulled out some ID and explained that they were agents working for FACT, the Federation Against Copyright Theft. FACT is a trade organisation dedicated to the protection of the intellectual property of its members. It's a kind of intelligence agency. The game was up.

Presumably, FACT had built up a hefty dossier, which contained a ton of incriminating evidence to be used against us, and they handed it all to Greater Manchester Police, who set about seeking arrests. They arrested my friend. That was easy. But I was thousands of miles away in Australia, so they raided my mum's house and arrested her instead. Even now, after all these years, it breaks my heart to think of my mum, a good, law-abiding, decent woman, who had never been in trouble in her life, being arrested and held in a cell.

Mum had nothing to do with our cable cubes enterprise. She knew nothing about it. She wouldn't have had a clue. God knows what must have gone through her mind when two officers from

Greater Manchester Police knocked on her door. It's a terrible ordeal for anyone to have to go through, but they knew what they were doing. Arresting my mum was a ploy to put emotional pressure on me to come home and face the music. I jumped on the first available plane to the UK. What else could I do? It was checkmate.

They dropped all charges against my mum, and she never had to spend a night in the cells, but, as you can imagine, she was not impressed with me. It takes a lot to make Mum angry, but this wasn't a case of me staying out all night or bunking off school. My antics were in a league of their own. Fortunately, I was granted bail. Yes, what I had done was criminal, but I was no threat to the community, and where was I going to run? I'd travelled halfway around the world to accept responsibility for my actions. There was nowhere for me to go.

My solicitor told me to be prepared for the possibility of a prison sentence, even though it was a white-collar crime, and I had plenty of time to stew because it took around two years for the case to come to court. I pleaded guilty to two counts of incitement under the Computer Misuse Act 1990, and my friend was convicted for the lesser charges of selling unauthorised decoders contrary to the Copyright Designs and Patents Act 1988 after selling a total of thirty-two devices.

A VERY CLOSE SHAVE

I came very close to getting a prison sentence. The judge said that he wanted to make an example of me to deter others from doing the same because the prosecution had really hammered home their message of how widespread this kind of copyright theft or fraud was becoming. What saved my skin was the fact that, since being arrested, I had built a successful career for myself as a web developer and was clearly going straight.

My defence lawyers successfully argued that if I was sent down, I would not only lose my job, but such a sentence could mean the difference between me continuing down the path of becoming a productive, law-abiding citizen or someone locked into a future of criminality. The judge agreed, and I was given a twelve-month suspended prison sentence, an order to complete two hundred hours of community service, which was the maximum amount you could be given, and a £600 fine. My friend, whose defence lawyers said he'd only played a minor part in the fraud at a later stage, was also ordered to complete two hundred hours of unpaid community work and was fined £400 for his part in the scheme.

As I had a full-time job, I had to serve my community time during the weekends. They had me cutting wood to make bird cages and pulling litter out of the river. I was grateful for the community service and attended the sessions with a willingness to work and a positive mental attitude. My probation officers told me they identified more potential in me and installed me in a charity shop where I spent the remainder of my time sorting clothes in the back office and making friends with the endearing elderly volunteers who, in the main, ran the shop. I think they were a bit unsure of me at first, but with time – and we had plenty of that – they began to soften. Once they had got to know me, they appreciated my gift of the gab and realised I was a good kid at heart, and I could tell they had grown quite fond of me.

I recognised that I had reached an important crossroads, and this was a pivotal moment in my life. It was the moment I decided that I was going to focus my skills and talents on making a success of my life through legitimate means. Dabbling with crime had almost cost me my freedom, and there was no way I was ever going to take that risk again.

CHAPTER FOUR

WORK HARD TO PLAY HARD

By the time I had reached my early twenties, I had learnt some significant lessons. I was developing a clear understanding of my strengths and, following my close scrape with the authorities, I was determined to figure out how to use my talents to succeed legally.

While I had certainly displayed some entrepreneurial spirit, my lack of direction had almost cost me my freedom. Many of my earlier exploits had been more akin to projects that I had felt compelled to follow up on rather than attempts to make a serious amount of money. My curiosity had got the better of me, I had shown a lack of judgement and things had got out of hand. Isn't that what being young is all about – making mistakes, learning from them, and finding one's feet?

There were two sides to my character that needed to be reconciled. On the one hand, I loved to have fun and could be mischievous. I was always up for a challenge. However, on the other hand, I was never afraid of hard graft, and when I gave something my attention, I gave it 150 per cent. In fact, throughout my formative years, my hard-working nature complemented my more free-spirited side perfectly. I guess you could say I always worked hard to play hard, and sometimes those things were one and the same.

For a working-class lad, computers and gaming were expensive hobbies to pursue, so I had to find ways to earn money.

Grown-ups often mention how they did a paper round when they were kids. But from around twelve years old until I was sixteen, I did *two* paper rounds – one first thing in the morning before school and another later in the afternoon after school. Paper rounds don't pay well, and never have done, but by doing two of them, I was able to make around £20 per week.

It was the nineties, remember, so in terms of spending power, it was like having over £40 per week in today's money. I could have easily splashed out on a top-selling music CD and a computer magazine, and I would have still had a few quid in change. But when you are careful with money, as I was, it soon adds up, and then you can buy the things you really want. I might not have taken to maths at school, but I understood one thing with crystal clarity – the value of money.

If there is one thing that every child should get to grips with from a young age, it's how to handle money and appreciate the value of it. As a parent, one of my biggest concerns is whether my own children value money as much as I did when I was their age. I am not sure it's that easy for children who are growing up with more wealth to truly understand the value of money. My children have more than I did when I was a child, but I try not to overly spoil them.

Psychologists refer to something called 'delayed gratification' – the ability to forfeit an immediate payback today for a greater reward tomorrow. By teaching children to be patient and save rather than spending what they have on impulse, we can better prepare them to succeed in the long term. I was always careful with money and still am. Being wealthy has not changed a thing in that sense – I know the value of money absolutely and will never take it for granted. There's something else that's never changed ...

THE SKY BLUES

I have followed my beloved Manchester City Football Club for my entire life and was a season ticket holder from the age of eleven. Back then, I used to watch the game from 'The Kippax', which is what we called the standing terrace at Maine Road, Manchester City's old ground. I would stand in the same spot each week, in what was known as 'Windy Corner'. As it was an uncovered area of the stand, Windy Corner was exposed to the elements and could be a pretty cold place on a Saturday afternoon in January, but it gave the best view of the pitch, and there was always a little more room.

I'm proud to say I was following Man City when they were still in the second division. I am certainly no glory supporter, and I still remember the buzz of them winning the play-off final against Gillingham at Wembley Stadium in 1999, which saw them being promoted to the First Division – an iconic moment for the club.

The atmosphere was electric. A couple of my best mates from school, Ian and John, travelled down to London with me as they were also big City fans, and we made a weekend of it. That was a big thing for us back then because we hardly ever used to venture far from Manchester. It turned out to be a truly historic event for the club, not only because City got promoted but because of how they won the game.

With just ten minutes to go before the final whistle, Gillingham managed to score two goals in quick succession, which put them 2–0 up. The clock was ticking, and our players were doing everything they could to get back into the game, but with every passing second, the situation looked increasingly hopeless for City. In fact, by the last few minutes of the game, at least a third of the 35,000 or so Manchester City fans, including my mates, had given up and left. I stayed, on my own, as I have always believed it's not over till it's over, and not quitting in the face of almost certain defeat is a sign of true character. At the same time, I was fully aware City were going to need to do something special to turn it around. And then they did!

Incredibly, we scored two goals in the last few minutes of injury time. I couldn't contain my excitement and was hugging and high-fiving strangers as though I had known them all my life. It was really a special moment and one that I will share with my grandkids—a genuine 'I was there' moment. The game went to extra time, but after another thirty minutes, neither side had scored, so there was still no clear winner. In the end, we won 3–1 on a penalty shootout. It doesn't get much more exciting than that. If we had lost that game, who knows where Manchester City would be now. I'm pretty certain we would not be one of the elite clubs in Europe as we currently are – everything happens for a reason.

At sixteen, I was fortunate enough to get some part-time work selling pies at Manchester City's ground on match days. It meant I could get to see my team and earn money at the same time, which felt like a win-win to me! The pay was only around £15, I think, for the match day, but again, my ability to manage money well meant I could make every penny count, and it was certainly more fun than doing the paper round twice a day.

While I have been reminiscing about old times, I've been struck by an interesting observation. As my life unfolded and my business took off, so did my status within Manchester City Football Club. What started as the cheapest season ticket you could buy, which was for The Kippax in 1990, evolved into a seat at the North Stand as I became a little better off – and also because standing at football grounds was phased out following the Hillsborough disaster of 1989.

Once Myprotein became more successful and robust, I was lucky enough to be able to have a seasonal corporate box, which was great as I could take up to ten guests to each game to enjoy the fruits of my labour.

Eventually, I gave up my seasonal box for a table for two in the Chairman's Club at Manchester City's new home, the Etihad Stadium. I am still as passionate as ever about Manchester City, but I don't get to go to every home game as I live abroad and it's not possible logistically. That said, I go to a lot of the European away games and the odd home game when travel allows.

THE THRILLS AND SPILLS OF MOTOCROSS

In 1993, I hit the age of fourteen, and I think it is fair to say in hindsight that I started going off the rails. That was the year I met the very popular and hilarious Carl Boon while on work experience at an IT company in Stockport. Carl had managed to ignite something within me – I came out of my shell and started to feel much more confident. Although I still loved gaming, I was getting my thrills from motocross as I charged through my mid-teens. Some might have called me an adrenaline junkie. I was enjoying hanging around with the cool gang and behaving mischievously. Look, we weren't housebreaking or bullying others – far from it – so don't get me wrong. But we were drinking (lager, alcopops, and vodka in my case), smoking cigarettes and taking the softer variety of recreational drugs.

It was my cousin Lee who got me into motocross. He was around eight or nine years older than me and I was an only child at that time, so I kind of looked up to him as a big brother. We used to travel around the north-west of the England, looking for the best courses. One of our favourite spots was under Barton Bridge, near where Manchester's Trafford Centre is now. The bridge was surrounded by wasteland and a sewer works, which was perfect for scrambling, and it was such a popular pastime that the land was criss-crossed with the trails of the hundreds of bikes that had been ridden there.

It didn't take long before I was so hooked on the sport that I'd acquired a bike of my own – another expensive piece of kit I needed to find the cash for. I never had any paperwork for the bikes I owned, and since I was only fourteen at the time, I had no driving licence either.

My first bike was a Honda CR125, which set the standard for motocross at the time, and it was as quick as a whippet. The CR125 had a 125cc, two-stroke engine and was designed for off-road racing. Honda stopped making them in 2007. I will never know why because it was a great bike. As I became more experienced, I progressed to a Husqvarna 250, but I've forgotten what the exact model was. What I do remember is that although it was still only a relatively small bike on paper, with a 250cc, two-stroke engine, it was a beast of a machine that was capable of absolutely savage performance and the engine noise was incredible. The 500cc version, which I had the good fortune to take for a spin later in life, was insanely scary to ride.

I've always had quite a methodical mindset, and I get a buzz out of looking at a problem and figuring out a way around it. I enjoy that feeling of progress you get as you crack new territory and know you are improving. But when it came to scrambling, it was more the thrill of getting carried away by the speed and adrenaline that hooked me in – 100-mile-an-hour living at its best!

While most other kids were either walking or using public transport to get around, I used an Aprilla 125cc bike to get from Mum's house to Dad's. I still didn't have my motorbike licence, but by sticking to various bridleways, parks and fields, I was able to do the three-mile trip almost entirely off-road.

If motocross taught me anything, it reinforced my 'feel the fear but do it anyway' attitude. There were too many times when I was so caught up in the moment that I went ahead with a jump or some other dangerous stunt with nothing but blind faith, instinct and a determined mindset to get me through. Fortunately, I lived to tell the tale, but at times my motocross skills were seriously tested.

Even as an adult rider, there have been times when instinct has overridden fear – riding through thick spray while overtaking a large HGV on a wet and windy day, for example. If you want to succeed as an entrepreneur, you have to learn how to deal with fear. I am not saying you have to get yourself a motorbike or behave recklessly – I take every business decision extremely seriously – but your instinct will tell you when something is possible. Fear will never tell you what's possible. It will only ever try to deter you from fulfilling your true potential.

My love of motorbikes never really left me, and I continued riding until 2011 when my first child was born. It felt like the right time to hang up my helmet, as I had become increasingly aware of how dangerous it is to ride motorbikes, especially on UK roads.

WEEKENDS WERE FOR PARTYING

At weekends, a crowd of us would hang around in 'East Av' park – our name for East Avenue Park – and various other spots to listen to music, get high and mess around. One of the most frequented was a shed at the bottom of the garden at one of my best mates' parents' house. Ross, who is still one of my best mates today, had a pool table in his shed. The whole gang of us spent many a night in there, playing pool and partying.

At the time, Manchester was at the epicentre of something massive, musically speaking, and we felt that we were a part of it. I am not talking about the Stone Roses, Oasis and all those indie bands that were taking over the world, even though it's cool that they came from my home city. Nope – we were into dance music, and by the time we were able to gain entry, we swapped the cricket club for getting wasted in Manchester's legendary Hacienda nightclub.

One of the best days of my youth was the day we all finished school. I went straight to the park to party with my mates, and we ended the day by piling into the Hacienda until the early hours, before going over the road to the infamous Café Loco to wind down until the trains started running again in the morning.

Looking back, they were really crazy times. Upstairs at Café Loco, we were the youngest people by a long way and didn't realise that some of the people we were mingling with were gangsters. The café was closed down in the end, following a gangland shooting that left at least one person dead. Luckily, we weren't there that night! Generally speaking, we never had any aggravation while we were there. In hindsight, I think a lot of the older people looked out for us because we were polite, up for a laugh and not cheeky. We were respectful, and they were in turn. They'd kind of taken us under their wing.

I used to love the 'Hac', as well as other Manchester haunts such as Sankeys, but I also had some great nights at the legendary Back to Basics in Leeds. We'd usually get to Leeds by car, which could be an adventure all by itself – a bunch of teenagers drinking, smoking and listening to very loud dance music while a mate, the nominated driver, tried to stay focused on the road.

One night, there were seven of us who wanted to go to Back to Basics, plus the driver, who was a friend of Natalka's. The only problem was that he drove a Fiat Cinquecento. How were all eight of us going to get to Leeds and back in a Cinquecento? It felt wrong leaving some mates behind, so don't ask me how we did it, but somehow, we all managed to squeeze into that car. It wasn't the most comfortable ride I've ever experienced over the 'Pennies', but we got to Leeds and back in one piece.

If we weren't at a dance club, local pubs and inner-city bars were the other places we enjoyed drinking in. These days, brandy and Diet Coke is my go-to drink, but, back in the day, I'd sup most things except lager – that became off limits after drinking a few too many Stellas at a school disco. It made me extremely unwell, and I still don't like the taste of lager or beer. That has stuck with me.

Our nights often ended at a party in someone else's digs, and we pulled many an all-nighter. Some of those parties could be pretty surreal, like the time when we went back to the North Manchester flat of a local professional boxer, who will remain nameless. His pet bird – I can't remember if it was a budgie or something larger and more exotic – had escaped from its cage and was flying all around the room, narrowly missing our heads. What made the situation even more amusing was that you could almost gauge how battered each person was by their reaction to the bird.

The boxer was stumbling around the room, desperately trying to catch the poor thing so he could return it to the safety of its home. Some, who were more awake and high-spirited than everyone else, were smiling, laughing and pointing at the ridiculousness of the situation. Then there were those who were so engrossed with their conversations and the music, they were unaware of what was going on. Others had crashed and were oblivious to everything. It was like a sketch from a comedy show.

Someone picked up a baseball bat and was gesturing as though they were going to swing for the bird, much to the amusement of one or two of those in the room – he *was* joking, I think. Thankfully, the bird was finally reunited with its perch as I certainly wouldn't have been OK with the baseball bat approach, and nobody else would have been either. For the record, no animals were hurt or injured at that party, although I am sure a few young partygoers woke up with severe hangovers the next day!

We had some mad times that I will never forget, just as I have never forgotten the people that I shared those experiences with. There are those who say that money is the root of all evil and it's hard to maintain friendships if you become wealthy. Let me put something on the table now, so it's out there.

DON'T MIX MONEY AND FRIENDSHIP

I have never claimed to be a leading philanthropist as of yet, but when my monies become more liquid, it's something I aspire to for sure. And I am not into pretending to be holier than thou and telling others they should use their wealth to save the world as that is a very personal matter. Genuine acts of charity are often the ones you don't get to hear about, and charitable people should never have to explain their decisions to anyone. I have tried to deal with wealth in a balanced and discreet way.

On the one hand, I believe in treating people sensitively and with respect. Most people are not looking for a saviour to wave a magic wand. They just need some support and encouragement, and maybe a safety net, while they figure out things for themselves. On the other hand, I have learnt that if someone asks for money directly, it is better to say 'no' and explain the reason why. If you value the friendship enough, it's simply not worth risking it for money, as a friendship is worth more. I've learnt the hard way that money can kill even the most solid relationships with friends and family. I must be doing something at least a little right because the vast majority of the hundred or so people I call my mates are the same ones I used to spend time with when I was younger and had nothing.

My oldest friends come from all walks of life, which I believe is a reflection of my natural tendency to be able to mix with anyone, whatever their background and culture. When it comes to running a successful company, people skills are of paramount importance. You have to adapt to the situation you are faced with. One minute, you could be talking to potential investors or the CEO of a company you are planning on doing the next deal with. Next, you could be dealing with an issue with your cleaning staff, and I mean no disrespect to cleaning staff – they were key in Myprotein, for example, as we manufactured food, and never once did we have any issues around food hygiene. I guess I am what some might call a social chameleon but certainly not fake or two-faced – two characteristics I dislike. I consider myself more adaptable and empathetic.

Playing wasn't only about partying. I had a serious passion (and still do) for electronic music, especially house and techno, and I was just as enthusiastic about creating it as I was about listening to it. The biggest name in the DJing world at that time was Technics. When dance music was starting to explode in the early nineties, the club standard turntable was the Technics SL-1210 MK2. The 1210 was state-of-the-art, but a pair of them and a mixer had a price tag to match – well over £1,000 or over £2,000 in today's money. That's a lot of cash for a teenager to find on his own, and it was certainly not something my parents could afford, not that I would ever have asked them to buy me anything as expensive as that anyway.

Determined to get my hands on my own set of 1210s, I took on extra work behind the bar at what was then known as the Nynex Arena (now called the Manchester Arena). At weekends, I also worked late into the nights in a kebab shop in Stockport city centre, which was no fun at all after pub and club kick-out time. It was a lot of graft, and it seemed to take forever, but after three months of incredibly hard work, I finally had enough money to get my hands on a brand-new, shiny pair of 1210s that I still own and use to this day!

Once I had my own decks, I was DJing as much as possible, at private parties with my mates and in any venue that gave me the chance. As I've said before, I always had the ability to enter the zone and hyper-focus on the things that I was genuinely interested in, and it was no different with music. If I had not pursued an entrepreneurial career, I believe I could just as easily have ended up as a professional producer and DJ.

JUST GO FOR IT

In 1998, when I was just eighteen years old, I spotted an opportunity to feature as a headline DJ at a major techno gig in Finland, and I was determined to grab it. In those days, the way to get a gig was to produce a 'mixtape', which I did by recording a live mix onto a cassette. I'd then duplicate the tape and send it to promoters in the UK and Europe. I might have told promoters in Europe that I was the resident DJ of a prestigious club in Manchester, as further encouragement to persuade them to hire me, but, as it happens, I didn't need to. This one promoter from Finland emailed me and told me he loved the mix I had sent him, and he offered me the opportunity to headline a gig he was managing. He paid for the flights, the hotel and all other expenses, and I got a fee of £500 on top, which I was absolutely delighted with; I would have done the gig for free! That was the first of many international techno gigs. Another important lesson – if you don't go for it, you will never know whether you could have got it.

Remember, fear is a liar. Thank you, Carl, for that pearl of wisdom. Don't let the fear of rejection stop you from doing the things you are meant to do. It would have been easy for me to doubt myself, given my high school results.

I have always had the capacity for working hard to achieve goals, but the best kind of work is the kind where you earn money doing something you already enjoy doing. DJing was definitely something I enjoyed doing, and I knew how to get paid for it. I have always embraced the 'work hard to play hard' philosophy, but, as you will find out in the following chapters, I developed a habit of making money by doing the things I loved to do. If you're not doing the things you love doing, it's not too late to start!

CHAPTER FIVE

A DEVELOPER IN THE MAKING

By the time I was sixteen, I didn't have much to show for the five years I had spent in high school, except for a decent character reference that said I was a good-natured, bright kid who had potential, a D in science and a U in IT. But I knew I had to do something with my life, so I enrolled with Stockport College to study computers. Given my exam results, they didn't expect much from me at college, so they put me in the lowest group.

After ten days, it was obvious I was not going to be learning anything I didn't know already, and I was bored out of my mind, so I went to my tutor and asked if I could be moved to the upper group. He flatly refused. I explained that I had already put a lot of time into teaching myself at home, and I pleaded with him to reconsider, but he still wouldn't move an inch. That left me with no choice but to leave, so I walked out of college and never looked back.

For the next six months, I had no sense of direction. Life was a blur of motocross, house music, club nights and the numerous jobs I did to keep me going. I was going nowhere, and I knew it. What I needed was something positive to pour my energy into – something that would ground me and give me the foundation to build a future. I just wasn't sure what I was looking for, until I discovered a new passion for . . .

WEIGHT TRAINING

An advertisement in the local newspaper caught my eye. A new gym called David Lloyd was opening in Cheadle. It looked really smart and spacious, had all the latest equipment, and they were offering a 50 per cent discount to the first five hundred members. Although I had been quite shy during my earlier years, all that had changed following my stint in work experience, and I can't say I lacked confidence in myself. Although I never thought of myself as particularly good-looking, I wasn't ugly either, and I was fit enough to look at. But at five foot nine (*and a half*) inches tall and around 10 stone (63.5 kg), I was certainly no Adonis. Going to the gym and training hard to bulk up would give my life more structure by providing goals that I could aim for, and it made me feel more like a man. It was empowering.

The gym ticked all the boxes that I'd thought it would, and, before long, I was training five nights a week and felt like a caged animal if I missed a single session. Training really felt like a matter of life or death, and if I missed a session, I would always make up for it by doing a bit more the next day or by adding a day on the weekend.

During those sessions, I focused on what I needed to do as part of my big-picture plan, and I gave that my full attention and dedication. Training was never far from my mind, I took it very seriously, and although I still liked to party on the weekend, I also paid careful attention to what I ate. I was spending a lot of time browsing through countless online forums, reading and absorbing tons of information on training and diet, so I understood how important nutrition was for stacking on muscle.

Signing up with David Lloyd proved to be a very worthy investment. Weight training is a rewarding pursuit because you can see progress as it happens. I was bulking up, gaining muscle definition, looking great and feeling positive about myself. But more than that, it had given me the focus and sense of direction I was looking for. I no longer felt like a dosser, and there was a renewed bounce in my stride. Had I not found the gym, I can honestly say I am not sure where I would have ended up or how my life would have unfolded. It gave me the step change in life that I needed. You could say I had become primed for success, and I believed in myself. It was time to keep my eyes open for a new opportunity so I could realise my potential.

A NEW JOB AT PANTEK

That opportunity turned out to be an apprenticeship with a company called Pantek, which specialises in software development. Pantek is still around today but has since rebranded to Solutions PT. I saw their advertisement in the front window of a careers shop that used to be situated near the old Grand Central shopping complex in Stockport. It was only a few doors away from the kebab shop I was working in. They were offering a modern apprenticeship that combined hands-on experience in a working environment with college-based learning and development in computing and software development. At the end, you got a National Vocational Qualification (NVQ), which was the equivalent to a college qualification but more practically geared towards the working environment.

Computers had always fascinated me, and software development and programming meant something to me because of my love of gaming. As I have mentioned before, my old neighbour and good friend, David, had been a keen and very talented programmer. Although he hadn't taught me much about software development, seeing what he was capable of had given me an appreciation for the discipline. I already knew how to strip down, rebuild, upcycle and even build computers from scratch. An apprenticeship with Pantek was exactly the kind of next step I was looking for.

There was only one problem: Pantek's application criteria. They were only considering applications from people who had achieved a minimum number of GCSEs at grade C or above and these had to include Maths, English and a science subject. With my grades, they weren't even going to look at my application form. It was frustrating because I was hungry for the opportunity and I knew I had the aptitude and the focus to succeed. There was no way I was going to allow a few bits of paper (or lack of them) to get in the way of me and the Pantek apprenticeship. I did the only thing I could do – I bent the truth about my GCSE results.

To be frank about it, I never expected to be called in for an interview. Even after they had spoken to me on the phone and invited me to their office, I was waiting for them to cancel. They had the contact details for my school. All they had to do was make a few enquiries, and I would have been found out.

Even as I made my way to the interview, I was trying to figure out how to explain away the fact that I didn't have any GCSE certificates to show them. Can you imagine how things would have turned out if they had spoken to me about GCSE maths during the interview? They never did. In fact, my results were never discussed.

During the interview, they asked me to talk about my hobbies and interests and to explain why I was keen to start an apprenticeship with them. They wanted to know what it was about software development that grabbed my attention, and they asked probing questions to find out what I knew already. The conversation very quickly started to feel like a friendly discussion between like minds, and I sensed that they were warming to me. I think they saw my genuine passion for computers, and knowing what I know now, I'd say it is vitally important to look for that when interviewing candidates. If I see someone's passion, it's a massive positive for me. You can teach many skills to a new member of the team, but you can't teach passion.

Around one week later, I received a phone call from the HR director and co-founder of Pantek, Mrs Bailey – the other co-founder was her husband, John. Mrs Bailey told me I had been accepted as an apprentice and asked me to look out for the relevant forms she had sent me in the post. She gave me a start date and congratulated me on being selected as a successful candidate. As I put down the handset, I experienced a surreal moment of mixed emotions – elation, excitement, pride and a feeling of accomplishment... blended with a subtle but very real sense that it could still all go wrong. Mrs Bailey was going to have to write to the school for a reference.

The issue of integrity is important to me. Yes, as a sixteen-year-old, I lied about my GCSE results in order to gain an apprenticeship. I hold my hands up, and you can judge me however you like for that. But I am no hypocrite, and I don't ask for one rule for me and a different one for everyone else. In my opinion – and as someone who built a global brand from scratch, I believe my opinion must count for something – it is wrong to elevate or dismiss individuals on the basis of their academic performance at such a young age.

Of course, we can't have doctors and accountants who are not suitably qualified running around misdiagnosing sick people and offering poor advice to businesses. I am not suggesting we throw away the idea of training and accreditation, but someone who is sixteen years of age is still at the start of life, and at that age, academic performance can be very misleading. There are a thousand and one reasons why someone who is extremely capable and multi-talented might not perform well in an academic environment. I am living proof of this, and as you will discover in later chapters, I looked for different indicators of potential when I built my team at Myprotein.

I am deeply grateful to Mr and Mrs Bailey for giving me the

opportunity to work at Pantek. It is one that served me well, and I hope I gave something back in return.

My school must have given me a great reference because everything ran like clockwork. I received the paperwork, signed my contract and started up with Pantek. Welcome to the real world, Oliver!

I had arrived, or so it felt as a wet-behind-the-ears young man walking into the offices of a high-tech company for the first time. My starting salary was £6,000 per annum or almost £15,000 in today's money – not bad at all for a sixteen-year-old – and I was getting a second bite of the education apple, supported by Pantek.

MAKING SENSE OF THE WORLD OF WORK

Initially, a lot of the conversations that took place around me went over my head, as I still had a lot to learn. It was almost like listening to people speaking in a foreign language with nothing but a dictionary and a few words of vocabulary to refer to. People rarely pronounce the words as you expect them to, they don't speak in the kind of perfect sentences you read in textbooks, and it all happens way too quickly.

At the same time, it was a pleasant working environment, and I was encouraged to learn at my own pace. As you can imagine, given that it was the 1990s, my hands-on learning and development included knowing how people liked their teas and coffees and where to file things, and one of the tasks I didn't look forward to was archiving. Pretty much everything was paper-based, so one of my regular tasks was to take the boxes of various papers downstairs into the basement. It was a real dungeon of a basement, with metal cages for storing all the archived paperwork – very dimly lit and full of dust. I spent many a day in there, organising and archiving the storage boxes properly. It's not something I can honestly say I enjoyed, but it was my responsibility, and I did it to the best of my ability. I concentrated on keeping my nose clean, having the right attitude, asking questions when the time was right and generally getting on with everyone.

These were my Hacienda years, so there were plenty of times when I came to work with a hangover or having not had much sleep, but my employers and colleagues were reasonable and flexible, and had realistic expectations as I was just sixteen and not commanding a C-level salary. I might not have been an A-star student, but I worked hard, listened to what others had to say and absorbed the working environment like a computer. I have a developer's mindset, so I appreciate systems and have an intuitive understanding of them.

My time with Pantek taught me valuable lessons. I came to understand the mechanics of how the business was run – I gained a big-picture perspective of how projects were dealt with and some of the processes involved. I also developed a solid grasp of how people work together and an understanding of office politics. I recognised which relationships worked and why they worked, and I also saw why some interactions were not effective and how these impacted on the workplace and on projects.

I have always been a people watcher. Figuring out how people tick uses a very similar set of skills to understanding how any program or system works. When you spend enough time watching and paying attention to details, you can identify strengths, weaknesses and triggers, and predict how people will behave.

The stuff that I learnt about operations and the social mechanics of how people worked together at Pantek proved to be invaluable later, when I set up and grew my own business. From a technical perspective, the apprenticeship provided me with a set of tools and a solid foundation, and I was able to use my own initiative and branch out and explore the specific avenues that particularly interested me.

While I was gaining valuable experience in the workplace, I was also going to Stockport College on a day release basis to study a Level 3 NVQ in Network Computer Operations initially and later a BTEC in Software Creation. Pantek provided their own training courses as well, such as the one they ran on InTouch Windows-based SCADA software, which related to control engineering.

The stuff I did at college and at Pantek wasn't exciting. A lot of my work involved getting different systems to talk to each other. While it didn't really capture my imagination, it was challenging enough, and it gave me a framework to work with. They introduced me to integrated development environments (IDEs), which are useful software applications used by computer programmers for software development. An IDE provides the developer with a comprehensive suite of tools for carrying out development work – a source code editor, build automation tools and a debugger, at the very least, but often other tools on top.

A PASSION FOR WEB DEVELOPMENT AND MY NEW BEST FRIEND – COLDFUSION

Once someone at work – a nice guy called Andrew, who was a real nerd and a superb programmer – had told me about the World Wide Web and I discovered websites, I was hungry to know more. That quest led me to several books, starting with one of the *Web Development Made Easy* kind of publications, although I can't remember the exact name. My reading evolved from simple books to more specialised ones that gave me detailed information about specific topics. Then I discovered the IRC chat rooms, and the fun really started.

Developers use different programming languages to build websites, depending on what they are looking for in terms of performance – a powerful yet cumbersome and not very user-friendly language; a really simple, high-level language that makes life easy but doesn't give the developer as much scope; or something in between.

I tried quite a few, including Perl, PHP and even Java. However, the language I kept coming back to was ColdFusion by Macromedia, which was later acquired by Adobe. I liked it because of its rapid development capability. It is an efficient language that is relatively simple to use and allows the developer to build a site much more quickly than, say, Java. You can add the functions you want by selecting the right building blocks of code and bolting them together – almost like putting together a prefabricated house instead of building one brick by brick. I am oversimplifying it, but it was easy to use compared to other programming languages, yet hard to master.

Purists turn their noses up at ColdFusion in many ways, preferring to use a 'cooler' language, but I am a pragmatist. Why spend time reinventing the wheel? Where do you draw the line? I loved upcycling computers, but I wasn't interested in building the processors. ColdFusion ticked all the boxes for me. It was a means to an end. Like any programming language, it took some time and effort to learn, but that was time well spent because it cut out a lot of the laborious donkey work that used to go hand in hand with programming in Java back then.

ColdFusion became my go-to language, later, when I started working as a freelance developer. I became an expert in ColdFusion, earning the title of a Macromedia accredited Certified Expert Developer. What is that well-known phrase – that with ten thousand hours of practice, most people can become an expert in almost any discipline? Well, I spent well over ten thousand hours coding in ColdFusion during my career as a developer. As well as working for others, I must have put tens, if not hundreds, of hours of my own time into building the first version of the Myprotein website, which I built from scratch and then maintained until 2009 when we moved to a different web solution. By then, the site was handling thousands of orders a day, so it certainly passed the test of time!

My knowledge of ColdFusion played a pivotal role not only in keeping me out of jail after my cable cubes misadventure but also by placing me ahead of the curve when it came to e-commerce. With the dawn of the new millennium, the world had entered a new digital age, and the way people were sourcing, selecting and buying products was changing at an astonishing rate. Whether the consumer wanted to buy a book or a ticket to the theatre, a revolution in buyer behaviour was taking place, and as an expert web developer, I was perfectly placed to exploit it.

By the age of twenty-two, I knew I wasn't going to succeed in life by selling grey imports or dodgy cable cubes, but I already knew how to build websites that worked and how to sell things online. All I needed to find was the right product.

CHAPTER SIX

UNDERSTANDING THE WORKING ENVIRONMENT

The apprenticeship at Pantek kick-started my career as a developer, which came in extremely useful later for building the Myprotein website and understanding how to maximise online potential. I was given a fantastic opportunity to learn and develop, and there is no doubt that it marked an important turning point for me.

Even on the first day, as a sixteen-year-old fresh out of school, I felt a hundred times more comfortable in the working environment than I had ever felt in school. It was much better suited to my way of learning than school had been. But I picked up more than technical skills during my time at Pantek. I learnt a lot about people, how they operate and how they interact with each other in the workplace. If you intend to grow a business that is bigger than you, you'd better take an interest in people because the people you hire will make or break your organisation.

When I joined Pantek, it was still a relatively small company with between fifty and sixty employees, so I didn't feel overwhelmed by the experience. Anyway, I was on the bottom rung as the newbie apprentice, so there was no real pressure placed upon me. My status could only improve. That said, whenever I passed any of the directors in the corridor, I'd feel a little embarrassed – humbled may be a better way of putting it – as they had far more knowledge and experience than I did, and they were at the top of the tree while I was just starting out.

People are just people. If you are at the beginning of your career, be mindful of that. Nobody is better or worse than you. They may be more technically skilled than you or have a more senior role, but once you find your path, there is no reason why you can't excel. And if you are the person at the top of the tree, try to be aware of how your employees might feel around you. At the end of the day, if they are too shy to speak out or they consider you to be some kind of deity just because you are the CEO, you are not going to benefit fully from what they can offer. Their potential will be stifled. The onus is on you to provide an environment where people can thrive for everyone's benefit. You can learn something from everyone, regardless of their rank or standing in life. Never forget that. We have two ears and one mouth for a reason.

For anybody entering the Myprotein offices, it would not have been easy for them to identify me as the boss. I never wore suits unless I had to attend an important external meeting. Most of the time, I wore smart casual clothing. This is what felt comfortable for me, and that's what's most important, I believe. It was the same for my whole team. They could wear what they wanted (within reason). Some of my directors felt comfortable in a suit. Other staff wore jeans and a T-shirt. I was very relaxed about dress code, which wasn't very commonplace in the mid-2000s.

I didn't make myself stand out with the most expensive shoes or a massive Rolex watch, and I came to work in a nearly new but everyday car. If you want to bring out the best performance from your team, leave the Ferrari and the Armani suits at home... at least until you have sold the business and moved on. On that note, any feeling of inferiority I experienced while at Pantek was down to me and me alone. The directors were down to earth. They were lovely people.

OFFICE POLITICS

Office politics is a fact of life in any commercial team environment. As long as the dynamics are not unhealthy, it is not necessarily a bad thing – just one of the consequences of bringing together intelligent, driven and competitive people into an environment where there are opportunities for people to thrive. Some organisations try to remove any sense of hierarchy, but this is usually an illusion. An admin person, as vital as they are to your business, is not going to get paid as much as, say, your top-performing salesperson or your marketing guru.

I'd say the environment at Pantek was a very healthy one, and I witnessed very little of what you might call back-stabbing. If it did go on, it was never aimed at me, but then again, I was only an apprentice. One of the things that struck me most about the people at Pantek, and other organisations I worked at later, was their different personality types. It is almost as though people run on different operating systems. One person might run on Apple's iOS system, whereas another might be running on Android. Where humans differ from machines is that we can compromise and change how we operate to fit a situation. Those who can do this well will always perform better within teams and know how to run a successful team.

Communication is a key skill – not only in terms of the language we use, but how we deliver it, when we deliver it and to whom. We must be flexible, and we must appreciate the operating system we are dealing with. There was an interesting range of operating systems running within Pantek.

Pantek's office comprised three floors. The most senior people were based on the top floor; the first floor was mainly for the accounts department, if my memory serves me well; and the ground floor, where I was, was the company's engine room. The development teams, admin staff and salespeople all worked on the ground floor. But the office also had a basement where the archives were kept.

One of the people I got to know on the ground floor was a guy called Steve, who was the manager of the support team. 'Ste', as most people called him, was around five years older than me and already established within the company, so he was someone I could learn from. He knew the ropes and was clearly quite career-focused. This was where he was meant to be in life, and he had a plan.

Ste and I got on very well, partly because we had similar interests. We both loved house music, and whereas I was only just getting into DJing, he had been doing it for years. I wasn't as career-orientated as Ste. Sure, I had really wanted to win my place on the apprenticeship scheme, and I was happy to be there, but this was my first proper job, and I was still so young. Had it not been for our passion for DJing and house, it's impossible to know whether we would have gelled in the same way.

Ste was always very patient with me, and he had a very gentle way of letting me know if I was distracting him from his work, which I quickly learnt to pick up on. Developers, on the other hand, could be a totally different ball game. I am not sure of the exact quote, but it's been said that it can take up to twenty-five minutes for a developer to become re-immersed into a task and back up to speed following an interruption. It's not surprising, therefore, that some developers can be quite prickly if disturbed!

The development team had its fair share of geeky characters, each with their own quirks and areas of expertise. Developers will often approach each other to ask for help and guidance with specific problems. Remember how I mentioned that ColdFusion allowed the developer to configure preprogrammed chunks of code to perform larger, more complex functions? Development teams often operate in a similar way. You could be stuck on one aspect of a project, but someone else might have already done that work. They would be able to tell you how to do it or even send you the code to fit into your own work. It would depend on what programming language you were using. Everyone bounced ideas off everyone else.

It wasn't all work and no play. Software developers have their own sense of adventure and their sense of humour can be a little off the wall. Overall, I'd say the atmosphere was pretty laid-back and friendly. My friend Natalka ended up working there as well. After leaving school, she'd been eagerly looking for work and ended up landing two job offers at the same time. It turned out that one of those vacancies was at Pantek. Natalka had no idea where I worked. Had she not told me about her job offers, she might never have ended up working with me, but I am glad she did.

I can't remember exactly how it came about, but I created a program that meant something would go running across Natalka's screen when she clicked the help button. She thought it was so hilarious, she persuaded me to roll it out to everyone else's computers, and I couldn't resist. Everyone loved it.

Another developer I've never forgotten – this was twenty-four years ago, remember – was one of the firm's elder statesmen who had been with the company since the day it opened. His name was John, and he was quite a shy and introverted man. Given his experience, he carried a lot of weight within the organisation, so you would only approach him if nobody else could help. Someone like John was never going to be rude to you if you asked him to help with a conundrum, but it had better be a good one. He had bigger fish to fry. That said, it was obvious when John was in the zone. You'd have to be half asleep not to see he was in 'do not disturb' mode, but when he came up for air, he was very approachable.

Not everyone was as polite or easy-going as John and Ste. There was a developer called Andy, who was one of the younger members of the team, and he was a bright spark with a passion for *Star Trek*. Andy was more outgoing than most developers, but if you needed to speak to him, you had to pick your time carefully. Don't get me wrong. Andy was a good guy – they all were – but like many highly intelligent and creative types, he had a volatile temperament. When something wasn't working as expected, let's just say he was very vocal in his outbursts towards his screen, and the whole floor would know exactly what he was thinking!

When you are seeing the same people day in, day out, and if you keep your eyes and ears open, you should be able to get a feel for how they operate quite easily. Some people are better at this important life skill than others. For those who aren't so good at it, you can't beat getting your head bitten off to learn when the best time is to approach someone.

Having started out as a shy individual and having grown up as an only child, I'd say my ability to tune into an environment and assess the dynamics was quite sharp. People-watching comes naturally to me. In fact, I appreciate differences in people, and I especially enjoy seeing how people react or respond to situations. The world would be a boring place if we were all the same, wouldn't it? Getting to know the various characters at Pantek wasn't overly challenging. I came to work, did what I had to do, learnt as much as I could from the experience and stayed out of trouble, so I never really got on the wrong side of anyone.

GOING SOLO

Once my apprenticeship had been completed, I left Pantek to work for myself as an independent web development contractor. From a working-with-people perspective, this was a completely different kettle of fish than being employed full-time by a software company.

As a contractor, you must be seen but not heard. You're expected to hit the ground running – in and out as swiftly as possible – causing the minimum disruption to the people who work there full-time. The people around you are not your teammates. They are your clients, and you are their guest. You can be friendly, but you must not become a distraction. It's best to keep your mouth shut, put your head down and concentrate on the job in hand. You are absolutely dropped in at the deep end, but the remuneration makes up for the pressure.

There's more heat on you from a technical perspective as well. You are hired to achieve a specific objective, and it is on you to accomplish the mission or give a solid account as to why the job can't be done. You are your own boss. And again, when you go to a site to solve an IT issue, you need to be mindful that you are not surrounded by your friends and colleagues. They need the problem to be solved urgently, and it's on you.

Being a contractor gave me the lifestyle that I wanted. I had the freedom to work my socks off for a while to bring the money in, and then take a sabbatical and live a little. That was one of the reasons I was able to take a trip to Australia with Gary. And I would have stayed in Australia a lot longer had I not been called back to the UK to face the music for my cable cube shenanigans.

I have always loved travel, and contracting meant I got to work in different parts of the country. For example, I remember being seconded to an office in Kendal, Cumbria, for three weeks. Not far from Windermere, it is a beautiful place to retreat to for mental space and solitary reflection. The countryside there reminded me of the Pennines. I was also sent out to a motorcycle insurance company down in Bristol. Contracting took me all over the place.

Although being self-employed gave me freedom and a sense of control in my life, there was one major flaw. I was twenty-three years old and wanted a house of my own, but in order to get a mortgage, I was going to have to show a lender that I was a solid bet. Life as a contractor had been fun, but I had to get a full-time job. I seized the chance to enjoy a little more sunshine and partying with a summer job, putting up posters in Ibiza – five months of absolute fun. That was my swansong – I like to think of it as my 'gap year' – before having to return home, knuckle down and focus on getting a mortgage.

A MEANS TO AN END

In 2002, I got a full-time job with 3T Productions, another software house, which specialised in web development for educational institutions and other public sector organisations. I was drafted in as a ColdFusion programmer, working as part of a team with five other developers – another diverse bunch of very interesting geeks.

We had a solid team leader called Ian – a Norwich City FC fan – who I enjoyed working for. Ian knew how to steer me in the right direction. He had a special kind of eye for understanding the bigger picture and was good at coordinating the team so we were all moving towards the same goal. Had I wanted to progress within the company, which I didn't, I am sure he would have supported me in that pursuit as well.

For me, working at 3T was a means to an end. I was not interested in working for a software company for the rest of my days, and I had no desire for a promotion. I just needed to be able to show the bank that I was capable of earning a steady income for long enough for them to give me a mortgage. Once that goal had been achieved, I would be out of there. That said, I did enjoy working at 3T, as I was being paid to do something that I was naturally good at and liked doing anyway.

One of my good friends there was a helpful developer called Jig, who had come over from India to work for the firm. Jig was a solutions person and a great person to discuss projects with. He was always happy to help and would give his time freely and generously. If he encountered an issue that was puzzling him, he'd take it home with him, research it online and move mountains to solve it. His approach was always very methodical, so he would know exactly what he needed to research to get past the obstacle. Even if it took him a while, he'd deliver. I don't know what he is doing now, but I am sure he must have gone very far in his career. He was a star performer.

I got to witness the more Machiavellian side to people at 3T. I got on well with the people on my team. We were easy-going, hard-working and passionate about coding and problem-solving. They also had a great bunch of personalities in the testing department – a friendly team of people who always seemed to be laughing and joking. However, it wasn't all sweetness and light. There were some individuals within the company who were more self-centred, and their focus was on how quickly they could progress to more senior positions.

The empire builders weren't interested in me and kept out of my business because it was obvious that I was not competing with them. My goal was to work to the best of my ability – why else would you spend time on anything – to learn more and sharpen my craft as a developer, and to tick those boxes for the mortgage lender. And again, I had the perception and the social skills to sidestep the politics, avoiding the worst culprits, so as not to be pulled into whatever scheme they were hatching to further their career, and disarming others by making it clear I was not playing the same game. I pulled my weight, and I didn't leave at 5.30 p.m. on the dot, but I'd rarely stay behind for more than an hour. After a year of working for 3T, I had my mortgage and my own two-up two-down house on Bilson Drive in Edgeley, Stockport.

Office politics can be toxic, but you don't have to be a part of it. If you have learnt anything from this chapter, I hope you have realised the importance of understanding people. I have a fascination for people, and later you will see how my passion for understanding others played a major part in helping me build a global brand.

CHAPTER SEVEN

MY EUREKA MOMENT

3T Productions was never going to be a part of my long-term future. I used to go to work, do what I needed to do and go home. I knew in my heart that I was destined for greater things, but at that time, I needed the fixed income so I could step onto the first rung of the housing market ladder and get my first mortgage. The firm was happy with my work, and I am sure I could have carried on working there, but, with hindsight, I know I wasn't giving it everything and was unlikely to progress there.

The people who progressed most quickly in my own company, Myprotein, were the ones who went the extra mile. They were typically the first in and the last to leave. Success is a team effort. Taking anyone on is a key investment when building a successful business. Hiring the right people is a great investment because they are the ones who will reciprocate – the ones who will go above and beyond to ensure your business is successful because they see your company's future as an important part of their future. It's a partnership.

I wasn't a clock-watcher, but I was no star employee, and I was definitely not an 'empire builder'. Everything about my job at 3T Productions was a matter of convenience, right down to where it was – a three-minute walk from where I was living, at Mum's two-up two-down terraced house. We lived on Stockport Road, one of the main roads that funnelled traffic coming into

Stockport from the outlying suburbs of Greater Manchester and Cheshire. Even if I stayed on at work for an extra hour or so, which I did sometimes, I'd still be back at Mum's long before most of my colleagues had reached their homes. Mum moved out of the house to live with her partner when I was around nineteen, so I used to have the place to myself. I'd have a quick bite to eat, relax for a bit to allow that to settle, and then it was time for me to indulge in what was fast becoming an obsession of mine – bodybuilding.

AN OBSESSION WITH BODYBUILDING

I might never have got into bodybuilding had it not been for David Lloyd opening a new gym in Cheadle. Although the David Lloyd brand had been around for ten years by that time, gym culture was not as big a thing as it is today, and I had never heard of them. David Lloyd is on the high end of the market, but when I first entered their Cheadle premises, I had no expectations. I'd never been to a gym in my life.

The new gym was part of an entertainment complex, with a few bars and eating establishments, including a TGI Fridays. The first thing that struck me was the clean, fresh and spacious feel of the place. Everything about it was state-of-the-art. The ceiling was very high, and the lighting was just right, creating the perfect bright and airy ambience. The air conditioning was fine-tuned to ensure that even though there was not the slightest whiff of a sweaty body, there were no cold draughts either. The temperature was perfect.

People were running, rowing, cycling and cross-training all around me, and as I explored my surroundings, I discovered every kind of gym equipment imaginable. David Lloyd had left no stone unturned in their mission to cater for their clients' needs, and my mind was blown by the range of contraptions available for working out every muscle you can think of. They had an indoor swimming pool and an outdoor one, and I used to enjoy swimming a few times a week to wind down after a workout. It often seemed a bit too chilly for me to consider the outdoor pool though.

Most of the machines used a pulley system to allow you to pull or push weight without the risk of injury, and they were configured to allow you to specifically target the area you were interested in strengthening. Other machines were designed to offer support while doing natural bodyweight exercises such as pull-ups or dips. But the part of the gym that really captured my imagination was where all the biggest, hairiest and scariest-looking individuals were grunting and seriously going for it – the free-weights area. If I'd had any kind of previous conception of what a gym was like, this was it. The people training there seemed to be the most focused, serious-minded individuals, and I wanted what they had. I knew I had come to the right place. This was going to become a kind of home from home, a place where I could retreat, gather my thoughts and reset my mind. Bodybuilding was something I could channel my energy into and provided me with the perfect mechanism for introducing discipline and focus into my life.

Bodybuilding became an all-consuming passion of mine. It involved far more than turning up at the gym, although that became an almost religious obligation. If I missed a session, I would feel uncomfortable and tormented until I was able to put the situation right by getting an extra session in at the weekend or training twice as hard next time round.

I was reading numerous bodybuilding magazines and sourcing as much information as possible from the internet in my quest for knowledge. Bodybuilding wasn't just a hobby to me. It was a way of life. Looking back on things now, I can see how my obsession with bodybuilding was just another manifestation of the same traits that helped me to succeed in business. There is no doubt that I have an obsessive personality, but while obsession is by its very nature an urge to dive deeper and deeper into something, I was always able to rein it in. If you are going to be obsessed about anything, be obsessed about something that will serve you well. And if you can't do that, figure out a way of making use of your obsession in a constructive way.

When I started bodybuilding, I was only around 10 stone, and I didn't have a spare ounce of meat on my five-foot-nine frame. I followed a simple, five-session weekly regime. Monday was chest, Tuesday was back, Wednesday was arms, Thursday was legs and Friday was for shoulders. I must have been around sixteen or seventeen years old when I first set foot in David Lloyd. By the time I was twenty-two, I had bulked up to around 13.5 stone of mostly pure muscle. I was stacked. My love of bodybuilding had to be balanced with my equally powerful love of partying, and I wouldn't change a thing – I could do both. Gym was for the working week. Partying for the weekend. Had I not had the partying to balance things out, I think I would have been huge. As it happened, doing what I wanted at the weekend took the edge off things and affected muscle gain.

Bodybuilding is an individualist's sport, but that doesn't mean you have to train in isolation or that you don't collaborate with others. I made a lot of friends in the free-weight area of the gym, and we used to have a good laugh together in between sets of reps. We'd spot for each other, and that built trust. For those who don't know, spotting is acting as the fallback position when someone is pressing or squatting with a large weight. They need to know you will be there to save them if their muscles give in. They are counting on you to stop them getting hurt. Weight trainers tend to have a lot of respect for each other because they are sharing the same journey.

As well as building a lot of body mass, I also significantly increased my strength and power. I was able to squat and deadlift double my own bodyweight and could easily press 100 kilograms for reps. If there is one thing I regret now, it's that I didn't spend enough time working my core and stretching. My bodybuilding days took their toll on my body, and I started suffering the consequences later in life with lower back problems and other joint issues. A knock to my shoulder when I was running didn't help. That left me with a damaged acromioclavicular (AC) joint. It wasn't the right kind of running either. I was on a night out, drinking. It showed me that I wasn't indestructible.

It is easy to get hooked on the gym. In my case, I needed something to keep me mentally focused, and it definitely delivered in that respect. Had I not been into my Friday and Saturday night partying, I probably would have taken bodybuilding even more seriously and perhaps even competed, but I enjoyed the balance. I still loved to go out on the weekend, which obviously hugely affected my gains. Bodybuilding was a way of life for me during the week. The weekends were for letting my hair down. But the gym was making me feel fantastic as well. Whatever your fix – cardio, gymnastic pursuits, weight training or something else – you can't beat the gym for de-stressing, and the kick of endorphins can become almost addictive. I got my kicks from doing low reps with very heavy weights, and that's something else I am paying the price for now.

Whatever anyone says about the way I trained, whether I should have stretched more, done more reps with lighter weights or spent more time on core work and stretching, one thing I know I got right was the nutritional aspect. It's a cliché, but it does the job – if you want to get the most out of a sports car, you have to fill the tank with the best fuel and lubricate the engine with the right oil, and our bodies are no different. We need all the macronutrients, as well as key vitamins and minerals, to stay well and run efficiently.

A THIRST FOR KNOWLEDGE

I was living in online forums, my favourite being MuscleTalk, and finding out everything I could about diet and nutrition. In a way, I became my own personal fitness instructor, discovering for myself how to train the body, feed the body and build the body quickly and efficiently. There are many aspects to nutrition, but one of the most important considerations for a bodybuilder is to ensure they have the necessary material for building muscle. Most of what you need, you can get from eating the right foods, but nutritional supplements are also a massive help.

The human body uses around twenty different amino acids to make the right proteins for muscle development. Creatine monohydrate, which is usually just referred to as creatine, is an excellent source of two of these: arginine and methionine. It is used to improve performance, boost energy and increase muscle mass while reducing the risk of injury during intense training sessions.

Branched-chain amino acids (BCAAs) are made from three amino acids: leucine, isoleucine, and valine. BCAAs are found in foods that are rich in protein such as meat, eggs, and dairy products. As part of a healthy diet, and in conjunction with other essential amino acids, BCAAs can improve muscle protein synthesis – which is a huge help for bodybuilding. They also help to reduce muscle soreness, especially when taken before a workout, and can lessen the effects of muscle fatigue.

There's only one way for humans to get BCAAs, and that's from eating the right foods, whereas we can produce our own creatine. However, creatine is widely considered as the king when it comes to muscle building, so it is no wonder that it is the most popular and studied nutritional supplement.

Creatine and BCAAs are excellent nutrients, and anyone who is serious about building bulk should be giving careful consideration to what they eat to support their training. However, in order to ingest the maximum amount of creatine and BCAAs to really build mass, you'd have to be eating an unrealistically enormous amount of food. And this is where nutritional supplements come in extremely useful.

As I became more knowledgeable about nutrition, it was only a matter of time before I'd be drawn towards supplements. There is only so much meat and dairy you can eat before the disadvantages start outweighing the benefits. You'd spend half your life eating or trying to digest what you'd eaten, and then there's the cost – high-quality sources of protein don't come cheap.

I'd been using supplements for around two years and I was seeing the benefits, but they were expensive. One of my staple supplements was a whey protein shake produced by what was then the leading sports nutrition brand in the UK, Maximuscle. (I used to get on very well with the founder of Maximuscle, Zef Eisenberg. Unfortunately, he lost his life last year while attempting to break a British land speed record. He will be sorely missed by many. RIP, Zef.) The shake would ease soreness, aid recovery, and most importantly, promote the creation of muscle mass via protein synthesis. Whenever I'd consider using a supplement, I'd read the blurb and study the nutritional values table to find out the benefits and assess its value versus its cost – effectively carrying out a crude cost-benefit analysis.

AND A HEALTHY CURIOSITY

It was a Thursday night, and if ever there was a time when I needed to increase my protein intake, this was it. Thursdays were for legs, and it'd been a heavy session. As I sat there in my mum's kitchen, drinking my pre-bed shake, I had the urge to find out what was in it. I was curious. What was the powder made from? I picked up the tub and read the ingredients, which were surprisingly simple: whey protein, flavourings, colourings and sweeteners, among a few other non-essential ingredients such as thickeners and anti-caking agents. Simple . . . except for one thing.

What the hell is whey protein anyway? I wondered. It was time to do a little Google searching.

Remember 'Little Miss Muffet', the old nursery rhyme? She was the one who was 'sat on a tuffet, eating her curds and whey'. At least she was until she got scared away by a spider ('who sat down beside her'). That nursery rhyme dates back to the very early 1800s, so imagine how many children must have heard it, but if they were anything like me, they probably never knew or asked what curds and whey are.

When rennet and certain bacterial cultures are added to pasteurised milk, the milk starts to go sour and clot. The clots are known as curds, and these are used to make cheese. The by-product of the cheese-making process, the liquid that remains once the curds have formed, is called whey, and this is full of protein.

Whey contains the complete set of amino acids and is especially rich in leucine, isoleucine and valine. In other words, whey contains many BCAAs, and it contains a healthy amount of calcium, magnesium and phosphorus, which are essential nutrients. It's also the most bioavailable form of protein, which means it is fully absorbed and utilised by the human body. What's not to love?

I'd made an important discovery and one that would alter the course of my life significantly. The powder that had been costing me a fortune was something that many dairies were still throwing away. I was determined to get my own raw whey and make my own protein powder.

This was my eureka moment.

CHAPTER EIGHT

A PRODUCT IN THE MAKING

It was 2003, I was twenty-three years old, and having been working for 3T Productions for around twelve months, I was about to put a deposit down on my first home on Bilson Drive in Edgeley, Stockport. I'd shown the banks that I had a fixed income and worked damned hard to save for the deposit. But, as I've mentioned before, everything I'd been doing was a means to an end. I felt sure I was here to do something bigger with my life than spend it as a developer in someone else's company. Don't forget the letter I'd written as an eight-year-old, stating how I wanted to be a boss and create jobs for people. It was a deep-rooted ambition of mine – maybe even hardwired into me.

Over the previous three years or so, I'd established myself as a pretty solid ColdFusion developer, and I had the skills and experience to build cutting-edge websites that were perfect for the new digital age of e-commerce. I knew how to build functional sites that were highly effective for selling online, but there was a missing piece in the jigsaw. I had not decided upon a product.

One of my main passions outside of work was the gym. Having discovered that the protein shakes I'd been paying through the nose for were actually made from something dairies would otherwise throw away – whey, a by-product of the cheese-making process – I sensed I might have found what I needed.

Whey is put through a process called microfiltration, which

removes fats and carbohydrates, and you end up with a very high-protein liquid – whey protein concentrate (WPC). The protein concentration can vary. The lower the protein concentration, the higher the lactose (milk sugar) level. The standard for nutritional products tends to be 80 per cent protein, but for people with lactose intolerance, a 90 per cent whey protein isolate (WPI) is better.

You might be surprised to know that for every kilogram of cheese produced, the dairy ends up with another 9 kilograms of whey. All that waste for such a small amount of cheese! They have to do something with it.

A penny had dropped. With dairies producing so much of this stuff, it was highly unlikely they were charging a high price for it. Protein powder shakes were not as much of a thing as they are today although raw whey powder was also being used by manufacturers of formula milk for babies. Either way, I sensed that I'd probably been paying well over the odds for protein shake mix. There was only one way to find out. It was time to make some calls.

STRIVING FOR TAKE-OFF

Even from the first phone call, it was clear that my gut feeling had been correct. Raw whey protein powder was easy to source and relatively inexpensive. On average, dairies were charging approximately £3 per kilogram. I'd been paying £30 for a '1 kilogram' tub of protein powder, which was actually only 2 lb – 907 g to be precise – and that included the flavourings, sweeteners, thickeners and other non-essential ingredients. Massive margin.

Dairies were selling the raw material whey protein powder in 20 kg two-ply sacks, which had a branded outer skin of paper and a waterproof lining on the inside. All I had to do was buy a couple of sacks, mix the powder with colouring, sweeteners and some flavouring and I would have a product. *Easy* ... or so it seemed. There was just one problem.

You couldn't buy just a few sacks. Dairies had tons of this powder to sell, and they wanted to get shot of it quickly, so they were selling it by the pallet load. There were thirty sacks to a pallet, or 600 kg in weight. Dairies were not prepared to break into a pallet because this would leave them with odd amounts to get rid of. As far as they were concerned, if someone was serious about business, they'd buy a pallet. I was extremely serious, but I didn't have £1,800.

If they could sell me a sack at £60, or even a few, I was sure I would be back for more. I had sourced the other ingredients, and with all things considered, I had calculated that I could produce an off-the-shelf protein powder blend for around £5 per kilogram. Even with a sale price of £10 per kilogram, I'd be able to double my money, and, at the time, as it was a food product, it was zero rated for VAT purposes. But the dairies I spoke to were having none of it. Buy a pallet or go away – they were the only two options. I was going to have to talk to my bank and see if they could lend me the money to start up.

I used to bank with HSBC, so I made an appointment to see one of their business managers in the hope that they might give me a £5,000 start-up loan. After a brief meeting, which lasted around thirty minutes, they flatly refused my application, and I was stunned. The UK's sports nutrition market was already worth tens of millions of pounds and growing steadily. I'd broken down the production process and clearly demonstrated that I had a business idea that was profitable. All I needed was the cash to get it going. Why couldn't they show just a little faith?

To this day, I will never understand why they turned me down, but it is their loss, not mine. They missed out because I immediately closed my account with HSBC. I'm not one to cut my nose to spite my face – and closing the account was inconvenient

– but I made an exception to the rule as there were plenty of other viable banking options. There was no way I would ever use HSBC again, and I haven't since.

As I also had an account with NatWest, I gave them a call to see if they might look at my application more favourably. Unfortunately, they also refused to give me a loan. Most businesses fail within the first year, and this is often because the demand is not there for their product and they run out of money. In my case, being well under the age of thirty was also a significant factor, but, on top of that, NatWest were not convinced that I was going to be able to break into the market, despite my product selling at a much lower retail price than every other brand already out there.

Even though NatWest wouldn't give me the money I wanted, they offered to extend my overdraft from around £150 to £500. It was something, and I was grateful, but I wasn't sure how such a small overdraft was going to benefit me. Even if I used the entire £500 in one go, I would still be £1,300 short of the cost of a single pallet of whey powder.

It felt like checkmate. Every dairy I had spoken to had insisted that I had to buy whey powder by the pallet load. The two banks that I banked with had refused to give me a business loan, so it was highly unlikely I was going to get a loan from anyone else. Banks make decisions based on a tick-box exercise and, unfortunately for me, I wasn't ticking the right boxes. But I didn't want to throw in the towel. The banks were not going to budge, so I was going to have to go back to the dairies.

Again, every dairy I called said the same thing – I had to buy a pallet. Even when I offered to pay much more per kilogram for a sack, they still refused. It just wasn't worth their while, they insisted. It created too much admin.

It felt as though I was banging my head against a brick wall. I'd made dozens of calls and was getting nowhere . . .

ANDY TO THE RESCUE!

Until I called a guy named Andy, late on a Tuesday afternoon. It must have been the tenth conversation I'd had that day, but this man said something I had not heard before.

'OK,' he said, and there was a bit of a pause, which felt like a minute but was probably just a few seconds. 'I can hear how determined you are to do this, but it takes more than enthusiasm to make a business work. Tell me how you are going to succeed. Why should I take a chance on you?'

It wasn't a 'yes', but it was an opening. Every other person I had spoken to had slammed the door shut and were only interested in explaining why they were not willing to open it. Andy was leaving the door open and asking me to explain why he should let me come in. My winning instinct came to the fore, and I could smell success. It was game on.

I knew exactly how I was going to sell protein powder. I'd be selling my products online, and I'd been working on a website to sell protein shakes ever since my eureka moment. Whatever you sell online, the logistics are mostly the same. In very broad terms, reach out and drive the right potential customers to your website, and when they land, make sure everything is designed to ensure they check out. You cater for their needs by offering choices. Make it easy for your ideal customers to buy from you. Convenience, quality, cost and choice. I'd already designed the wireframes for my website to ensure the conversion rate was as high as possible and make the customer journey a smooth one.

When I explained to Andy how I was going to reach my market and demonstrated my experience and expertise with e-commerce and online marketing, I sensed a shift in his attitude. I suspect he was a man who believed in giving people chances, but that in his heart he had expected me to confirm all the reasons why it was better to only sell to people who would buy in bulk. The result would be the same, but at least he'd know he had given me a fair hearing.

But I'd thought of almost everything, and I think he was genuinely surprised.

'Andy,' I said, 'sell me a sack, and I will be back in a couple of days to buy twice as much. You can bank on that. What do you think?'

Again, there was what seemed like a massive pause. I could almost hear his brain whirring on the end of the phone.

He let out a sigh, almost in resignation, as though he was not happy with the decision he had come to. It was almost a chuckle – at his own expense.

'You know what, Oliver?' he asked, rhetorically. 'I can tell you're determined to do this, and if I say no, I bet you will ring another hundred dairies. I will tell you something else. Every one of them will refuse. That's how it is. Why should anyone take a chance on you when they are already selling their quota to established companies?

'But I like you,' he continued. 'I have a good feeling about this, and you have a good vibe about you. I reckon you *will* come back in a couple of days to buy more.'

Another pause...

I tasted success and dived in for the sign-off.

'We have a deal?' I asked.

'You have to buy two sacks. I will sell them to you at the same pro rata price as a pallet, but if you are not back within a week to buy two more, I will never sell to you again. This isn't a favour. I am trusting you. Show me you can grow as quickly as you've said you will.'

And that was that. I had a deal, and I could hardly contain my excitement. *Stay cool, Oli*, I reminded myself. Self-control is important in business, and you have to show confidence. Had I not shown conviction and belief in myself, Andy would have become just another no-deal that Tuesday, and I'd probably be writing an entirely different book.

I will always be grateful to Andy for taking that chance on me. When I got to know more about him, I found out he was a Scout leader. It takes a special kind of person to inspire and develop young people.

Within a week, I had converted those two sacks of whey into sales and doubled my money. When I called Andy to place my next order, he told me he'd not had a shred of doubt that I'd be back within the week. 'You'd better get cracking and sell these quickly,' he added. 'I want you to buy a pallet by the end of the month.' This time, I could hear the laughter in his voice, and I knew I was going to be buying from Andy for many years to come.

CHAPTER NINE

BOOTSTRAPPED – DEBT-FREE WITHIN A WEEK

It had taken me just two days to convert the first two sacks of raw whey powder that I'd bought from Andy into sales. For every kilogram of WPC 80 (80 per cent concentrate) that I bought, I was making roughly £7 profit. The profit was slightly less if customers bought in bulk, but it was higher if they bought add-ons such as a scoop or flavourings, so £7 is an average figure.

The profits I made on those first two sacks were immediately reinvested into the business. By the end of the first week, which was the deadline Andy had given me to come back and buy another two sacks from him, I'd actually bought six or seven sacks. In fact, within seven days of launching the website, I was totally debt-free. Not only had I smashed the target that Andy and I had agreed, I had completely paid off my £500 overdraft. My business was bootstrapped from scratch.

Andy was the UK contact for a firm called Bacarel, which was based in Staffordshire. Bacarel was (and may still be) the exclusive UK distributor for Fonterra, which is a cooperative group representing over 10,000 dairy farmers in New Zealand. Whey protein wasn't the only protein I could buy from Bacarel, so I was able to offer a small range of different protein powders to my customers from the day Myprotein was launched. As well as whey protein concentrate (80 per cent), the others included milk protein concentrate, calcium caseinate and whey protein isolate (90 per cent).

Milk protein concentrate (MPC) takes longer to digest than whey protein, so it makes you feel full for longer and is ideal as a bedtime shake. It is an excellent source of protein that is effectively delivered in a drip-feed fashion due to slower absorption rates compared to whey protein, so in theory it helps to prevent your body going into a catabolic state during sleep. MPC has a less neutral taste and more body than whey protein as well, which some people prefer, and that is why it is often used as a key ingredient in smoothies.

Calcium caseinate is an extract of milk protein. As the name suggests, it contains calcium, so it is good for teeth and bones, but it is also extremely high in the amino acid glutamine, which makes it superb for muscle recovery. Here's a sample of what I said about calcium caseinate on the earliest Myprotein website:

Calcium Caseinate is a spray-dried dispersible milk protein, manufactured directly from fresh skimmed milk. The enhanced dispensability of this ingredient makes it extremely easy to mix and the flavour is less bland than other proteins due to the high amount of protein per gram.

Calcium Caseinate in more detail
Our Calcium Caseinate is high in calcium and low in sodium. It is easily dispersed in water and forms a stable colloidal suspension with high opacity.

It is extremely high in the amino acid glutamine, higher than both whey and soy isolate. Calcium Caseinate could also help other proteins become more digestible to [sic] *prolonging the time they spend in the intestinal tract.*

Calcium Caseinate is a great protein to supplement with right before bed or if one knows they will not be eating a high protein meal during the day as the protein synthesis will be notably slower than most other proteins. The recommended dosage for this effect is at least 30 grams of Calcium Caseinate in a serving. This will yield a high percentage of protein. Calcium Caseinate can be used to reach daily protein requirements easily.

This protein is also Halal certified.

Suggested use for Calcium Caseinate

Take between meals, 2 to 3 times a day.

Mix 3 heaped tablespoons (30g) of Calcium Caseinate with milk, water or fruit juice. For the best results mix with a screw topped mixer or a food blender.

Do you want to see the <u>amino acid profile</u> for Calcium Caseinate?

A few of the proteins were Halal-certified straight from the dairy, which was great as it gave me access to a wider range of consumers. It's worth noting no animals were killed for whey as it it was a veggie product; we just needed the milk! It was very important that I offered products for as many people as I could. That was always a key goal, and it was one that I delivered on as I grew the product range to include other religious requirements such as Kosher and, later on, products such as 'gluten-free' to deal with food intolerances.

A key mission of mine from the off was to offer the customer as much accurate information as possible and then let the consumer make an informed choice. This is demonstrated on the very first product pages, which included all the required nutritional details as well as the amino acid profile for each product.

One of the products we sold was guarana, which is extracted from the seeds of a South American plant that is naturally very high in caffeine. However, unlike coffee beans, it releases its caffeine content slowly. It is a natural stimulant, which makes it useful as an appetite suppressant and for providing a steady release of energy while training. Some even say it has aphrodisiac properties, but that was never something we highlighted as a selling point! It is said that Amazonian tribes have been using guarana for centuries to keep them alert when hunting.

I was also selling HMB (beta-hydroxy beta-methylbutyrate), which helps to reduce the breakdown of muscle and promote muscle gain. In other words, it is used by bodybuilders and other athletes to help maintain the structure they have built and to keep their muscles strong and healthy.

Ask anyone who has either blended or packed protein powders, and they will confirm that if you spend any amount of time in that environment, you end up covered in the stuff. It gets into your hair, your clothes and literally into the pores of your skin, so you end up smelling of whatever you have been working with. One of the problems with HMB, and this is a reason why a lot of people dislike working with it, is that it has quite an unpleasant smell.

Putting its distinctive odour aside, it's an excellent supplement to take. Here's what I wrote on the Myprotein website:

HMB (Beta-hydroxy beta-methylbutyrate) is an amino acid, but derives from the breakdown of Leucine, a part of normal dietary protein. HMB can be also found in certain foods like catfish, alfalfa and it is also a natural component of mother's milk but is scarcely found in a normal diet. HMB was discovered in the 1950s and has been studied for several decades but has only really become popular as a sports supplement around 1995.

HMB has been proven to slow down the breakdown of muscle protein as well as promote muscle gain, which means that it has both anti-catabolic and anabolic qualities. Early studies have shown that HMB supplementation also lowers cholesterol and helps strengthen the immune system.

HMB Supplement Benefits
In essence, the key benefits for HMB supplementation are:

- *Helps prevent muscle breakdown*
- *Increases lean mass gains*
- *Prevents muscle catabolism*
- *Speeds up muscle repair*
- *Decreases body fat*
- *Decreases blood cholesterol levels*

Scientific Studies into HMB (Hydroxymethyl Butyrate)
In a controlled scientific study, 41 male volunteers aged 19 to 29 were given 0, 1.5, or 3 grams of HMB every day for 3 weeks. The participants also lifted weights 3 days a week for 90 minutes. The results suggested that HMB could enhance strength and muscle mass in direct proportion to intake.

In another controlled study reported in the same article, 32 male volunteers took either 3 grams of HMB daily or placebo, and then lifted weights for 2 or 3 hours daily, 6 days a week for 7 weeks. The HMB group saw a significantly greater increase in its bench-press strength than the placebo group. However, there was no significant difference in body weight or fat mass by the end of the study.

Reference: Nissen S, Sharp R, Ray M, et al. 'Effect of leucine metabolite beta-hydroxy-beta-methylbutyrate on muscle metabolism during resistance-exercise training'. J Appl Physiol. *1996;81:2095–2104*

You will notice how I included not only the scientific source references but even outlined a summary of some of the research. As supplements were becoming more popular and the fitness industry was booming, there was a prevalence of less than credible claims being thrown around. I was not interested in promoting myths. Everything about the Myprotein brand was high quality – transparent, credible, well researched and effective.

By offering a broader range of supplements on the Myprotein site, there was something for everyone, although the most purchased product was a whey protein concentrate (WPC 80). As well as selling WPC 80, I also supplied WPC 75 (75 per cent protein) and 'whey protein isolate' (WPC 90 or 90 per cent protein).

From the day I launched my website, Bacarel was my one-stop shop for proteins. Andy was a great guy to do business with, and I continued using him for several years until I was buying up to 20 tonnes of whey powder a month from him alone, but, with continued growth, I had to find a direct source.

BUILD TRUST THROUGH STRONG RELATIONSHIPS

There is no substitute for strong relationships in business. Never underestimate the value of having suppliers you can trust not to overcharge you and that you can count on to give you the most reliable service. When I moved on from Bacarel, I successfully traded with another UK supplier, and I am not going to name them, but, after a few years, they revealed themselves to be less than savoury when they tried to blackmail me out of my own business.

Just to give you an idea of scale, our new supplier would not sell to us unless we bought at least a truckload of WPC 80. Myprotein had come a long way since I had persuaded Andy to sell me a couple of sacks! Even though we had to look elsewhere for WPC 80, we continued to buy other products from Bacarel, especially as we had such a strong relationship with the firm, although I think that by that time, Andy had passed away. RIP, Andy.

The quest for a large, reliable supplier of WPC 80 led us to the German dairy Müller. After the new UK supplier had tried and failed to blackmail us, we had to find a new source of whey protein, and that meant having to buy from America even though the British government charged a huge levy for doing so. They were protecting the interests of British dairy farmers, which is fair enough, but none of the British dairies could sell us the volumes we needed. In fact, as far as I was aware, up until we found Müller, no dairies in Europe could offer us the quantities we were looking for.

Fortunately, Müller had realised there was a massive market for whey protein powder and were determined to get a slice of the action, so they were about to open their new factory in Germany. We had detailed talks with Müller's most senior directors to discuss our whey protein requirements and powder specifications, which led to us becoming their first customer. We played a key role in helping them develop their first whey protein, following lots of new product development trials.

In the early days, I had very few overheads, which made bootstrapping the business more achievable, although I had to put an almost unimaginable amount of effort into it. Barely a moment passed when I wasn't focused on the business. The other ingredients, such as the flavourings, were not cheap per kilogram, but you only used a small amount for each kilogram of finished, blended product, and the only labour cost was my own time. The most significant monthly overhead was the fully serviced, small box room I was renting for around £250 per month, and that rent also covered electricity, water, rates etc. This was where I stored, mixed and packaged the products ready for shipping, although when it came to calls, printing out the labels and other admin, that was done at my new home, which I moved into around April 2004. It wasn't the best idea to move into my first home and launch Myprotein within the same month, but I don't like to do things by halves.

Everything else, including the containers I was using to send the powder to customers, was accounted for. The plastic bags cost pennies whereas the tubs were quite expensive, but by giving my customers the choice, they were in control of how their powder was packaged and if they wanted the tubs, they would swallow the extra cost. And anyway, I was careful to make sure I only bought what I believed I could sell, which was an ever-increasing volume as my customer base started growing at a steady rate. All I had to do was stay on top of things, but I ran an incredibly tight ship until the very end. Efficiency was key.

AGILITY WINS THE RACE

One of the key advantages that Myprotein had over everyone else was its agility, not only in its ability to adapt generally, but the speed at which new ideas could be brought to market. I could come up with a product concept in the morning, and it would be ready to go and made available on the website by the afternoon – no exaggeration. Everything was done in-house, from the printing of the labels to the marketing copy on the site. It was impossible for anyone else to keep up.

New product development (NPD) was something else that I just seemed to understand organically, so much so that I am dedicating an entire chapter to it later. We live in an ever-changing world, which means new threats and new opportunities are constantly emerging. The quickest to adapt will always thrive and become more successful than everyone else. I'd say I was pretty good at dealing with threats, but I excelled at spotting opportunities and developing commercially viable products that solved problems and plugged gaps in the market – something I could do rapidly and instinctively. I even came up with my own word for this – 'trendspotting'.

Another advantage that meant I could start selling from the moment I had bought my first few bags of whey was being able to build, maintain and update my own code and MySQL database to power the website. As a highly proficient web developer with experience in building sites for e-commerce, I was able to develop the website and back office systems for my brand long before I bought the first sacks of raw whey from Andy – before I had even settled on a name. I had two names in mind, Myprotein and Protein4U, and I believed they were both strong, but I went with Myprotein and have always felt it was the right choice. Again, having web development skills in-house added to the agility of Myprotein and saved a fortune in costs. Think about it – if you have to outsource, not only do you have to find someone who has the skill to build the features you need, you have to be able to get hold of them when you need them, explain your requirements in a way that they will understand, and then hope they can turn it around quickly. And for every hour they are working on the project, it is costing you money and giving your competitors more time to get there first. I was available 24-7 if needed.

I also don't think I could have 'bootstrapped' had I not developed my own site as it would have cost thousands to outsource. The only other way would have been to find a web development agency that would have wanted me to swap equity for development, but this would have ended up costing me millions in the longer term because of my diluted equity.

The Myprotein website was officially launched in May 2004, when search engine optimisation (SEO) was still very much in its infancy, but it was around that time that Google started to really clamp down on 'black hat' practices such as keyword stuffing and paid-for backlinks. From the start, every fibre of my business was about the user experience, and that included the website, which did exactly what it said on the tin. It gave my ideal customers – bodybuilders and people who took their health and fitness seriously – the kind of information they were looking for, written in plain English. More than that, I wanted to make sure I was streets ahead of everyone else in terms of the product. And all of that was good practice from Google's perspective, so my site became increasingly easy to find by people searching for nutritional supplements, and many other keyword searches.

UNDERSTAND YOUR CONSUMERS

I looked at the fitness market through the prism of what I call a 'swingometer'. The way I see it, you have your lifestyle clients on one extreme of the spectrum – they do a bit of running, spend some time on the cross-trainer, do a bit of yoga or Pilates and maybe a kettlebell routine that they have read about in *Men's Health* or *Cosmopolitan* – and on the other extreme, you have hard-core bodybuilders who eat, sleep and breathe their training and read *Flex* magazine. These days, people source information online, through their phones, tablets and laptops, but back then, printed magazines were much more popular.

Myprotein was designed to be focused on the hard-core gym goers, and one of the advantages here is that these people make sure they are educated on their subject matter. They know what they want and need, but are also open to new ideas – perfect for a cutting-edge brand like mine, which existed to supply the latest and highest-quality supplements. But there was another, smarter reason why I wanted to target this market.

Hard-core gym goers make the perfect brand ambassadors. How many people would listen to a newbie? I knew if I could get the hard-core weight trainers on board, everyone else would follow. They were the perfect influencers and ideal for referring new customers.

By focusing on the timeless, simple principles of good business – producing affordable but high-quality products that match people's needs and making it as easy as possible for them to buy them – I made sure my most effective and successful salespeople were my customers themselves. Word travels fast when you get it right, especially in a gym environment where fitness fanatics and bodybuilders go out of their way to exchange ideas and support each other. And I knew exactly what the right products looked like because I was an enthusiastic weight trainer myself.

To capitalise on this word-of-mouth marketing even more, I pioneered a win-win referral scheme, which turbocharged referrals. I will cover this more later, but this scheme was a game-changer and drove the acquisition of more than 30 per cent of all new customers to Myprotein, which is incredible as the cost per acquisition was pennies. This scheme is now a staple for all sports nutrition stores and many e-commerce sites globally. It is right up there as one of my most innovative business ideas, and one that I am most proud of.

A TALENT FOR DISRUPTION

I knew what products were out there, identified their strengths and weaknesses and usually predicted what was round the corner as well. The difference was that I had acquired the power to make the future happen before anyone else did, and do it better, because I was making my own protein shakes as we were totally vertically integrated. The brands that were already out there shared several vulnerabilities that I was able to exploit. In retrospect, I believe some of the main brands at the time were perhaps a little complacent, and maybe a few were also not wanting to upset their retailer customers by selling directly to the consumer. They never saw Myprotein coming, but the way I see it, disruption was inevitable in this marketplace as with all marketplaces. We need to always evolve.

Firstly, there was the issue of price. Serious bodybuilders were paying through the nose for a variety of protein shakes and other nutritional products. It wasn't just the price tag for the tub you had to think about. The amount of powder you had to use meant you went through a tub very quickly. I used to have three shakes a day. When you weigh it all up – making sure you were stocked up with a healthy supply of chicken, tuna, red meat and dairy products, and then buying protein shakes on top – hitting the right numbers for protein and other nutrients was a major expense.

Protein wasn't the only type of supplement that was consumed either. Other vitamins and minerals were becoming increasingly popular, and there were other powders available, such as creatine for stacking on natural mass, or glutamine, which is an aid for recovery. Then there was a whole bunch of other amino acids and nutritional supplements that were gaining attention and popularity on the back of high-quality, science-based research.

Of course, what no one else had figured out – and if they had, they certainly hadn't tried to do anything about it – was just how huge the profit margin was on these products. And although I tended to use the market-leading brand at the time, they weren't the only ones retailing at five or six times the cost price. That was the going rate. They weren't running a charity, and neither was I, but I knew I could sell a high-quality product with a healthy, sustainable margin and still sell powder at a fraction of the price of my competitors. I decided I was going to give the customer the absolute lowest price, while still making a healthy enough profit for my business to remain robust and sustainable.

While most of the people I knew complained about the high price of protein powders, what most of them hadn't noticed was the marketing trick the established brands were using, and most of them were doing this – selling 2 lb tubs. When people think of 2 lb, they tend to think of 1 kg, but that is inaccurate. A 2 lb tub of powder works out at 907 g, which is almost 10 per cent less than a kilogram.

I am not suggesting for a second that any of the main brands were selling any less than the amount they promised in their marketing or on their product packaging, but there was a lack of transparency, and transparency was – and still is – one of the key pillars of the Myprotein brand. When you buy sugar, you buy in kilograms, and it's the same for flour, rice, pasta, meat and nearly every other consumable product you can think of. We have been metric for years. And yet, when it came to protein powder, it was being sold by the pound – to a section of society who would be more aware than most of roughly (but not exactly) how many pounds there are in a kilogram. The typical protein shake customer is aware of what they are pushing, pulling or lifting. They take their training and their nutrition seriously. They will tend to equate two pounds to a kilogram – easy maths. To be fair, the main brands at the time were coming from the US where imperial measures were the standard.

KEY PILLARS FOR ACCELERATED GROWTH

Transparency was one of several key pillars that not only strengthened the Myprotein brand but also enabled rapid growth. The timing was great because of the rising interest in health and fitness generally The other pillars included the convenience of e-commerce, the idea of empowering the customer to make an informed choice and a no-nonsense marketing approach. These pillars tapped into what I saw as trends, or as I liked to describe it, waves that Myprotein could surf. It's all about being relevant to demand, and consumers wanted to know exactly what they were putting into their bodies, how it worked and what it would deliver – without the marketing buzz words. We were selling by the kilogram, and our customers would be left in no doubt that if they bought a kilogram, they were getting 2.2 lbs. These days, everyone in the UK and EU is legally obliged to label their products using metric measurements.

Another issue, which also links to transparency, relates to what people need and want to pay for when they buy a shake. Before Myprotein, you had to buy whey powder by the tub, and, whichever size you bought, you got a measuring scoop that you'd use to make the shake. I am sure I am not the only one who ended up with scoops all over my kitchen. What's the point? Sure, it's great for a first-time buyer as it makes it easy for them to get the mix right, but most people buying protein shakes are not first-time buyers. They only need a refill, not a starter pack.

I wanted to kill two birds with one stone – transparency *and* choice – so I didn't sell scoops with the powder. Those needing to buy a scoop could buy one for pennies. Most customers only wanted the powder, and Myprotein gave them the choice to do that. Typically, customers would buy a tub with their first order, and then they'd refill with bags. It was totally up to them. If they wanted a 500 g tub, they could have one, and if they wanted a 5 kg bag, that was fine as well. The customer could see exactly what they were paying for and how much value for money they were getting. It was a simple and efficient way to sell protein mix, and great for the environment as well.

Can you imagine how many plastic scoops were ending up in landfill sites? Plastic tubs were even more of an issue for the environment. And again, I must emphasise that I am talking about 2004, long before the single-use plastic debate of recent years had become a thing. Myprotein was consistently setting trends, not following them.

Myprotein was aimed directly at the consumer. I was not interested in using distributors or getting my products on the shelves of retail outlets or gyms in those earlier days. Those options would create more hurdles for me to overcome – not least getting my foot in the door in the first place, as the new entry in the market – and each of those layers would mean having to bump up the recommended retail price so the other organisations in the chain could have their slice of the profits. That seemed like a waste of time and expense when I could use the internet to reach my customers directly. Selling to the people who were using the product made much more sense to me, and that is where I believed the future of commerce was heading.

OFFER CHOICE

One of the most important factors that contributed to the success of Myprotein, right from the start, was choice – based on clear, transparent and honest facts. Flavour is an obvious example. Not everyone loves chocolate. The fact that people had been paying for a plastic scoop they didn't need was less obvious. But I wanted to take choice further. *What other choices can I offer to Myprotein customers?* That line of enquiry led to a whole range of options that others hadn't thought of. When considered collectively – the product range, scoop or no scoop, sweetener or no sweetener, packaging options, flavours, etc. – Myprotein was offering the consumer unparalleled choice.

Whatever choices I came up with, they were always easy to

implement. Selling directly to the consumer via my website meant I was only accountable to my customers and myself. I didn't need to persuade some gym owner or health food shop to put their trust in my new strawberry-flavoured protein shake and give it shelf space. All I had to do was to add it to the website's 'MySQL' database as a new product, and it would auto-generate on the front end. Now, this may sound like common sense to you, and you may wonder what's so fresh about any of this. Things have changed a lot since 2004, and a lot of the change we see in the nutrition space was driven by innovations that I came up with for Myprotein.

Offering the maximum level of choice evolved into a truly innovative concept that I called the 'Customiser', which allowed for far more choice than flavour. The Customiser gave customers the ability to create their own mix of calcium caseinate, milk protein concentrate and whey protein concentrate. They could decide whether to use dextrose or maltodextrin as the main source of carbohydrates – maltodextrin is not as sweet as dextrose but was considered slightly more slow-releasing, which enabled a steady supply of energy.

Likewise, Myprotein customers could choose between creatine, guarana extract, HMB or l-glutamine, or they could decide upon a mix of all four! And if they preferred a tub to a sealed bag, that was fine too. It was all about choice, right down to the kind of sweetener, if any, to be used – aspartame or sucralose. When it came to flavour, they could choose how much to use. Did they just want a hint of vanilla or a full-on assault on the taste buds?

For every flavour (chocolate, orange or strawberry) and for each kind of sweetener, customers were given the option of 'extra' or they could choose 'none' – an acquired taste, admittedly. Just as some people like one sugar with their cup of tea while others prefer none, I wanted to apply the same rational thinking to nutritional supplements. None of us are the same. Every person is different.

Off-the-shelf products are made for a generic person. How can you treat an 18-stone, semi-professional bodybuilder and an 8-stone, sixteen-year-old newbie the same? You can't. It's a simple as that, and I didn't think it was right – hence 'My' protein.

I am particularly proud of the back-end processes that operated in the engine room of the Myprotein website. The back end is something the customer never sees, but it is crucial for the production team and warehouse to function efficiently. From stock control to customer orders, the back end manages everything. I gave the Myprotein system the rather mundane and descriptive name of 'SAS', which is short for 'Secure Admin System', but without the SAS, we wouldn't have been able to function. If I had not put the thinking and effort into making the back end as slick as it was, right from the beginning, we would never have been able to cope with the huge spike in demand. It was tight and efficient and functioned just as well with thousands of orders per day as it had when the first orders were processed in our first week. I built it with very clean and scalable code, using the best practices in ColdFusion and SQL to ensure the site always ran fast. As a developer, I never cut corners with code and always coded the right way, even if it was maybe a bit more laborious to do it that way on most occasions.

I had no special equipment for blending the powders. The factory was me, myself and I. If one hundred people wanted one hundred different types of shake, I had to hand-produce one hundred different shakes, pack them and send them off. As you can imagine, especially for someone who struggles with arithmetic, the last thing I wanted to be doing was working out how to put together a 5 kg mix that contained 75 per cent whey powder, 17 per cent milk powder, 5 per cent dextrose, 3 per cent creatine and a specific amount of flavouring and sweetener.

It would have been a nightmare had I not created the algorithms within the SAS to do all the maths for me. Once a customer had placed their order, a docket was produced that could be printed out, listing exactly how many grams of the various ingredients I had to use to match their exact requirements. It was beautiful, worked like clockwork and was 100 per cent bespoke. The site acted as the perfect order taker, offering people the kind of choices that mattered to them, making it easy for them to customise their own powder and providing me with a childproof mechanism for preparing the orders precisely.

Here is some of the old website text that I have managed to find in the archives:

Sports Supplements Tailored for You

You have just found a completely new & unique concept for supplying high-grade, raw Sports Supplement products to you in the UK. We also pride ourselves on being the best value, highest quality & most reliable source for Sports Supplements (Creatine, L-Glutamine, Guarana), Protein Powder (whey protein, milk protein, caseinate), Carbohydrates & other Sports Nutritional Products for the bodybuilder, athlete, power lifter or sports person at direct prices – with a twist! <u>*So, What is This Twist Then?*</u>

The underlined text was hyperlinked to another part of the site where they discovered they could customise their order. There was also a link to the Customiser in the side menu. As I said, the site was built with convenience and customer choice in mind. What if the customer was not sure what they needed? It was easy for me to look at things from the customer's perspective because I understood the product. I wasn't just selling Myprotein shakes. I was using them.

So, in the side menu, there was a section called 'Shop by Goal', and all they needed to know was what they wanted to achieve. They were offered four choices:

- Build muscle
- Bulking
- Energy recovery
- Fat loss

Those who wanted to build muscle would be offered a selection of products that were relevant to them. It was ridiculously easy for people to buy what they needed to achieve their goals. I left no stone unturned.

No matter how magic the product was or how well the website functioned, you may be wondering how I managed to get the message out there so quickly. How did I convert those two sacks of whey powder into protein shake sales within a few days of buying them? Well, it certainly wasn't by telling all my friends and family about the business. Even though I believed in my product and was using Myprotein supplements myself, I hate asking people for favours, and telling everyone in the gym about Myprotein would have felt like putting pressure on them to buy from me. That's not my style. I told a handful of my closest friends and family at most. Ironically, when the brand started to grow and the people around me started using Myprotein supplements, one of them clicked that I was the founder, so they approached me – not the other way round.

How I marketed Myprotein is a chapter within itself, but before I get to that, let me share with you just how physically demanding those early days were.

CHAPTER TEN

'SIXTEEN-HOUR DAYS'

Whenever you hear anyone talking about how they started their own business, they will often mention long hours and hard graft. Phrases like 'sixteen-hour days' are bandied about like confetti, as though you have to be glued to your business almost 24-7 if you want to succeed as an entrepreneur.

If you have been there and built a business from scratch, you will already know the kind of Herculean effort that is required. If you have built a successful business without tons of hard work, do let me know and I will buy *your* book.

For those who haven't dipped their toes in the entrepreneurial waters and are hoping I will tell you there's an easier way, sorry to disappoint you, but there probably isn't – not at the beginning anyway. I love what I do, and I was always passionate about the industry I was in and the products I produced. You have to be. With passion comes commitment and a drive that goes beyond having to do something because it's your job or because it pays the bills. Unsurprisingly, many entrepreneurs continue to work sixteen-hour days (and longer) because they *want* to – not because they *have* to. That said, when you're running a business, you need to be available when issues arise, and depending on your business, that could mean any time during the day or night. I built a global brand, which was available 24-7 – people were buying and using my product during every hour of the day and night, so an issue could arise at literally any time.

What did my sixteen-hour days look like? The hard work started around six to nine months before launching Myprotein, when I still had a full-time job with 3T as a web developer and was spending my nights building my website. I had a nine-to-five job, but I'd often work until 6 p.m., get home by around 6.15 p.m., have something to eat and then hit the gym. So, I wasn't even starting on my website until almost 9 p.m.

Some people are done by 9 p.m. or at least are too tired for the mental concentration required for coding, but, to be honest, that was when I was at my most alert and could naturally settle into the zone. I've always been more of a night owl than an early bird, so it wasn't unusual for me to hit the sack in the early hours.

Even in 2004, front-end web design was not as sophisticated as it is now, and it has not stopped evolving, but I am a developer – not a designer – and my main concern with web development was how a site functioned. Efficiency is very important to me, in every aspect of my life. That doesn't mean the design and aesthetic feel of the Myprotein website wasn't important, but my number-one priority was to ensure the right people could easily find the best solution for their needs. I made the user journey as easy, straightforward and intuitive as possible. In case you are wondering what inspired me to go with Myprotein's distinctive blue colour scheme, apart from being associated with my favourite football team, blue is typically considered a masculine colour and the largest market for my products in 2004 were men. It must have been a good call because the branding has certainly stood the test of time.

TIME FOR A 'BIGGER BOAT'

Once the site was built and I was ready for launch, the real fun started, and I experienced several wake-up calls. Firstly, there was the realisation that my kitchen was not going to hack it as a factory. I'd received some whey protein samples from Bacarel, along with several samples of creatine, guarana and l-glutamine that had been sent to me by a functional ingredients distributor. It was obvious I was 'gonna need a bigger boat', as even one 20 kg sack of whey protein was clearly going to take up too much space for the kitchen of a two-up two-down, small terraced house. Even if I had found the space to work in my kitchen, I am confident that the powder would have permeated everything else in the room. Meals would never have tasted the same again! It was time to look for a larger storage and blending space for Myprotein.

I knew about a large multi-use light industrial and office facility within walking distance of my house – twenty minutes away if that. Strangely, it was where Pantek was located, where I'd first worked as a sixteen-year-old. It had the feel of an old mill, and I believe it had previously been occupied by an engineering company. Either way, it had been bought by an organisation called EZ Space, and they'd built partitions to divide the interior into separate storage spaces. I knew I needed to rent somewhere but didn't have the capital to stretch to a long-term lease, so I was going to have to balance need with affordability. As it happens, I landed on a bargain and ended up renting a small serviced room for around £250 per month, fully inclusive. It ticked a lot of boxes for me.

It was walkable from the 3T offices as well as from my house, and that was super-important given that I was going to have to bounce between my house, 3T's offices and the warehouse. I simply wouldn't have the time to spend on longer journeys.

Having an 'office' of my own also meant I had a legitimate postal address rather than my own home or a PO box number. And, most importantly, I had somewhere where raw materials could be delivered to and stored instead of having a house full of proteins and amino acids.

Once the website was up and running, the whey powder deliveries were happening and orders had to be processed, the shape of my sixteen-hour day changed, but the intensity didn't, and the hours got even longer. That was another wake-up call. When one challenge is dealt with, another one presents. There is no such thing as an even keel in business. If there isn't a problem to solve, you should be looking ahead for the next improvement or the next opportunity to be seized upon. One of my rules, which I adopted right from the beginning, was that the day was not over until I had done three positive things.

A guy called Danny at Parcelforce, who I would like to think of now as a friend, used to call round to the office every day to collect processed orders for delivery to Myprotein customers. Danny did everything he could to help me, including making sure that my office was the last place on his list. As I was in full-time work, I couldn't get to the Myprotein office until around 5.45 p.m., and the absolute latest that Danny would collect deliveries was 6 p.m., so I was cutting it fine.

Prior to launching Myprotein, even when I was working on the website until late into the night, I didn't clock-watch and it wasn't my style to leave 3T at 5 p.m. on the dot, but once my own operation had started, I didn't have much choice. I had to dive out of work by 5.15 p.m. at the latest, get to the warehouse and get the packages ready for dispatch. They needed to be boxed, sealed with packing tape, labelled and ready to go.

Then I had to be there to hand them over to Danny personally. Nothing could be left to chance. I couldn't just leave a stack of boxes in the corridor for Danny to collect. We'd agree on how many boxes were being sent, the manifest would be signed off, and that was that. Typically, the next day, I would have another bunch of happy customers – at least those who opted for the next-day service rather than the two-working-days service. Yes, that was yet another choice I offered Myprotein customers, but it certainly wasn't the norm at that time.

The only way I could have the packing ready for Danny was if I had already prepared everything else in the morning. The exact mixing ratios for each order were calculated in the back end of the website. All I had to do was print out the order, and then I had the address details and production docket on one piece of paper. A single order could be anything from a 1 kg bag of protein to a more complex bulk order for various products. And guess whose job it was to do the mixing and preparation. That's right – it was mine, and I had to make sure that job was done before I could go to my full-time job at 3T. I was in for another wake-up call.

My new day started at 5 a.m., and I would have to be done and dusted – literally in my case, as it was almost impossible to do the job without getting caked in powder – by 8.45 a.m. By the time I was sat at my 3T desk at 9 a.m., I had already put in almost four hours of work for Myprotein. You might be wondering why I didn't do the prep work in the evening. It wasn't possible. Once I had handed over the goods to Danny for delivery, I would walk back to my house for a bite to eat around 6.15 p.m., have a rest and I'd be in the gym by 7.15 p.m.

That was my 'me-time'– pumping iron in the gym for one hour – and then it was back to business with Myprotein. I will be covering my marketing strategy in much more depth in a later chapter, but suffice to say it involved spending a lot of time online, generating and contributing to discussions on forums and other internet platforms.

INCREASED ORDERS AND LONGER DAYS

Email enquiries came through thick and fast. Myprotein grew rapidly and consistently from day one, and not a single day went by when orders didn't come in, so I was kept extremely busy with admin and customer service. Then there was the website, which I was constantly maintaining, updating and improving. So, I had to work late into the night. Seriously, apart from my intense gym workout, which was the closest I got to relaxing, my life was 100 mph and non-stop. I could have called this chapter 'Twenty-hour days', and it wouldn't have been too far from the truth most of the time.

Another reason why it was better to print out the orders in the morning was because I wanted to ensure that as many orders were processed as possible on a given day. Had I done the printing at night, I would have missed a chunk of next-day delivery orders and those customers would not have received their orders in time – not ideal.

I have only presented you with an outline of what a day in the life of Oliver Cookson entailed. Living it was an altogether different experience and one that I want to share with you. Even in the first week, I processed between 80 and 90 kilograms of protein into customer orders. It doesn't sound like a lot, but unless you have done the job, you will have no tangible understanding of what that involves, so I am going to break it down.

The Myprotein storage room was oblong with a large window that almost spanned the entire length of the room. There was a heavy-duty, stainless steel table under the window, and that's where I would work. On one side of the table, I placed the fresh orders to be blended. In front of me, there were two weighing scales – a smaller, more sensitive one for the sweeteners and flavourings, which gave readings to the nearest tenth of a gram, and a larger one for protein, which gave readings to the nearest gram.

Every order was unique and had to be processed precisely. The various protein sacks had to be placed on the floor around me, while other ingredients such as the colourings and sweeteners were on the table in front of me. I used to buy creatine in 25 kg cardboard drums that had a plastic, waterproof inner lining. The creatine drums were too big and cumbersome for the table, so that would be another resource I would have to stoop down to reach from the floor.

In the last chapter, I referred to a hypothetical order for a 5 kg mix containing 75 per cent whey powder, 17 per cent milk powder, 5 per cent dextrose, 3 per cent creatine, and a specific amount of flavouring and sweetener. What did the process of producing that mix involve?

The order printout told me exactly how much of each raw material I needed to add into the mix. That was the easy bit. For those who don't want to do the maths or root around for a calculator, this is what those percentages look like in grams and kilograms:

3.75 kg whey powder

850 g milk powder

250 g dextrose

150 g creatine

A very small and precise amount of flavouring and sweetener

We offered a choice of whey powders, so depending on whether the order was for WPC 75, 80 or milk protein, I'd have to select the right sack. Either way, I had to bend, stoop or squat down to scoop up what I estimated to be the right amount, and then I'd have to weigh it. Getting the right amount might mean having to toss some back into the sack or having to reach down for a little more, but it had to be precise. Then it was the same again for the milk powder, dextrose and creatine. It was a very labour-intensive process, but due to the customised nature of our service and the infinite variety of potential stock keeping units (SKUs) available, it was impossible to make stock and everything had to be made to order in those early years.

Customer service is everything. If you get that wrong, you are not going to survive, let alone thrive and grow. If my customers had asked for a specific mix of powder, that was exactly what they were going to get. And look what happened to Myprotein. It thrived and it grew – quickly.

Once the individual ingredients had been measured, they were placed into a large 10-litre mixing tub for blending by hand. This meant picking up the tub and shaking it as vigorously as possible for a good thirty seconds or so – for as long as it took to ensure every scoop had the same composition.

Blending was at least as important as accurate measuring and ensured customers were getting a consistent mix with every scoop. The mixing tub held around 5 kg of whey, so for larger orders I would have to repeat the mixing and blending process several times. It might not seem like the most physically demanding task for someone working out five nights a week, but the effect was cumulative, and after hours of repeating this process dozens of times, you'd know about it.

The finished blends were packed into food-grade plastic bags and labelled to show the contents. These were double bagged, sealed with cable ties and then packed into boxes. I used a very simple three-box system. Typically, orders of 5 kg or less were packed into small single-walled boxes. Orders weighing upwards

'SIXTEEN-HOUR DAYS'

of 5 kg but less than 15 kg were packed into medium single-walled boxes, and for larger orders up to 20 kg, I used large double-walled boxes. This system stood the test of time, and we were still using these three boxes when we were dealing with over a thousand orders per day.

MY FIRST HIRE – MUM

For the first three months, I was still working full-time, which meant I was having to deal with an ever-increasing amount of order processing and mixing and had no extra time to do it. There was no room for manoeuvre, so the pressure and the intensity built up steadily, and I had to match it with determination, resilience and hard work. And once it became impossible to keep up with that pressure, I left my job at 3T to focus all my attention on Myprotein. Initially, I was doing everything myself, although after a month or so, my mum started helping at weekends. By January 2005, I'd taken her on full-time as 'chief blender', a job that she described as helping her grow muscles she never knew she had. She only did this role for a while until we employed some full-time production staff, and then Mum got back to a desk and ended up working in accounts.

Mums are a godsend, and mine certainly was. She took a 75 per cent pay drop when she swapped her office-based job as a secretary in central Manchester, a career she'd enjoyed for nineteen years, to come and work for me. I ran a tight ship from the start, and Mum was the only person apart from me who was authorised to sign off purchases. She worked hard for Myprotein until the day I sold it, and I will always be indebted to her. You can't buy trust and loyalty.

As Myprotein grew, EZ Space gave us the option of upgrading to larger rooms, until we ended up with an operations space of around 400 square feet, as well as our own storage space in the basement. Whereas Pantek had used the basement for archiving data reels in steel cages, we were using ours for storing pallet-loads of whey protein.

Our main room, where we did all the blending, was on the second floor of the building, but the storage area was in the basement and there was no elevator. When deliveries arrived, I had to carry them by hand from the ground floor to the basement. Every time we needed a new sack, I would have to go down to the basement and haul it up to the second floor. Again, you might think carrying a 20 kg sack of powder up three flights of stairs is no big deal for a strapping young man who works out, but it's no fun when you have to do it many times a day.

Deliveries could be particularly challenging. There were thirty sacks to a pallet, and every one of those sacks would have to be taken down to the basement. Usually, the pallets would arrive on a tail-lift wagon. The back of a tail-lift wagon opens out and doubles as a powered elevator for lowering goods from the trailer to ground level, so you don't need a forklift. This made life easier for me because we didn't have a forklift back then, or even one of those pallet trucks that lets you pick pallets up at ground level and pull them around manually.

On some occasions, pallets were delivered by wagons that didn't have the tail-lift mechanism, so the cargo would have to be 'handballed'. That would mean cutting into the external wrapping of each pallet and unloading the sacks one at a time. Handballing involved climbing into the wagon, shifting one or two sacks to the edge of trailer, jumping down to ground level so those sacks could then be lifted from the trailer and placed at the entrance of our building, and repeating this process until all the sacks had been unloaded. It was back-breaking work, and once that job was done, the whole lot still needed to be moved to the basement!

Shunting sacks of whey and drums of creatine was hard work, and I hated it, especially the handballing days, but I gritted my teeth and got on with it. Who else was going to do it? Nobody if you are a team of one. I was careful to instil that ethos into the company culture as the Myprotein team grew. Unless one person is responsible for a given task, nobody is. We were lean, and when something needed doing, we just got stuck in. Everybody knew what they had to do. There were no passengers. But do you know something? I am glad I went through that. By the time we were employing over a hundred staff when I sold the company, there was not one single job that I hadn't done.

From a leadership perspective, that kind of experience is extremely valuable. It empowers you to take control of any aspect of the operation if an unexpected spike occurs, and that wins respect. I always believed in leading by example. Having that experience also gives you meaningful insight into what is possible, so you set realistic goals for your team.

When a member of my team told me something couldn't be done, I could show them how it could be done because I had done it. On other occasions, I showed my staff how the same job could be done in half the time or with far less effort. Let me be clear: I am not claiming to be superhuman here, but when it's your own business and you have built it from the ground upwards, you have a vested interest in finding the most efficient way of doing things – or you should.

While hairnets, aprons and gloves all contributed to an even cleaner environment for handling food, they didn't prevent the powder from being absorbed into every fibre of our clothing and right through to the skin. In the early days, when I was stood on my feet for hours as the sole blender, weighing, mixing, shaking and packing orders, I didn't even have time to shower before shooting off for my full-time job at 3T. As I mentioned before, anyone who has worked with HMB powder will tell you it has a very distinctive, pungent and quite unpleasant smell. By the time I finished my shift at Myprotein, I could be caked in the stuff. I can only imagine what my colleagues at 3T must have thought. None of them ever mentioned it to me.

NOT FOR THE FAINT-HEARTED

Building a business from scratch is not only hard work physically. It is also mentally challenging and can easily become the only thing you think about from the moment you wake up until you go to sleep. But if you are selling to people all round the world from an e-commerce platform, things can go wrong at any time, even when you're sleeping.

The Myprotein website didn't store any credit card details or other sensitive financial information, and that kept us beneath the radar of serious hackers. We used Sage Pay to process payments in the early years, but as the volume of orders increased, their system was prone to crashing, and our customers wouldn't be able to use the site. Every time that happened, we were not only losing orders, it was damaging our brand. The last thing I wanted to see was my potential brand ambassadors complaining on forums about not being able to buy from the Myprotein website.

One of my worst days ever happened around two years in, when I was trying to enjoy a holiday in Spain, near Marbella, with a few of my good mates. The system was up and down for two days, with some outages lasting hours. Imagine the impact of the site going down for this long. Without the site, the business was effectively dead. Once I realised what was going on, I had to rush back to my apartment and was glued to the screen almost continuously until the situation was resolved. It was a nerve-wracking time.

Something similar happened years later, when the website was being updated and we were migrating everything to a warehouse management system. Things did not run as smoothly as I would have liked, and we were unable to process orders for a while. Nightmare. You know what they say – the bigger they are, the harder they fall. Growing does not necessarily shield you from threats and challenges. Everything gets upsized, including the risks. The stakes just keep getting higher. If you are starting out and your website goes down for any length of time, it has an impact but nothing like the impact it will have on a pan-European brand!

It's another one of those clichés that you will hear about entrepreneurs, but, in my case, it was especially true, so I am going to say it. When you've launched a business, and it is growing at a terrific pace, you can feel as though you are in the loneliest place on earth as you keep stepping further away from the cliff edge on a tightrope. That's exactly how it felt.

I had one thousand and one things on my mind at any one time, and it felt as though I was carrying the weight of the world on my shoulders. When faced with challenges, there was no one I could turn to, not even my mum. It was my business, and I had no business partner, no mentors, no non-executive directors, or even friends who had the relevant experience.

It is easy to look at the revenue figures and EBITDA values, note the phenomenal growth of Myprotein, and think it must have been plain sailing, but it wasn't. Remember, I was barely in my mid-twenties, and I often felt stressed out with the pressure of keeping it all together – one wrong move, and it could all become pear-shaped.

I could almost have written a separate book on sixteen-hour days because I cannot stress enough how hard you must be willing to work to succeed. From the website to stock control, from sales and customer service to logistics and manufacturing, I was responsible for the whole operation, and even when I took people on, it was still on me.

It might appear as though the company was charging ahead like a bolting horse, and I was hanging on to the reins with one hand, trying to keep control. But businesses don't grow rapidly by accident, and no matter how much it might sound like I was a victim of my own success, I was hungry for that success, and I was doing everything I could to make it happen. The growth of Myprotein was driven by some very smart marketing decisions.

CHAPTER ELEVEN

NO-BULL MARKETING

An idea, a great product and even a huge market for whatever it is that you're selling are not enough to ensure success. I am sure thousands, perhaps millions of ideas, products and services have failed to take off – not because they were not good but because the right people were either unaware that they existed or didn't know enough about them to make an informed choice.

The magic ingredient is marketing. When you know how to reach the people who will benefit from whatever it is that you are selling, and you know how to paint the picture in their minds so they can recognise and feel the value of your product, they will buy it. It's as simple as that. And when I use the word 'value', that means giving them a reason to use your idea instead of somebody else's. Without the value, you are just another voice in a noisy room.

KNOW WHO BUYS YOUR PRODUCTS AND HOW TO REACH THEM

From the start, I instinctively knew how to reach my customers. These days, people talk about creating a marketing avatar and building as detailed a picture as you can of your ideal customers. Some even go so far as to call them names:

'This is Chantel. She posts selfies on Instagram, loves upmarket coffee shops, watches films on Netflix at least three times a week, and tunes in to *The Real Housewives of New York City* . . .'

That's all very well for some large organisations, but if you are a sole trader starting up a brand on your own, that's an overly complex approach. You should understand your customers instinctively and know how you are going to serve them. In my case, I had a natural and deep affinity to my customers. It was easy for me to empathise with them. I was a Myprotein customer!

Although I have spoken a lot about my passion for bodybuilding, and there's no doubting that I took my training very seriously, I wasn't a bodybuilder – not in the true sense of the word. I was a weight trainer. In my opinion, a bodybuilder is not just someone who wants to bulk up as I did. They eat, sleep and breathe the craft of building the perfect physique for competing. Bodybuilding is an all-encompassing discipline that covers training, diet, fasting, posture, and other preparation for competitions. That was not a route that I wanted to go down, but I understood it. I knew the mindset of the bodybuilder, and I could relate to it. I knew how they trained, what they ate, what made them tick and where they shared and gained knowledge. I knew what they wanted. More importantly, I knew where they hung out online when they weren't pumping iron. They were spending time on the same online forums as me. One of those forums was called MuscleTalk, and this played a crucial part in Myprotein's marketing strategy from the very beginning.

In the days before the rise of Facebook and similar social media platforms, people used forums to meet and engage with other people with similar interests. MuscleTalk was a popular forum for people interested in all things muscle-related, whether they were serious bodybuilders or weight-training enthusiasts like me. Visitors could either read the posts of others or they could create an account, personalise their profile, and post articles of their own.

The site was divided into numerous subforums, so visitors could easily find the topics that were important to them. At the time, those topics included food and nutrition, competing, posing and supplements. The aim of the site was to provide a platform for discussion, where information could be shared and exchanged. When I logged on, I spent most of my time in the supplements subforum.

I was never interested in becoming another ego on the site. That's not my style. Even though I am not as shy as I was when I was a child, I don't go out of my way to be the centre of attention. I set up a MuscleTalk account in the name of Myprotein, and I linked my profile to my website. There was no photo of me. In all the years that I used that forum, nobody ever knew who I was or what I looked like. They didn't even know my name, and they didn't need to.

Around about the time I launched Myprotein, a new feature was introduced on the MuscleTalk site, which allowed members to pay to post a 'sticky' topic. A sticky topic would remain highly visible at the top of the page, even after other posts were added. MuscleTalk was promoting a low-cost trial, and sticky posts were available for tens of pounds, so I snapped one up. It worked, and I made an immediate return on the investment.

I am not sure if I was the first to book a sticky post, but I was one of the first to sell whey protein powder supplements directly. The only similar advertisement was from a really friendly guy called Steve, who ran a consortium called The Whey Consortium. I think Steve was a gym owner who had bought a few pallets of whey for himself and his gym members and was flogging large sacks to other gyms and their members as well. It was a much more raw consumer offering than what

Myprotein was selling, so although we obviously served a similar space, I am sure Steve will agree he was focused on the bulk selling.

As soon as I posted a sticky post, the website's traffic would explode, and the orders flooded in. I had no direct competition. Although some of the other brands had a presence on the forums, they were mainly aimed towards retail clients and could not compete with Myprotein on price or choice. We were the only real direct-to-consumer brand around.

Having a sticky post didn't stop me from engaging in my other activities on the forum, so I was still posting other discussions and getting involved in conversations started by other members. Once the orders were processed and other members started using Myprotein, that became another topic of conversation in itself. People were either thanking me for a great product or recommending my brand to others. An unstoppable momentum was being generated, and I was hooked by the excitement.

Barely thirty minutes went by at any given time, an hour at most, when I wasn't logging on to the MuscleTalk website to catch up on things. It was a highly addictive activity because everything I did would generate a response and there were multiple ways to stimulate more buzz. The sticky posts didn't just direct people to my site. People would ask questions and post other comments, and that created more engagement. And the more interaction and discussion there was, the more sales were generated. That's what made it so addictive. I was like a teenager who had posted a selfie and was now hungry for likes, except I wasn't concerned with vanity. I was watching my business grow, and the sales figures were rocketing.

I was excited and driven to keep the momentum going. The positive feedback, the daily orders and the constant interaction weren't just signs of things to come in terms of revenue growth and brand popularity. I had created this, and the time had finally come when I could see the results of all that hard work. Myprotein was my baby, and I was watching it thrive. It was the ultimate validation, and I was on a high. Letting people know about Myprotein and investing time and money to shout about it on MuscleTalk was the acid test.

VALUE YOUR CUSTOMERS – SERVICE SPEAKS LOUDER THAN WORDS

For at least the first five years at the helm of Myprotein, I was still hooked on forums, and I admit it probably took just as long for me to learn not to take things personally. When I say Myprotein was my baby, it felt like a part of me, and if someone criticised the brand or its product, I felt it. You have to care about what you do. Of course you do, and if you receive criticism, check yourself; is it valid, can you improve, have you dropped the ball or overlooked something? Always strive to improve, but don't let ego get in the way. I don't care who you are, there is always room to improve, and if you are not sure how then positive criticism is a blessing. This becomes easier to see when you learn to put emotions aside and deal with complaints rationally.

Sometimes people would complain about things that were outside of my control – issues with the postal service, for example, because the driver had passed the parcel to a neighbour they didn't get on with. When something like that happened, my first thought would be something along the lines of, *How is that my fault?* I would want to politely suggest that they take that up with their local postal service, but obviously I wouldn't follow through and say that. As we grew in size and popularity, I am sure some comments aimed at us were from fake profiles that had been set up by would-be competitors, but I'd treat them with the same courtesy and respect I'd show any genuine customer. The customer is always in charge, and my standard response was to apologise and say how sad I was that their expectations had not been met. But I soon cottoned on that even this kind of issue presented me with an opportunity to go the extra mile in terms of choice.

Once the parcel had left my offices, there was little I could do to take control of the situation. Sure, I could track its progress and so could my customers, but if the driver who knocked at their door was inappropriate or knocked once and left it on the doorstep, I couldn't physically stop them. What I could do was let Myprotein customers choose the parcel delivery firm, so I gave them two options – DPD or Parcelforce. It was such a simple move but magical at the same time. By passing the choice on to the customer, I was almost controlling the uncontrollable. They would make the decision based on deeply personal experiences and feelings that I didn't need to know or understand. By offering them the choice, they felt more empowered, and I received fewer complaints about delivery after that.

Sometimes, the problem was on our side. It didn't happen often, but given that the factory was me and all orders were prepared by hand, it was possible for a customer to get the wrong order or an incorrect weight. Myprotein's customers felt a strong connection to the brand. I was building a following or a tribe, so a lot of the feedback I received came via forums.

Where something had gone wrong on our side, I'd try to identify the weak point in the process and set up a system to make it less likely to happen again. A great example of this was the 'check weighing' system. After an order had been processed, the weight would be written on the box and documented on a packing sheet, showing all the orders of that day. That way, if someone claimed their order was missing products, I had something to refer to as I had 'check weighed' the whole box.

We are all human, and everyone makes mistakes, so if it turned out the customer got it wrong, I'd still replace the order.

You will always get your try-on merchants, but I believe it is better not to use a mallet where a gentle push will do the trick. Even if I suspected foul play and the packing sheet showed the correct weight had been recorded, I would let it go the first time. If the same person tried to do the same thing a second time, I would deal with the issue gently but effectively, using my records to prove my case. It didn't happen too often.

Most of the feedback and discussion on forums was positive and constructive. People would pose questions and explore avenues or make suggestions on how products could be improved. They might ask if I had thought of adding a new supplement or flavour to the menu. Sometimes they'd ask why they couldn't find something they wanted, or they'd refer to the latest research. I would give all reasonable suggestions serious consideration, and if someone asked me if I'd read a research paper that had thrown up some interesting findings, I'd take a look.

The vertically integrated set-up of Myprotein gave us incredible agility, and I could respond to new information quickly. If I liked an idea I'd heard or if I'd come up with one of my own, depending on what it was, I could turn around a new product within one week, one day or even one hour. Most of the new products I launched were inspired by posts in forums, primarily MuscleTalk. Forums provided me with an effective way of keeping my finger on the pulse of my customer base. And I was creating brand advocates who would staunchly promote Myprotein to all of their friends and defend the brand if anyone else said a word against it. Launching new products and posting special offers and other promotions amplified and accelerated the process.

One of the ways I had gained such respect and authority amongst the weight-training and bodybuilding community was by sharing knowledge, but I learnt very quickly that it was better to leave the details to the experts. Whenever I posted about new findings, I'd do so with strict caveats, but that was not the case for everyone using the forums. When it comes to the world of sports and exercise, misinformation and snake oil salespeople are everywhere – anything to sell the product. I didn't want to be associated with any of that.

When it came to how I promoted Myprotein, I took a no-bull approach to marketing, doing everything I could to empower my customers to make informed decisions. This was another way of adding value. Giving people the information they need to make intelligent decisions is more likely to lead to results and customer satisfaction because you are managing expectations at the same time. The brand went from strength to strength.

A REVOLUTIONARY REFERRAL SCHEME

Another way of offering value is to reward loyalty, and to thank brand advocates for supporting your brand and encourage them to do it even more. Long before I launched Myprotein, I had thought about the most effective ways of generating leads and promoting the brand. It seemed obvious to me that the best way to do this was to leverage customer loyalty, so I set up a revolutionary referral scheme. And it is no exaggeration to use the word 'revolutionary'. The system I set up was the first of its kind and possibly one of the best ideas I ever came up with.

When someone signed up to the Myprotein website, so they could place orders, they were assigned an MP number. As Myprotein's first ever client, my MP code is MP1. Today's customers would have MP numbers in the millions if the current website were using the same unique ID system! This number acted as the customer's personal referral number and could be used by others in exchange for a discount on the Myprotein website.

I would send them an email to let them know what their code was and how it could be used, and I sent them a supply of referral cards with their order. By writing their MP number on each card, they had a mechanism for offering others a discount on Myprotein products:

'Use this card and get a 5 per cent discount off your first order.'

The card gave instructions on how to redeem the code for discount on the website. However, the MP code also told me who the referrer was, so they could be rewarded for promoting my brand. It was a win-win-win solution – the referrer benefitted, Myprotein benefitted and whomever they referred us to benefitted as well. Beautiful.

Whereas the MP code could be used by new customers to gain a discount, the referrers were granted 'reward points' that they could redeem with their next order. Referrers gained five reward points for every pound spent using their MP number. Five reward points were the equivalent of a five pence discount off their next order with Myprotein. So, if someone spent £40 on their first order, which was more or less the typical order value, the referrer would earn 200 MP reward points or the equivalent of £2 credit, which would be added to their account for them to spend on their next order.

When you consider that customers were sent twenty of these MP discount cards with every order, it is easy to see the potential for making a lot of money. If you love a product anyway and you know you can benefit from 5 per cent of first order expenditure of twenty other people just by spreading the word, you are going to hand those cards out like there's no tomorrow, and that's exactly what happened. I even knew of one person who was using his full-time job as a cashier in a well-known health shop to actively promote Myprotein over the other brands available. Let me be clear and add that I don't condone that behaviour, just as I would never encourage people to stuff referral cards into lockers in gyms. I was selling a superb range of products that people loved and felt loyal towards, and I am sure the majority of referrals were from friend to friend or from a gym owner to their own members.

I launched other methods for people to refer, such as A5 posters, so gym owners, for example, could let their members know, and there was even an emailable link. Customers were so loyal to the Myprotein brand, they were not only singing its praises on all the forums, but they were posting their unique referral links in public posts and driving traffic to my website.

These days, people talk about social media posts going viral, and that is the best way to describe how the Myprotein referral scheme exploded. Customers were emailing me to ask for more cards. This goes to show that even now, in our world of technology and huge audiences, word of mouth is still one of the most effective and powerful ways of marketing that we have. We trust the people we know, and we buy from the people we trust. It's as simple as that, and when you know how to harness that power, you can grow a brand more quickly than you might believe possible.

Everyone benefitted from the referral scheme, but the biggest winner was Myprotein because every reward point redeemed, and every penny saved, came off the back of money being spent on Myprotein products. The brand's customer base was growing at more than an exponential rate. It was incredible, and I can say that right up until I sold the brand in 2011, roughly a third of all new customers came from referrals.

THE MYPROTEIN FORUM – BRINGING THE DISCUSSION TO MY WEBSITE

I decided to set up my own sports nutrition forum on the Myprotein website. Thousands of websites host their own forums for their most loyal customers to chat and exchange ideas, but this was unheard of in 2004. I am confident that I was one of, if not the first to do so. Other business owners thought I was crazy:

'Why do you want to do something like that, Oliver? It's asking for trouble. Anyone who wants to complain is going to be able to make trouble for you on your own doorstep. Your competitors will be laughing.'

I disagreed. After all, I had not achieved what I had by following the crowd and only doing what other people did. Besides, the forums I had been using had become saturated with adverts and marketing posts. I wanted my own marketing space that I was in charge of, and given that I had a large, almost cult-like following, I knew I could build the environment I wanted very quickly.

Again, my instinct was right, and the Myprotein forum rapidly grew into a seriously useful hub where our most loyal, hard-core followers could gather to discuss all things fitness-related and add content of their own. Forum discussions do well on Google searches, so the forum was attracting traffic organically from searches as well.

The forum did indeed provide a platform for dissatisfied customers to air their views; however, I never saw this as a threat. It was an opportunity. Very few people want to complain about stuff for the sake of it, and if someone were obviously 'trolling' the forum, other members would soon put them in their place. Unhappy customers complain because their expectations, which are usually reasonable, have not been met. By giving them the platform to voice their concerns and acting on those concerns swiftly, I was demonstrating a remarkable level of transparency, and everyone could see we were a brand that listened to our customers.

I was building a community where I could nurture, communicate with, learn from, and better serve my customer base. It was another win-win situation. Customers knew they were being listened to, and Myprotein was constantly improving its service. The forum continued to grow steadily, becoming increasingly busy, and eventually had over a million posts.

People wouldn't have been congregating on the Myprotein forum and actively promoting our products had the quality not been there in the first place. Customer loyalty is driven by quality and value. To those people who told me that launching my own forum was a bad idea, if that is how they feel, I suggest they take a good, hard look at their products and services. If you are investing in excellent customer service, you will have nothing to fear or hide from.

THE EARLY DAYS OF ADWORDS

As more businesses embraced the internet revolution and started selling online, Google became increasingly important as a vehicle for driving traffic to websites. Numerous search engines had risen and fallen in the battle to become the go-to place for finding things online, but, by the time I launched Myprotein, Google was the clear winner.

In 2004, Google's online advertising concept, AdWords, was still very much in its infancy, having been launched only four years earlier. AdWords was less complex then than it is today, but a very powerful and intelligent tool all the same, and I immediately recognised the opportunity to use the platform for growing Myprotein. For the uninitiated, here's a childproof explanation of how it works.

When you search for anything in Google, the first couple of listings at the top are paid-for advertisements and will have the word 'Ad' written in bold next to the website address. These advertising campaigns are set up in AdWords, Google's own advertising platform. The results you will see beneath those advertisements are organic listings that have made it to the first page of the search because of factors relating to search engine optimisation (SEO).

I set up an AdWords account and created a text advertisement, which would link through to the Myprotein website. That advertisement would only show on pages that were displayed to people who had searched for whatever keyword or key phrase I was targeting. If someone was searching online for 'whey protein', for example, it was highly likely they were looking for a protein supplement. Typically, Myprotein advertisements were simple and to the point:

Premium Whey Protein/£10/kg | Next Day Delivery
Multiple flavours to choose from. 5-Star rated.

Depending on the industry concerned and the keywords and key phrases being targeted, the competition to appear on page one of the search results could be fierce, so businesses would 'bid' for a price per click – the price you would pay per click-through from the text advertisement to your website, based on the keyword or key phrase you were bidding for. If the keywords or key phrases you wanted to be found under were more sought-after, the bid price would be much higher.

With AdWords, you only paid for results, on the assumption that you were bound to convert some of your click-throughs into sales, so if you wanted to be the first in the queue for those click-throughs, you had to pay more than the competition. Google effectively ranked the sponsored listings according to the bid amount being paid. Those who paid the most would appear on the top of the first page of search results for the key terms they had bid for more frequently than anyone else. Those who paid slightly less might still appear on the top of the first page, but less frequently than the advertiser who had outbid them. Advertisers who spent less again would be more likely to appear in the right-hand margin, and depending on how much they had bid, they would be placed higher or lower on the page. How much you paid determined your place in the pecking order.

I was quick off the mark when it came to using AdWords, at a time when very few were selling whey powder directly to the consumer online, so the bid price for search terms such as 'whey protein' was still fairly low. I had almost no competition and was bidding pennies per click rather than pounds. If the highest bid was only thirty pence, for example, it was easy for me to offer thirty-one pence to win the bid and ensure my advertisement would always appear at the top of the page.

Even those with a basic understanding of business recognise that the most successful entrepreneurs know their numbers. AdWords provided a suite of tools for finding out how many times the advertisement had appeared (impressions) and how many times it had been clicked on, so the click-through rate (CTR) could be calculated. You could also see how many of those click-throughs had led to a sale, which would give you the cost per acquisition (CPA) – how much it was costing to acquire a new customer using Google AdWords. I didn't want to pay for existing customers who were using Google to find our website, so I excluded anyone searching for the Myprotein brand by name as a 'negative keyword', and that brought the true CPA down further by filtering out brand searching.

There was a lot more to AdWords than picking one or two strong keywords or key phrases relating to your industry and then throwing all your money at those. For a start, if everyone did that, they'd all be bidding for the same limited selection of words and phrases, and those bids would become very expensive very quickly. You could save money and greatly reduce the CPA by aiming for the keywords and phrases that were less popular – also known as 'long-tail keywords'. Bidding for 'whey protein powder' would be less expensive than 'whey protein' because people are less likely to search for 'whey protein powder', but those that do are still ideal prospects.

I built my AdWords campaigns from scratch, starting with keyword research. Having decided on a selection of keywords to investigate, I would use AdWords' suite of tools to find out how often each word or phrase was searched for and how much it would cost to bid for it. The key was to balance the popularity of the search term with the bid price for targeting it. If a long-tail keyword was so obscure it was rarely going to be searched for, it wasn't worth bidding on.

Having decided upon which keywords I was going to focus it was time to apportion the advertising spend accordingly. AdWords allowed you to set spending limits for each keyword that you bid for, which was a fantastic idea because it meant you could plan your advertising spend strategically. It also stopped you from overspending if the click-through rate of one of your keywords suddenly shot through the roof.

Once I had chosen the right keywords, placed my bids and decided how much I was going to spend on each one, I had to make sure that people who saw the advertisements would want to click on them. Technology and hi-tech tools will only take you so far. Improving the click-through rate was down to copywriting skill, and that was my job as well. However, Google allowed you to add in a variation of the copy for the same advertisement, and its algorithm would determine which version had worked best using 'A/B test principles'. This feature meant you could fine-tune your copy to maximise the advertisement's effectiveness.

AdWords campaigns needed to be monitored carefully because the situation was constantly changing. The bid price for search terms was in a state of flux, so even though I would set my bid price at the start of the campaign, if people started bidding more for the same keywords, the advertisements I had set up for that word or phrase could be displaced from the top spot.

Secondly, I had to keep a close eye on the conversion rates relating to each keyword. Google uses a 'pixel' to measure how many click-throughs are converted into orders for a given keyword. Every time someone clicked on an advertisement without placing an order on the site, I was spending money for nothing in return, and my cost per acquisition was rising.

With my campaign manager hat on, I had to decide whether to throw more money at each bid, known as 'bid pushing', or withdraw spending from it, known as 'bid pulling'. I got a buzz from managing AdWords campaigns in the same way I had enjoyed creating sticky posts in the bodybuilding forums. It was exciting and addictive. Winning meant increased profits.

In the early days, the CPA for targeting 'whey protein' was less than £3. It's a different world now. People are savvy, the industry has boomed and there are many advertisers all tapping into the same pie. The main brands are all established, and every brand has its share of the market. These days, you would be lucky to have a CPA of £25, so it takes significantly longer to gain return on the investment. Typically, it now takes a few orders to recoup the cost of acquiring the client, but when I was in the market, I could make an excellent return on their first order.

Over the years, Google's AdWords tools have become increasingly sophisticated, allowing marketers to fine-tune their campaigns with incredible precision. People coming out of university with marketing degrees pay for courses to learn how to use AdWords, and it takes skill and experience to master. However, I was there from the start, so as AdWords has evolved, so have I, to the point that I consider myself an expert.

From 2004 until 2009, I was the only person who had access to Myprotein's AdWords advertising campaigns. Nobody else was allowed near the Myprotein AdWords account, not even with a set of very specific written instructions. I knew my customers and the business better than anyone, and I understood how to get the most out of AdWords in terms of gaining the optimal CTR and CPA – reach and profit – however, this wasn't infinitely scalable!

In 2009, we engaged a dedicated AdWords agency. The handover was very gradual, but when it came to giving up control of the AdWords campaigns, that process had to be particularly slow and methodical. Around 40 per cent of Myprotein orders were coming from AdWords, so that was a major part of our overall marketing mix. AdWords, the groundbreaking referral scheme and SEO were the cornerstones of Myprotein's marketing strategy and, collectively, these three helped generate around 80 per cent of new business.

GETTING TO GRIPS WITH SEARCH ENGINE OPTIMISATION

Whereas AdWords provided the platform to jump the queue and be seen at the top of the most relevant pages for the keywords of your choice, having the right SEO strategy could put you on the first page without paying Google a single penny. But it wasn't, and isn't, easy. SEO is an art that takes time, patience and strategic thinking.

When someone types a word, phrase or sentence into a Google search, Google wants to ensure it finds the most relevant, high-quality and up-to-date results to match the query. Why? Because its entire business model depends on its ability to deliver meaningful and useful results in the blink of an eye. If it can't do that, users will find another search engine that can, and the advertisers will follow. Once you understand that concept, you can immediately grasp why Google is constantly seeking to improve its algorithm and what you need to do to keep up. Understand the spirit of the rules, and the letter of the rules will naturally follow.

Google ranks pages for relevance, and the process is both simple and complex at the same time. It follows very simple principles to rank websites but has to use a versatile and complex algorithm that looks at a huge range of variables to do the calculation.

At the most basic level, a website will be assessed on its content. Does the text in the site match the search request? Perhaps it does. However, if the site has not been updated for six months, its content could be out of date. Likewise, if the content is not well written – not easy to read or riddled with spelling errors – it will be judged to lack credibility.

How easy is it to use the site? Has it been optimised to adapt to the device it is being displayed on or does it offer a poor user experience (UX)? Other factors include how it is linked to the wider online discussion for the keywords and key phrases being searched for. How relevant is the site to the overall conversation? For example, if the site relates to best-practice marketing techniques for 2021, then you'd expect it to have a regularly updated blog section to keep people informed of the latest trends and developments. And if it contained any content of value, you'd expect other sites to refer to it. That brings me to a concept called PageRank (PR), which, up until around 2011, was a highly significant metric in understanding how your website would be ranked by Google. Here, 'Page' is a reference to the name of Google's co-founder, Larry Page, as opposed to a web page. PageRank is a measure of a site's authority, not a page's.

The more relevant your site was judged to be for the keywords and key phrases relating to its content, the higher its PageRank would be. Now, think about this: if you wanted to know where to buy a second-hand car, and a few of your friends offered you advice, you would be unlikely to listen to the one who had driven three different disasters over the last three months. Their advice would lack credibility. They would hold no authority. However, the one who had been driving the same old, second-hand car, which had not failed an MOT for four years, might be a better person to talk to.

'What year's your car? Ten years old, isn't it? And you paid peanuts for it. I've never known you ever to have an issue with that motor. Where did you get it from?'

By the same token, if your marketing website is mentioned on a directory site that lists every kind of business you can imagine, whether they are top class or bottom of the pile, that is not going to count for as much as being referred to in a BBC online article about marketing trends. The BBC website carries the maximum level of authority, so if there is a link to your site from there, that reflects well on your site's authority, and its ranking will improve. You could say a 'backlink', as it is known, from the BBC website will give your site a huge boost in authority according to the Google algorithm – or mega ranking juice, to put it bluntly.

At this point, it is worth mentioning the difference between 'black hat' and 'white hat' SEO. It's all very well understanding that adopting SEO best-practice principles will bring results – developing and maintaining a high-functioning, user-friendly, regularly updated site that is informative and highly relevant to the industry it relates to – but if your site is new, it is going to take a long time for Google to realise how fantastic it is. So, webmasters go out of their way to figure out how to boost their Google rankings by any means possible. Just as a sole trader will sometimes try to create the illusion that they have a massive office in the city centre, to boost their credibility, SEO experts do the best they can to show Google their websites are the most relevant search results in their industry.

White hat practices include all the things that Google wants you to do – creating excellent content, being respected enough in your field that high-authority sites want to link to your site, creating cutting-edge blog articles that show you as a thought leader, etc. In other words, putting a lot of time and energy into building up your authority the squeaky-clean way.

Black hat covers all the underhand techniques to make Google think your site is much more relevant than it really is – keyword stuffing, paid-for backlinks and other shortcuts that go against the spirit of good SEO.

The reality is that black hat SEO will reflect poorly on your site in the long run, and when – not if – Google catches you out, your site will be kicked so far into the long grass of search results that your long forgotten MySpace page will be more likely to show up in a search than your website. But at the same time, it is logical and reasonable to want to follow Google's algorithmic thinking as closely as possible and stay ahead of the curve in terms of showing its algorithm how important your site is to the industry it belongs to.

SEO is very different now, in 2021, than it was a decade or so ago. Things have moved on, but the art of SEO still boils down to striking the balance between playing perfectly to Google's algorithm and the possibility of unintentionally overstepping the mark into black hat territory. From an SEO perspective, the forum I created on the Myprotein website turned out to be a stroke of genius because instead of having to even think about paying others for backlinks, I had a whole army of followers who were constantly pointing people to my website. And they were discussing Myprotein on many of the most highly relevant and authoritative sites. The referral scheme links created many more organic backlinks which also worked hugely in my favour.

My focus had always been on creating a high-functioning, fully optimised, efficient and easy-to-use site for anyone wanting to find the right supplements for their training objectives. The content was clean, well written, concise and highly relevant to my industry. In a nutshell, I had developed a site that was naturally compatible with the principles of white hat SEO. This was down to the ethos of the brand rather than any deliberate attempt to do things with SEO in mind.

You could say it was organically Google-friendly; however' a gentle nudge to help rankings was not going to get me a Google penalty. I paid bloggers to write high-quality articles that were optimised for the keywords and key phrases I wanted to target. In other words, keywords were blended into the text to ensure the optimum level of 'keyword density' without impacting on the article's natural flow and readability. They would then submit these articles to the editors or content managers of high-authority websites in the hope of being published. The blogs were well written, informative and designed to offer value, but they also contained carefully placed backlinks to the Myprotein website.

We targeted high-ranking Domain Authority (DA) websites, including '.edu' sites, which are among the highest-ranking, top-level domains. Domain Authority is another ranking metric, which is not part of Google's algorithm but gives an accurate indication of a site's authority. Sites such as these would only publish the best articles, so although I was paying for blog articles, nothing I was doing was underhand. I was giving myself the best fighting chance of getting noticed by asking people who were far better at writing optimised articles than I was to reach out and win some organic backlinks for Myprotein. This practice is known as 'SEO outreach'.

I enjoyed the cat-and-mouse game of keeping up with the ever-changing Google algorithm. Every now and then, Google would announce a major update, which was often the equivalent of turning the world upside down. Those who had seen it coming, such as myself, would already be prepared for the new algorithm. Others would tumble from the front page of Google to the internet's version of oblivion. For many, that meant the end of their business as their lifeblood had effectively been cut off. No shop window, no sales funnel and no enquiries. No business!

Learning about SEO wasn't a chore to me. The same elements that had fascinated me about hacking as a teen appealed to me when it came to beating Google's algorithm. I immersed myself in online forums and SEO think tanks, where I could learn the latest techniques for optimisation. There will always be code makers and code breakers, and they push each other to progress and evolve. In many ways, they are two sides of the same coin – innovators, strategists and intellectual combatants. It all comes down to what side of the fence people want to sit on. I found SEO interesting and rewarding in the same way that I loved building AdWords campaigns. It gave me a channel for combining my technical and creative skills to achieve measurable results that meant something in the real world – more traffic, more sales and more revenue. You will not be surprised to hear that this was another role I passed on with care when I employed a marketing director and then a dedicated agency in 2009.

USING EMAIL TO EFFECTIVELY REACH CUSTOMERS

While the aim and principles of marketing will always remain the same, there are many methods for achieving marketing objectives and these are constantly changing. Another marketing tool that I used to grow Myprotein was email. These days, email marketing has become a tougher nut to crack. People have become a lot more choosy about what they will accept in their inboxes, and anti-spam filters have become so sensitive that even the most important emails can be rejected if the subject line has not been well thought out. And, of course, new legislation such as the EU's GDPR regulations have placed even tighter controls on how email data can be stored and used.

Email marketing was a small but important part of our overall business development strategy, and our approach was so squeaky clean that it would have passed today's GDPR regulations with flying colours. Our customers signed up to receive emails when they registered with the Myprotein website, and given the close relationship we had with our customers and the loyalty they showed towards our brand, they were usually delighted to hear from us. But we never launched any kind of email marketing campaign until 2005 when the brand was around a year old.

When it comes to email marketing, you have to strike a balance between maximising the amount of revenue you can generate and the risk of irritating customers. With that in mind, I took a very cautious approach to contacting people via email, so I only sent one or two newsletters per month. In hindsight, I believe I should have done a lot more email marketing, and I often feel the same about affiliate marketing.

Many businesses outsource affiliate marketing to agencies that have access to thousands of affiliate marketers whom they can cherry-pick to target the right groups. That was never something I was going to do because I wanted to stay in direct personal control of the Myprotein brand – one poor decision can adversely affect a brand's reputation for a long time – but I didn't have the time to invest in understanding and implementing an affiliate marketing campaign.

Once I recruited a very talented marketing director, Mark, in 2009, who was heading up the marketing department at Rightmove at the time, email activities were gradually increased and became smarter. The database was segmented to enable more accurate targeting, and we started sending out specific weekly offers to different groups. Weekly became twice-weekly, twice-weekly became thrice-weekly, and now emails are sent out daily. As I said, the climate has changed quite dramatically in regard to how emails can be used for marketing. The fact that it is still working for Myprotein is testament to the effectiveness of building up a database slowly and carefully, and having the right feel for how you can use it for marketing purposes without alienating your customer base. The brand must be doing something right!

USING PRINT – LEAVE NO STONE UNTURNED

While Myprotein was ahead of its time from an e-commerce perspective, I understood that to maximise reach, you have to explore all avenues to your market. There were still plenty of people reading printed publications such as *Muscle and Fitness, Men's Health, FHM* and other men's lifestyle magazines. Now, some of them would also be spending time reading about fitness online, but what about the ones who weren't? I wanted to reach them as well. That's where print advertising entered the mix.

I hired a freelance designer to help with design, and I dipped my toes in the water with an eighth of a page advertisement in *Flex*, in 2004 if my memory serves me right. Over a period of time, having built a relationship with the advertising manager, I gradually upgraded to quarter-page advertisements, then half-page, and so on, until eventually I was booking the inside front cover.

Print advertising never delivered the measurable results of other marketing mediums. Yes, I appreciated that, from a branding perspective, Myprotein couldn't afford not to be seen in the relevant print publications, but I was always cynical about how printed advertisements benefitted our bottom line. For that reason, print never gave me the same buzz as my other marketing activities. There was no sense of achievement, nothing to measure and no indication that they were doing any good at all. Where's the fun in that? The conversations with Mark, the new marketing director, around how much we should spend on print were always 'lively'.

THE POWER OF TELEVISION

Around 2005, I applied for a place on *Dragons' Den*, but I had no intention of taking investment from anyone. Of course, I'd listen to any serious offers, but my primary goal was to leverage the opportunity for marketing; the show's viewership peaked at 3.4 million that year!

At such an early stage in Myprotein's journey, investors would have wanted me to sell equity too cheaply, especially on that show. That said, if I was going to appear on *Dragons' Den*, I wanted to be given at least one good offer.

My application was successful and, following a series of interviews, I was scheduled to feature, but I withdrew from the show a few months before filming. While the publicity would have been great for Myprotein, and I am confident that at least one dragon would have put in a bid, I was just too busy, and I was focused on running the business. Remember, you can always change your mind, even after you have already started a ball rolling.

People often ask me how I would feel about appearing as a dragon on the show. I am sure it would be a lot of fun, but I couldn't dedicate the time. Who knows? Maybe I will appear as a guest some time, if they invite me.

BOOTSTRAP YOUR MARKETING

I am proud of what I achieved as a marketer, especially as I had never been on a single marketing course. You could say I bootstrapped my marketing in the same way that I bootstrapped my business. Marketing is widely recognised as being hit and miss.

It is easy to get it wrong and spend a lot of time, effort and money for nothing in return. When I reflect on my approach to marketing, I can honestly say I got it right most of the time. And I didn't just figure out what other people were doing and then do that better, although it is fair to say I became an expert in disciplines such as paid search marketing and organic SEO. I trailblazed. Others have followed.

If there is one takeaway that anyone reading this should remember, it is to recognise the importance of creating as many routes to a sale as you can. Leave no stone unturned in ensuring you can reach as wide a market as possible and that anybody looking for your products and services will land in your shop, on the end of your phone or on your website.

I stayed connected to my customer base and focused my energy on developing new products that addressed their needs before anyone else did. And I made sure that however they were engaging with the world of sport and nutrition, they would find out about Myprotein and how our products could benefit them. I created multiple 'landing pads' for people to buy from my brand, and I believe that was one of the key drivers of Myprotein's growth and success.

CHAPTER TWELVE

INNOVATIVE THINKING – DISCOVERING NEW IDEAS THAT WORK

Plenty of things happen to us and around us in life that we have absolutely no control over. It is a waste of time to get hung up over things we can't do anything about, and time is too precious to waste.

At any given moment, we are faced with a junction, and there are many directions we can take. Sometimes, these micro-decisions seem insignificant in the grand scheme of things. However, wherever we are today will have far more to do with the decisions that we have made than force majeure, and that includes the micro-decisions that we might not have thought were important at the time they were made. The older we are, the more time we have had to seize control of those decisions and put ourselves on the road that we choose. And it is never too late to realise that.

Micro-decisions are not only about taking action. They also relate to how we react or respond to the world around us. I am not a psychologist, and I am not going to claim that emotions are a choice, but I believe that what we do with our emotions and how we respond to them is entirely under our control. Everyone gets angry, but not everyone shouts or lashes out or smashes up their room. Everyone gets kicked in the teeth sometimes, and it can feel as though life is hopeless, but those who stand up, regardless of how futile it might seem, and choose to believe they can make things better, often turn things around.

We can be the directors of our lives or the victims of circumstance. That is one choice we all have to make. I made mine in business, and it paid off.

I will be honest and admit that I have been impatient for as long as I can remember, and that mostly boils down to being intolerant of time being wasted. It's precious, and I want results now. To be fair, however, I make a conscious effort not to allow my impatience to negatively impact on others. I will be discussing leadership later, but what I will say here is that those who have worked with me and for me would happily verify that one of my key ways for motivating others has always been to lead by example.

Most people who know me would also probably add that I am a hard example to follow in terms of hitting life at 100 mph and working long hours. If you want to bootstrap your life and your business, it helps, and that's why I devoted an earlier chapter to showing how hard it really is. But I have never inflicted that upon or expected it of others. After all, the way other people behave is another one of those things that we can't control. We can only hope to influence how they control their own behaviour.

My feeling of impatience might be so deep-rooted that I can't eradicate it from my psyche, but what I can do is control how I respond to it. My response to impatience and the desire to make the best possible use of time has been to look out for ways to save time at every opportunity. This mindset affects every decision I make, from the major life-changing choices to the seemingly insignificant micro-decisions. All my choices point in one direction: efficiency. That doesn't mean I am anti-social either. It means I choose who I socialise with, how I socialise and when I socialise. Making conscious decisions is one of the keys to success in life. Understanding how to make your natural traits and tendencies work for you is yet another example of bootstrapping. I believe any trait can be turned into a positive force for good.

My obsession with efficiency has been a major factor in driving me to think differently and come up with innovative ideas that I could develop into tangible time and money savings. My desire to save time and money extends to the people I serve, and it forms the backbone of great customer service.

There is a famous quote, which is usually credited to Einstein: 'The definition of insanity is doing something over and over again and expecting a different result.' Whoever said it was bang on the money, and that's my point.

CURIOSITY IS THE KEY TO DISCOVERY

I am not special, not superhuman, and I am certainly no intellectual giant. I studied and put a lot of time into learning things, but the choice to think differently is one that any of us can make at any time – *what if?* That's all it takes. If you don't ask the awkward questions, you might never see the alternatives.

Throughout my story, there are examples of situations where the ideas I came up with were not rocket science but came about because I asked basic questions and had an open mind as to where my questioning would take me. That's where curiosity is crucial. People who always think they are right will only ever question opposing perspectives. Question everything. It is human nature to have a perspective and to feel attached to it, but nobody is right all of the time, and if there is a better way of doing something, I want to find it.

When curiosity, questioning and recognising trends come together, that's when the most lucrative opportunities arise. Ideas come in all shapes and sizes from the bizarre to the hilarious, and they won't always work, but you have to value every single one of them. If you don't explore new ideas, you won't find the clever ones that will work. That's what innovation is – discovering new ideas that work.

'TRENDSPOTTING'

Even 'trendspotting', the term I coined to describe my passion for, well, spotting trends, came about from identifying patterns – something that only happened because of my natural curiosity. You spot patterns by paying attention to changes taking place now and seeing how those changes relate to what has happened before. Predicting how things are changing allows you to identify potential threats and opportunities before you reach them. If you see them earlier than everyone else, you have the chance to stay ahead. It's one of the reasons I have grown to love history. Earlier in this book, I quipped that understanding the French Revolution was never going to make me rich, but, for sure, it would help a leader to determine whether they were on the path to being overthrown or celebrated.

In terms of new product development, innovative thinking can stem from being one step ahead on a predictable curve. Other times, it is more a case of being one of the first to recognise that a significant change in direction is taking place and choosing to explore that road before anybody else does. In my case, I pioneered and set new trends, and that's something I am extremely proud of, but again, it doesn't make me a genius.

In all three of these cases, whether developing a trend, catching a change in direction, or creating a whole new avenue, the mechanism is the same – curiosity and a quest for making things better.

I was not the first to make a sports nutrition supplement or to buy whey powder and develop a product from it. Neither was I the first to build an e-commerce site. Where my thinking proved to be innovative was in recognising the opportunity to be the first in my marketplace to use the internet to sell to the consumer directly. And being vertically integrated made it possible for me to seize opportunities quicker than anyone else.

By the time I launched Myprotein, like-minded individuals had already started gathering in online forums to discuss whatever it was they were into and to learn from one another. The new era of the informed consumer was on the horizon. I spotted it and saw it as an opportunity to market Myprotein by joining in the discussion and developing better products by listening to what was being said.

As I pointed out in the last chapter, the core principles of marketing haven't changed, and maybe never will – true principles tend always to be true and can be generalised to any situation – but how they are implemented will change. Perhaps there will come a time when it is possible to interact with computers via thought. The nuts and bolts of marketing will still be the same, but the trailblazers will recognise they need to be creating the right multi-sense thought concepts to capture the imagination of their customers. Again, innovation is not rocket science. Everything you need is already there, waiting to be discovered.

BUILDING A WEBSITE FROM SCRATCH
– ONE BRICK AT A TIME

Once I had concluded that the way to go was via the internet, turning my attention to the website and how it could function was a natural next step. There are two approaches you can take to anything. One way is to accept the fact that most questions have already been answered and avoid reinventing the wheel. The other method is to go back to the drawing board, start with what you want to achieve and meet the challenge with a fresh pair of eyes. I applied both principles, by starting with the existing best practice and looking at how I could improve upon it.

At the start of this chapter, I stressed the importance of every decision, even the micro-decisions. Opting for a bespoke website was a major decision, and some might wonder why anyone would choose to build a website brick by brick in a text editor. Building a website from the ground up is extremely time-consuming, and it is demanding for anyone who can code. Can you imagine producing a structure as large as a house by stacking dominoes? Similar scenario.

I knew what I wanted to achieve, but at that time there were no suitable e-commerce frameworks available. Whichever angle I took, I was going to have to build many of the functions and features I wanted from scratch. Hiring another developer or an agency to do it was never an option either. It would have cost tens of thousands of pounds, which I didn't have. And anyway, why would I want to pay someone else to do something I excelled in and enjoyed doing?

I am a big believer that some of the most innovative ideas are driven by the challenges we face. The more demanding the challenge, the more creatively we have to think about meeting it.

It was going to take an enormous amount of time and effort, but I intuitively suspected the pay-off would be huge. By taking the brick-by-brick approach, I could implement any feature I wanted. It gave me the scope to ask the what-if questions and to think differently. It opened the door to creating an innovative website that could work exactly as I wanted it to, without compromise.

There are various stories about a lumberjack's perspective on cutting down trees. The story goes that the lumberjack said something along the lines of, 'If I had ten hours to cut down a tree, I'd spend eight hours sharpening my axe, one hour to cut it down, and an extra hour to admire my work.' Some say that story goes all the way back to Abraham Lincoln, but I am mentioning it because it illustrates my point about the value of time perfectly. To use the same analogy, in terms of the time I spent building the website compared to how effective it was when I launched, I spent nine and a half hours sharpening my axe and cut down the tree in ten minutes.

Then there was the Customiser. Is it really so difficult to deduce that consumers want choice and convenience? Surely that is an elementary consideration for anyone with the most basic knowledge of marketing and customer service? And yet, what I observed in the market in the years prior to Myprotein was a lack of choice and minimal customer service.

To be fair to the other brands operating at the time, part of the reason they were slower to offer the maximum level of choice was because they were primarily selling to retailers who were serving a captive audience. There was an element of complacency as well because they each had their share in a rapidly growing market, and they had solid relationships with the retailers and other distributors they were selling to.

IF THEY IMITATE YOU, YOU'RE DOING SOMETHING RIGHT

So, again, that decision to create a bespoke website for selling directly to the consumer almost made improved consumer choice and better service a foregone conclusion. That was the disruptive factor, and it made everything else possible. However, once you go down the trailblazing route, something else becomes inevitable – imitation.

Other brands, such as Bulk Powders, soon followed my lead, and in their eagerness to catch up, many of these brands tried undercutting Myprotein, which is normal practice for me-too brands that are trying to win market share. I am not having a pop at any of them here. Business is like a game of chess involving multiple players. It is ruthless because every customer that you win means one less for your competitors unless they can do something better to draw them away from you.

I would launch a new product, and others would immediately start work to create their own version. That said, by the time they had developed a product of their own, I had usually brought other innovative products to the market. It was cat and mouse, but I always stayed ahead, I believe, because of a difference in mindset – curious, open-minded and customer-focused.

When you have put the time, energy and thinking into developing a new product, why should you sit back and allow your competitors to benefit? Staying ahead was an effective strategy for staying ultra-competitive, retaining customers and winning new ones, but I wanted to minimise losses to the copycats who were undercutting Myprotein. I wanted to develop my own price-matching solution.

There is nothing unusual about the principle of price-matching, and there was nothing new about the concept in 2004 either. Unfortunately, one of the downfalls of selling on price, which is no good for anyone in any market, is how it drives down prices and profits. In a way, the customer benefits least because price wars put pressure on brands to place more focus on selling cheap instead of offering the best products and services.

An excellent example of how to go about price-matching is John Lewis's 'Never Knowingly Undersold' message, which the brand has been using for almost a century. Those words are chosen carefully to show that the company is aware of what others are offering and that it endeavours to offer greater value for every pound spent. It's a very positive message that assures customers rather than encouraging people to shop around or play brands off against each other. It oozes confidence.

THE ONLINE PRICE MATCHER

My own invention, which I am proud of, was the 'Online Price Matcher'. There was nothing special about the principle on which it operated – Myprotein would beat anyone else's price by 10 per cent. What made it innovative was the way it was implemented. Price-matching was becoming a time-consuming and exhausting process. Claims came through from different directions. Some people made comments in forum discussions, and others sent through emails. I had to acknowledge the messages that came in and manually check their claims out online.

I was also concerned about the people who couldn't be bothered claiming their discount. Some of them might just go with the cheaper option, so I needed to kill several birds with one stone – make it easier for the customer, minimise the hassle for me, and add a little John Lewis into the equation by assuring Myprotein's customers that we had it covered and they were unlikely to find a better price.

The Online Price Matcher took care of all three issues efficiently and effectively – my kind of solution. This feature allowed the consumer to type in the URL of another brand, and they would be told which price matches were available for that website and how much the same products would cost from Myprotein after the discount had been applied. Life was easier for everyone.

The text for the Online Price Matcher is shown below:

> ## *Online Price Matcher*
> *Have you found a cheaper price for one of our products or ingredients elsewhere on the Internet? If so, why not use our Online Price Matcher which will search our database for any known price matches.*
>
> *Just enter the URL of the website below and press "Find It!" to search.*
>
> *Website URL:*
> *Don't enter "http://"*
> *(i.e. www.amazon.co.uk)*
>
> *If the price match you are looking for isn't already added, then please contact us and we will add it right away.*

Consumers had one easy-to-find and easy-to-use portal rather than having to contact us, and if they were entitled to discount, it was all taken care of automatically. As for the kind of consumer who might not want the hassle of checking prices, the Online Price Matcher gave them a very strong message: we had confidence in our own ability to match prices. They didn't need to shop around; we had it covered.

The website also featured a Price Match Promise on the home page. Those who clicked on that would be taken to a frequently asked questions (FAQ) page, where Myprotein's price-matching promise was spelt out along with all the necessary caveats – the competitor had to be EU-based and offering the same quality of ingredient. I was careful to stipulate that prices would not be matched for products on a competitor's site that were not in stock or could not be shipped that day. Price-matching is all about comparing like for like, and that's why it didn't apply to our formula or custom blends either.

There were lots of other caveats, and they were all fair. Without terms and conditions, I would have been inviting abuse, but like any small print, it was there for those who wanted to dig.

The first thing people noticed when they visited the Myprotein site was the price promise and the price-matching feature. The strategy and the psychology worked well, and Myprotein's customer retention rate rose significantly. We were not contributing to a price war. We were preventing one.

Incidentally, I tried hard to cover every possible question on the FAQ page, from how we were able to offer such low prices to questions relating to food intolerances, allergies and packaging. Myprotein had been forward-thinking in its approach to packaging from the get-go, by giving the customer the choice to purchase powder in a bag or in a tub, for example. Another packaging initiative I launched before anyone else, which is now commonplace, is the resealable stand-up pouch. This had a cylindrical base to allow it to stay upright and a resealable edge at the top.

The stand-up pouch offers all the benefits of flexible packaging – cost-savings for the customer, lower production costs and reduced environmental impact – without the disadvantages. You can place the pouch onto a work surface, just as you can with a tub, and it is easy to dip the scoop in when making a shake. As the pouch is resealable, its contents stay dry for longer, protected from contamination, and you don't need to worry about leakage when it is stored. Flexible packaging is also much easier to store and ship than tubs or boxes.

Using stand-up pouches forced me to think innovatively about how products would be labelled. The way I got round the challenge was by using preprinted branded pouches that already carried Myprotein's generic branding information. Specific nutritional information was added using transparent labels when each order was blended and packed. The end product was branded, bespoke, and professionally finished. It was a slick operation, and we were the first company to offer this kind of packaging. Everyone else followed, and now stand-up pouches are pretty much industry standard and have been adopted by brands operating within many parallel industries as well.

'THE CUSTOMISER' – RAISING THE BAR IN CUSTOMER CHOICE

One of Myprotein's main selling points was choice – choice of packaging, choice of ingredients and how they were mixed, and customers could even decide whether they wanted a plastic scoop with their powder. The site's pièce de résistance in the early days, which embodied everything that was great about Myprotein's choice proposition, was the Customiser, which allowed customers to create their own bespoke powder to suit their training needs.

Customers appreciated being able to create their own bespoke supplements, but given that a typical order would be for at least 5 kg, they'd be stuck with whatever flavour they had chosen until it was time to reorder. I got round this issue by offering them the option of 'whey protein natural', which was 100 per cent pure whey protein powder with nothing added or taken away – no sweetener and no flavouring. They could purchase the sweetener and flavourings separately.

Whey protein natural is a very versatile product because you can do what you want with it. You can use it to fortify foods such as porridge or smoothies with protein if you want, or you can make the shake just with water and add naturally sweet ingredients such as stevia or honey to give you the sweetness profile you desire. It is entirely up to the individual. By the way, while I find the taste of raw whey protein quite neutral, some would describe it as an acquired taste. One of the small details I included in the Myprotein website was a guide to tastes, which was fully explained in the FAQs.

Our customers would buy the flavours and sweetener they wanted, and this meant they could buy in bulk while enjoying the luxury of a different flavoured shake every day. I'd taken a landing pad – the option of buying plain protein powder because some people wanted that – and seized upon the opportunity to offer even greater choice and better service.

CONSTANT INNOVATION

As I was selling flavourings as a separate item, in powder form, I reflected on whether further cost savings were available. I wondered how these flavoured powders were produced, and whether I could break things down further, so I called Martin, who was the MD of Claremont, which was my preferred flavouring house at the time. He explained that the flavours were supplied to Claremont in liquid form but were sprayed onto a powder, which was then dried to produce a more stable product. The finished product was better for storage, lasted longer and was easier to transport.

I still used the powdered flavourings for blending, but for customers who wanted to buy the flavourings separately to add to whey protein natural, I sold them the raw liquid, which I branded and trademarked as 'FlavDrops'. FlavDrops provided tons of flavour. They were so highly concentrated, customers only needed a couple of drops for a shake, or they could add more to taste. By cutting out another step in the manufacturing process, it was a more efficient way of giving Myprotein customers more choice, more flavour and more value. And again, it was a simple idea, but I was the first in the world to do this. Why hadn't anyone else thought of doing this? They had not asked themselves the question, *How is this flavouring made?*

Weight trainers and bodybuilders look for different kinds of sports nutrition supplements depending on their goals. When they are trying to gain weight, they tend to buy whey protein or milk protein with added carbohydrates, which come in the form of maltodextrin or dextrose. However, these carbohydrates have a high glycaemic index (GI), which means they produce a spike in blood sugar levels. High-GI carbohydrates are neither healthy nor any good for weight gain, unless somebody wants to get fat – blood sugar that is not used is quickly stored as fat – and sugar spikes are dangerous for diabetics as their bodies cannot deal with sugar. I wanted to find a healthier and more useful alternative.

The first thing that came to mind was oats, but the problem with oats is that they are not naturally soluble. At that stage, most people would have dismissed this line of enquiry, and this is one of the main points that I want to get across in this chapter about innovation. The thought processes that I used are learnable. I asked myself whether I could make oats more 'drinkable' by grinding them down into a fine powder. There was only one way to find out. I gave it a go with a mortar and pestle, and it worked!

Having tested the hypothesis and discovered that oats could be ground to produce a lower-GI alternative to dextrose or maltodextrin, I was faced with another challenge. Grinding oats down by hand was not a practical solution, so I was going to have to find a miller. That search took me all the way to Scotland where I found an oat mill that was able to use a milling process to grind down the oats.

I was able to offer Myprotein customers a far superior carbohydrate. It had a significantly lower GI for slow-release energy, and it was water soluble. All it needed was a name, so I went for something simple and wholesome – 'Ultra Fine Scottish Oats'. They did what was promised on the tin and a new product was born. I was paying pennies per kilogram and selling for pounds.

It was a win-win scenario because the customer was getting a higher-quality, healthier carbohydrate that they could have as part of a supplement or on its own as a nutritious meal. This became a top-selling product and was later rebranded as 'Instant Oats'.

Anyone who's seen Sylvester Stallone's iconic boxing film from 1976, *Rocky*, will remember the famous scene where he rises at 4 a.m., staggers still half asleep to the kitchen, opens the fridge, cracks open five eggs into a glass and necks them raw. Raw eggs are synonymous with protein, and I am sure weight trainers, bodybuilders and boxers around the world followed Stallone's lead if they weren't doing it already. The best part is the white of the egg as that is where the protein is, so these days that's what bodybuilders and weight trainers are into.

Now, apart from the fact that drinking raw eggs is a grim experience, there are two main problems. Firstly, there is the possibility of salmonella food poisoning, which can lead to serious illness and even death in extreme cases. The other issue is an ingredient known as avidin, which inhibits the body's ability to process the egg's protein. Cooking an egg properly will kill salmonella and neutralise the avidin, but some nutritionists argue that cooking reduces the egg's nutritional value. Given all of these factors and the complexities of producing something that could be shipped, stored and consumed safely, raw egg whites were not on my radar as a viable product.

Around 2006, I went to a huge food ingredients exhibition to find out what was new on the horizon. After all, our customers wanted the cutting edge of food ingredients. Remember, curiosity is one of the cornerstones of innovative thinking. If there were any other sports nutrition brands there, I didn't see them. The other delegates were large restaurateurs and huge manufacturers that were producing food for the supermarkets. I loved attending such exhibitions, even though spending all day on my feet, visiting one stand after another, was a tiring experience. To put it bluntly, I would be done in by the end of the day. The effort was worthwhile though, because knowing what was out there gave me an edge and I got the chance to speak to lots of people and forge useful relationships.

RAW EGGS WITHOUT THE RISKS

One of the more interesting stands I visited featured a large barrel, which contained litres of specially treated egg whites. The stand belonged to a French company that was supplying ingredients to mass producers of meringue. They had patented a technique for pasteurising egg white enough to neutralise the avidin and kill any salmonella, without 'cooking' the egg and taking away any of its raw qualities. The end product was something that offered all the benefits of raw egg whites with none of the disadvantages, and it could be stored at room temperature for up to six months. This was a next-level product.

There was no doubt about it, I could see the potential for raw egg whites, except for one small issue – Myprotein ran a powder operation, not a liquid one. The French company was used to supplying the product in what are known in the industry as intermediate bulk containers (IBCs), but I didn't want huge vats of the stuff in Myprotein, so that was never going to work for us. However, if they could provide me with more manageable units, such as 1 kg consumer-ready bottles, I felt this could be another viable option for the Myprotein customer.

Numerous conversations followed, many ideas were discussed and bounced back and forth, and the company sent me a variety of containers to check, but there was always something not quite right. What I needed was a plastic bottle that was light, durable and wouldn't leak in transit. I wanted something that looked good and was well sealed, so it had to be the right shape and made from the right material. I was sure we would discover the solution in the end. Optimism and determination are a must if you want to succeed as an entrepreneur. It is too easy to quit, and then you just end up following the leader like everyone else.

In the end, my optimism was justified because they eventually presented us with the perfect container. It was like a plastic milk bottle, but more durable. It was definitely worth the wait, and I had a superb product for Myprotein, although supplying us meant they had to totally reconfigure their production line! Unlike untreated raw egg whites, which have an unpleasant gloopy consistency, Myprotein's new product had a more viscous, almost syrupy feel to it. The bodybuilders loved it, and it blew up.

They were able to purchase thirty-two raw egg whites in one 1 kg bottle, packed with natural protein and other goodness. There was no risk of salmonella, they could keep it for months, it tasted great and was easy to drink. Consuming six raw egg whites in the morning, after a workout, had never been so pleasant or safe. We had developed a flier of a product.

I knew other competitors were bound to follow, but the company I was dealing with was the only one of its kind. Anyone wanting to buy this pasteurised egg white would have to come to this company, and they had a patent on it so no one else could copy them. I secured my position by including an exclusivity agreement in the purchasing contract, so no other sports nutrition brands could buy from them. It was the first time anyone in the sports nutrition market had done this, to the best of my knowledge, and this became something else that my competitors copied. It meant there was a race to discover new ingredients, new products and new ideas, but Myprotein usually won.

I had a knack for bringing ideas to the table that were ahead of their time, but I have only really talked about the ones that worked. On some occasions, I couldn't get an idea across the finish line. We can learn just as much, if not more, from things going wrong or from failing to cross the finishing line, as we can from the sensational victories. You could say the victories only serve to confirm our theories. They prove us right. The defeats, while painful, teach us things we didn't know!

To finish this chapter, I want to share an innovative concept that I never quite managed to complete, although some elements were implemented in a kind of advanced beta form.

AUTOMATED DATA ANALYSIS

Around 2005 or 2006, I read a book about three marketing metrics – recency (R), frequency (F) and monetary (M). By that time, the 'RFM model' was not new, having been introduced to the world of marketing by Arthur Hughes in the mid-1990s.

To give a very brief and simplified explanation, RFM analysis involves segmenting the customer base according to recency – when did they last buy something; frequency – how often do they buy something; and monetary – what is their typical spend when they buy something. Understanding these metrics allows marketers to predict buying behaviour and also identify ways of encouraging people to buy more.

In principle, staying on top of RFM metrics, on a customer-by-customer basis, allows marketers to notice changes in customer behaviour. If someone's RFM metrics suddenly change because they are spending more, or they are buying things less frequently, why is that happening, and how can marketers capitalise on it? The RFM model, therefore, is an excellent tool for optimising sales and developing campaigns to maximise engagement with customers.

I could see how the RFM model could help me drive sales and engagement. For example, if I could easily identify those customers whose buying frequency had dropped, I could launch a campaign to re-engage them, encourage them to buy more, or, at the very least, find out what had changed. Strategies could be developed and implemented to respond intelligently to specific behavioural triggers.

The last thing I wanted to do was trawl through stacks of numbers and analyse them manually. I recognised the value of the RFM model, but there had to be a more convenient, accurate and efficient way of utilising it. There was, and it seemed obvious to me – automation.

Every Myprotein sale left a data trail because it came through the website, so the figures were all there to be measured and analysed. To my knowledge, there were no other tools out there for automatically applying RFM analysis to data. If anyone had thought of the idea, they hadn't done anything about it – not within the nutrition space anyway – so I was going to be one of the first.

I built a separate tool for segmenting the Myprotein database according to RFM principles, and I developed an algorithm that could predict when a customer was likely to return, what they would buy, and how much they would spend, etc. When customers behaved unpredictably, an appropriate trigger email would be launched to respond to the change. What I had created was a data warehouse for processing, interrogating and understanding big data.

My data analysis tool came close but never quite delivered the functionality I was after. I had wanted to create something that was constantly humming behind the scenes, taking care of everything automatically. However, I had to run it manually once or twice a week, and it was time-consuming. Even though I never managed to accomplish the mission, I put the hours in and continued with it almost as a labour of love. It was a puzzle I enjoyed trying to solve.

On reflection, given that I was developing this idea around 2006, this whole concept was well ahead of its time. Had I finished this project, I am sure it would have grown the business significantly, perhaps exponentially, by strengthening loyalty, increasing cross-selling, and boosting the spend per customer.

I have shared with you some of the innovations I am most proud of, but there were many more. Once I had decided to think differently and follow my ambitions rather than settling for what was already commonplace, the scene was set for plenty of new challenges, and therefore opportunities to innovate, to arise. It was a brave step to take but one that paved the way for Myprotein to be widely credited with creating a new market while becoming the number-one sports nutrition brand globally. It has since been described as probably the most innovative sports nutrition company ever.

Exploring new ideas is not something you should be afraid of, and it can be fun. Try to find ways of turning your weaknesses into strengths and making strengths even more valuable. Don't be afraid to look for the solution for the toughest problem. I turned my lack of appetite for doing arithmetic into a strength by building algorithms to do calculations for me. The Customiser told me exactly how much of each ingredient to blend together for an order. And who would have thought someone who really wasn't comfortable with maths would be one of the first to build a big-data analysis tool?

Let challenges drive you forward. Ask questions. Listen to the answers with an open mind and ask more. These are the traits of the innovative mindset.

CHAPTER THIRTEEN

STRATEGY: BE LIKE WATER

Pick up any business book you like, and I can almost guarantee you will be advised that you need to write a business plan. You might have already written one, started one or feel guilty because it's just an idea in your head right now.

Writing a business plan is a great idea, and speaking as an investor, when I come across start-ups looking for investment, I expect them to have one. That said, if they haven't prepared one, I wouldn't hold it against them. I'd simply ask them to come back to me when they had something concrete to present. Why would I not just turn them away? Because I didn't have a written business plan either. I wasn't the first self-made entrepreneur to succeed without one, and I won't be the last.

Not having a written business plan doesn't mean someone doesn't have a plan or isn't prepared. I have a passion for learning and self-development. The fact that I could go through the school system and leave with only one GCSE and yet go on to become an expert in business, ColdFusion, SEO, NPD, Google AdWords and marketing, for example, illustrates how different people absorb information in different ways.

When it came to gaming, learning about computers and programming, I did it all on my terms. Some people like learning early in the morning. Others do better during the afternoon or evening. I was always a night owl. Schools are regimented institutions. Children are expected to start at a set time, which is usually quite early in the morning, and stick to a timetable. That was never going to work for an autodidact like me. Not only do different individuals have their own optimal times for learning and development, but we all have our own preferred approach to learning as well.

Psychologists say that we each use a unique mix of kinaesthetic, visual and auditory modes of learning. While we all use all three approaches, people tend to rely on one or two dominant modes: feeling, visualisation or talking things through. I believe I mostly process ideas visually and kinaesthetically. When it came to the Myprotein website, I knew what it was going to look like, and I felt the customer experience that I wanted to deliver through the site.

Speaking of web development, the best code is clean and efficient, with no unnecessary elements, and every piece of code you write should be serving a purpose. I love efficiency, so you will not be surprised to learn I am very similar in conversation. I tend to say what needs to be said, at least in business situations, and I prefer people to give me top-level summaries unless I want to delve deeper into something. Of course, everyone's different, so I don't expect others to show the same brevity. Words are only a means to an end for me as opposed to a way of figuring things out. I use them to communicate and to receive information from others, but the way I play with ideas in my head is by seeing them in my mind's eye and feeling my way around.

Maybe it's because I spent so much time alone as a child that the auditory mode of learning became less important or that might just be how I am hardwired. Either way, writing a business plan wasn't on the radar. For whom was I going to write one? I didn't need to see one, and I wasn't asking anyone else for help. Sure, I spoke to the banks in the early days, but they were dismissive from the start of the conversation, so having a written business plan would have made no difference whatsoever.

Again, I need to emphasise that I bootstrapped my business. If you want someone to invest in your idea, you will need to put together a business plan. They may not ask for it straight away, but if the right boxes are ticked for them to want to take a closer look, they will want to see a plan. On that note, business plans need to be realistic. Overinflated growth figures that appear to have been plucked from mid-air, or as former Chancellor of the Exchequer Kenneth Clarke once put it, belong to 'the Dolly Parton school of economics – an unbelievable figure blown out of all proportion, with no visible means of support', are a turn-off for any investor or loan provider.

If I didn't have a written business plan, what kind of plan did I have? Remember, as an eight-year-old boy, I'd written a letter to my teacher declaring that I was going to be 'a boss'. I don't remember writing that letter, but what I do remember from being that age is that if anyone asked me what I wanted to do when I grew up, I'd always say 'a businessman'. I wanted to be a businessman. I believe that having that target in my mind at such a young age was a kind of plan in the making. A seed was planted.

Later, in my teens, when others asked me what I was going to make of myself, the only thing I was certain of – and I did know it somehow – was that I was going to be a millionaire before the age of thirty. How did I know? Was I psychic? No. Again, I believe this was the beginning of a plan. At the time, I never had a coach or mentor, but I have come to understand that the starting point for anyone trying to achieve success is to knock down the invisible walls of their mind. Fear, doubt, lack of imagination and a lack of ambition are all barriers to success. The first part of any plan has to be having the right mindset.

I was always a highly driven individual, but only when the right buttons were pressed. That's where knowing what you want is vital. If you don't know where you want to go, you're not going to be that enthusiastic about putting one foot in front of the other. When I needed to raise funds to buy the things I wanted, I didn't write down target figures or how many hours I was going to have to work to hit them. It was much more instinctive than that. I focused on the obvious – find a way of making money and do as much of that as possible – and I went for it, whether that meant working two separate paper rounds, working in a kebab shop or behind a bar.

OK, once I had got that ball rolling, I probably did a few calculations to estimate how long it would take to accumulate the money I needed, but the point is that writing down the figures or knowing how long it would take wouldn't make it happen any faster. I knew what I had to do, and I did it. When it came to working hard and earning money, my lack of patience came in extremely useful. I wanted the results yesterday, so I would do whatever it took to get to where I wanted to be as swiftly as possible.

Action is what you need for results. It is better to start without the perfect plan than not to start at all, as long as you have mulled things over enough to know you are not risking disaster. You have to strike the right balance between being a go-getter and being reckless. Those two things are not the same.

DRIVE, FOCUS AND DETERMINATION

Another important part of any strategy is to have focused determination. If your heart's not in it, how can you hope to succeed? Whatever kind of project you want to start, you have to be ready for the challenges, the sixteen-hour days and the things that go wrong. The most successful entrepreneurs are driven.

When I started building the Myprotein website, there was no long-term plan. I had a product, and I instinctively knew the value proposition. Myprotein was going to offer more value by delivering the best possible quality at the keenest price, wider choice, greater transparency and superb customer service. I knew what I wanted.

As a customer, I could empathise with the people I was building Myprotein for, and everything I was doing was to provide a more convenient way for them to purchase the perfect products for their specific needs. I didn't need a better plan than that. How I felt about my customers and what I knew they wanted was my North Star, and that was the science behind every decision I made.

So, while there was no written business plan, what I had was a sense of being on the right track. Building Myprotein was what I was supposed to be doing. All my life, I had known I wanted to be a businessman, and I'd been hungry for success. I had the confidence, the self-belief and the determination to succeed. But more than that, knowing exactly who my customers were and what they wanted meant that I knew where I was going.

You could say I was practising the art of planning without planning. When you have a strategy, planning almost takes care of itself, brick by brick, and it lets you remain agile and responsive to change. But what was my strategy?

When I first reflected on how I built Myprotein, I didn't recognise a strategy as such, but the more I have pondered the question, the more I have realised that the strategy was so close to me as to be in my blind spot. The strategy was my mindset. When everything you do comes from the core of who you are – how you think, how you feel, what you value – you can't go wrong. It's not something you have to learn or adopt. It is who you are.

THE 'BE LIKE WATER' PHILOSOPHY

In many ways, my mindset could be expressed as a philosophy – be like water – and when I applied that philosophy to building a sports nutrition brand, Myprotein was the result. It was the embodiment of my values. I could devote an entire chapter to my affinity with water, but I will keep my explanation brief.

Water always takes the route of least resistance. Next time you find yourself looking out of the window on a rainy day, take a moment to notice the water droplets on the glass, and watch how they find their way down the pane. You can't predict their route. It's as though they feel their way there. Moment to moment, they find the path of least resistance.

Knowing what my customers wanted and tuning into their needs made selling to them as easy as giving sweets to children. I focused on my customers, and I empathised with them. That kept me on the path of least resistance and made everything else possible. Myprotein was sensitive to change and was able to evolve at a quicker rate than other brands.

Osmosis is the process by which water naturally moves from an area of higher concentration of water to an area of lower concentration of water. My way of moving into areas of low concentration was to spot new markets and create them. By the time other brands were able to follow us, we were already dominating and our base in that market would be rapidly expanding. Myprotein naturally flowed into the spaces where it could offer value.

In the last chapter, I spoke about micro-decisions. In the long term, it is persistence, patience and small incremental steps that pay dividends. Water is gentle, cleansing and soft, but manages to cut shapes into coastlines and produce the smoothest pebbles from the most jagged-edged rocks. This profound impact on its surroundings doesn't happen overnight. It is the result of a slow, steady and never-ending process. Determination and perseverance are the keys.

Looked at close up or in small amounts, water seems to be passive and offers little resistance when poked or prodded. A cupful of water will easily fragment into many droplets when it is thrown into the air. But it's apparent lack of strength is an illusion. Water has the power to burst through the strongest barriers if there is enough of it and the pressure is high. However, one of its most hidden strengths comes from buoyancy. It can lift the most incredibly heavy objects. Think of oil tankers, cargo ships, aircraft carriers and cruise liners. The fact that they float seems to defy logic. By leveraging the loyalty of Myprotein's customers, I was able to grow the business at an astonishing rate, generating huge amounts of momentum and gaining new customers almost virally. Their loyalty provided the buoyancy to lift Myprotein to even greater heights.

As discussed in the last chapter, one of the secrets of innovative thinking is to be able to explore new ideas and experiment with them. The art of innovation involves being able to let go of expectations and preconceptions based on past experience. You have to think outside of the box and look at things from a fresh perspective. Water washes away and cleanses. We use water to purify the vessels we drink and eat from. In the same way, if we can empty our minds of the known, we make room for the innovative thinking that comes from being open-minded and curious.

Along the same lines, water is able to absorb substances such as sugar, salt or other liquids. It is transformative. The materials it absorbs change their form as they are dissolved, and its own possibilities are expanded. Sugar makes it sweeter, and plain water can become an energy drink. Salt enables it to withstand higher temperatures without having to change to its vapour form. When added to the powders that Myprotein sold, water became a wholesome and tasty sports nutrition supplement! It is the mediator, the relationship builder, the master negotiator or the chair that can handle the most energetic discussions. It facilitates interaction.

No matter how busy I am, how successful I become or however many zeros there are in the bank account, I am always receptive to new ideas. Everything we see around us started as a thought. Imagine how boring life would be without the power of creative thinking. The concepts we are exposed to, that we absorb, often change us forever. Just as water can allow vessels to move from one continent to another, to be like water is to be able to bring people and ideas together to realise new possibilities.

Almost any of the qualities of water that you can think of can be applied to how we approach life, business or problem-solving. But there is one quality that I haven't mentioned yet. Above all else, water enables life. Without it, nothing can survive. It nourishes, protects, freshens, refreshes and heals. It is Mother Nature's miracle cure. My mindset was like water, and that provided me and Myprotein with all the vitality we needed to thrive.

KEEP MOVING FORWARD

I've always had a naturally methodical approach to things, and I constantly look for ways to improve systems to save time. This systematic perspective meant that things mostly ran smoothly, even though I was rushing around like a lunatic. Building the website was painstaking and time-consuming, and while I wouldn't say I didn't jot down a single note, I knew the site's structure inside out, so I always knew what to do next and why.

Once the site was launched, things happened at such break-neck speed that it felt as though I just had to hang on for dear life and make sure I didn't fall off the horse. At the same time, I was spurring the horse to run faster and jump higher. It was one of the most exciting and invigorating times of my life.

I didn't have the breathing space to be able to take a step back and ask where I wanted to take things. But that didn't stop me from doing everything in my power to grow the business further. Finding new ways to reach new customers and sell more was something I enjoyed immensely and found incredibly rewarding.

You can't afford to stand still in business. That could be the moment that you lose your edge and allow your competitors to catch up. One small lapse in concentration could mean missing a threat or an opportunity. It is a race, and there is no finishing line, so you have to keep moving, growing, learning, assessing and future-proofing. As soon as you feel as though you can take your foot off the gas, that is the prompt for going back to the drawing board and asking yourself what you can do to improve and where you want to take things.

As Myprotein took off and the revenue figures were skyrocketing, we hit several key milestones that gave me cause to reflect on how well things were going and where it might all lead. For example, I will never forget the day, late in 2005, when Danny, our Parcelforce driver, came round to take the deliveries but couldn't fit them all in his van. We placed the items in the back as creatively as we could, to get the most out of the space. Then we did the same with the front passenger seat, but no matter what we did, we could not get everything in. Danny had to call a colleague of his to come over at short notice with another vehicle. That was probably one of the first times it hit me how fast we were growing.

Myprotein was, and still is, a lean and highly profitable cash cow. Within three years of trading, we were looking at seven-digit annual revenue figures, and over the next couple of years, I started to wonder how I could safeguard my own personal future. With that in mind, I wrote myself a dividend cheque for the sum of £1 million. I was just twenty-eight years old.

Becoming a millionaire had been an ambition of mine since my teens, but it might surprise you to know that I wasn't super-elated or jumping in the air with raised clenched fists like a lottery winner. For a start, unlike a lottery winner, I'd worked damned hard to make that money. It was the result of persistent effort and smart thinking. And unlike a goal at a football game where the ball has been kicked back and forth until suddenly your team manages to break through and score, I'd seen the revenue figures steadily climbing, month on month, year on year. Technically, I had been a millionaire on paper since the age of about twenty-six, so it was half expected.

In a way, hitting that milestone was the start of a journey, not the end. I wasn't extravagant with my money, so I wasn't about to throw it all away on women and cars, but I was doing all right. For the first time since I'd started, I could focus attention on Myprotein's long-term future.

ONE EYE ON THE ENDGAME

Even though I have always been a self-starter, I'd never really read any books on strategy. The business books that I had read had mentioned the importance of having a business model that worked and then making it work in practice. Well, I definitely had a business model that worked, and I'd nailed the execution. It was 2009, and for the first time since I'd launched Myprotein, I considered my exit strategy.

I approached a corporate finance company to find out more about the process of selling the business. They told me I couldn't sell the business because it was too dependent on me. The only other people working for Myprotein were middle management, office staff, the warehouse team and production operatives. If I took a week off, there was nobody to steer the ship. On that note, from the day I launched Myprotein to the day I sold it seven years later, I didn't take more than seven days off in a row. I think I only had three or four holidays throughout that entire period.

The corporate finance company said they needed to know the business could run without me, and they suggested recruiting a senior management team to gradually take over control from me – on their watch. They said something to the effect that they didn't believe I would be able to do it on my own.

Nothing more needed to be said! There was no way I was going to let that happen. It was my company, and if anyone was going to build a senior management team, it was going to be me. That meeting changed my perspective and, for the first time, I had a clear vision of what it looked like to cross the finish line and step away from Myprotein.

Until then, all the various systems I had in place had kind of evolved by themselves. It had been an instinctive process because that is how I tick. If I was going to hand over control to a team, no matter how competent, experienced and well chosen they were, I was going to have to document all of Myprotein's operations, protocols and KPIs.

That process involved a lot of reflection – another feature of being like water – and it allowed me to see how far I had come, not only in terms of growth but how Myprotein had evolved operationally. I could see the business plan retrospectively. Having the right strategy had allowed the right plan to unfold, and this brings me back to the question considered at the start of this chapter – whether or not you need a business plan.

These days, I am running between fifteen and twenty projects at any one time, some of which I might write about in future books! Do I have a written business plan now? Sure I do, but I am in a different place to where I was in 2003 when I was preparing to start Myprotein.

In 2003, I was a twenty-two-year-old man and I had to take calculated risks, but I am older, wiser, and more mature now. I don't need to, or wish to, take the same kind of risks I was taking in my early twenties, and I have the luxury of being able to step back and take my time. I also recognise that writing a business plan is considered best practice. That said, even with so many more balls in the air than I had when I launched Myprotein, I only write very top-level decks.

Throughout this book, I have talked about the importance of staying agile. Whatever plans you make, be ready to change them. Anything can happen, and although I am sure the majority of my current projects will be successful, it is wise to be just as ready for failure as for success.

Once I had made up my mind to make an exit, I didn't ramp up the pressure on myself by aiming for a sell-by deadline, but I set a one-year timescale to 'groom' the business, ready for sale. That said, my original plan was never to sell it all. In later chapters I will be sharing that process with you.

If you take away anything from this chapter, it is to understand that while strategy is essential for navigating the challenges you will face when growing a business, it doesn't have to be complex or even written down. It can be as simple as knowing the purpose of your business and making sure every single decision you make is driven by it.

CHAPTER FOURTEEN

STRIVING FOR CONTINUOUS IMPROVEMENT

In the last chapter, I described how my strategy for building Myprotein was underpinned by my mindset. I had always had the ability to concentrate intensely, but as I got older, I recognised the power of thought and made more of a conscious effort to cultivate the right way of thinking.

Our thinking determines our reality, but since many of our thoughts seem to arise unconsciously, it makes sense to develop the right conditions to encourage more useful thinking. Or, as Marcus Aurelius wrote in *Meditations*, 'Such as are your habitual thoughts, such also will be the character of your mind; for the soul is dyed by the thoughts.' That's what I mean by mindset. Try to make constructive, positive and creative thinking more of a habit.

My father immigrated to the UK from Iran around the time of the Iranian Cultural Revolution of 1979. It must have been a period of great upheaval for him, having to leave everything behind to start a new life in England. One part of his Persian culture that he brought with him was his love of backgammon and, of course, the wonderful cuisine. Although backgammon is played all over the world, it is an extremely popular pastime in the Middle East, and it is not uncommon to find people playing it in coffee shops and other public places.

Like most dads who want to bond with their children while passing on wisdom, my dad taught me how to play backgammon, along with another passion of his: chess. I will always be grateful to him for teaching me these games because they are excellent tools for helping people sharpen their analytical skills. Thank you, Dad!

What came first, you might wonder – the chicken or the egg? Did I always have an analytical mindset or did my early introduction to strategy games push me in that direction? Maybe it was a bit of both, but I believe playing chess and backgammon provided a vehicle for refining traits that were already there. As I've already pointed out, if something didn't grab me, I found it very difficult to apply myself to it. In fact, I would be highly unlikely to even try unless there was a compelling reason why I should. Clearly, strategy games tapped into my psychology on a number of levels.

Firstly, I love challenges. Actually, it is fairer to say I can't stand being beaten. If you put the right challenge in front of me, I will want to hit it head-on and succeed just to prove it can be done. A lot of people allow themselves to be beaten at the first hurdle, which is usually induced by fear. It's another cliché but one that's worth inserting at this point: Henry Ford said, 'Whether you think you can, or you think you can't, you're right.' I have always believed in myself, and that attitude has served me well.

Secondly, I am incredibly impatient. When you combine a strong aversion to losing with a lack of patience, what you get is a mindset that is determined to learn how to win as quickly as possible. Backgammon and chess are the perfect practice arenas for this kind of mindset. In each case, the outcome of the game is determined by skill and strategy rather than luck.

Although backgammon involves the use of dice, it isn't the numbers that are thrown that determine the outcome, so the best player usually wins. How the players choose to move their pieces will have a far more significant impact. After all, fortune cuts both ways, so by the end of a game both players will experience their fair share. I believe the law of averages always prevails.

When you think about it, backgammon is a powerful metaphor for life, isn't it? People often say life is just like chess, but anything that happens in chess is down to the two players involved. Life throws all kinds of curveballs that are totally outside of our control. However, as is the case with backgammon, it is usually what we do with what we have that makes the biggest difference.

There was no way I was going to allow my dad, or anyone, to repeatedly thrash me at any game, so every time I made a tactical error, I learnt from it. By the way, when I say I can't stand defeat, that doesn't mean I am a bad sport or sore loser. I am just being honest enough to say I play to win and take the task seriously, but not too seriously. Once the game's over, you have to learn from it, wipe your mouth and move on.

Many people enjoy playing games for the sake it, but I can't relate to that. If I am going to do something, I am going to give it my best shot, and if I decide to pursue it further, I will strive for constant improvement. There are a million and one other things I could be doing to relax rather than wasting time on things I will never be good at. That's why we watch box sets or listen to music, isn't it? I would rather invest my time in activities that allow me to learn, grow and develop.

FOCUS ON THE THINGS THAT COUNT

One of the keys to success when it comes to learning and development is recognising where to focus attention. I am not religious, but there is a commonly known appeal for wisdom that ties in nicely with the point I want to make: 'God, grant me the serenity to accept the things I cannot change, the courage to change the things I can, and the wisdom to know the difference' – Reinhold Niebuhr.

Another way of putting this is to recognise where improvements can be made. Mental arithmetic was not one of my strengths. Focusing time and energy into becoming a better mathematician would have yielded a much lower return on investment than learning how to write code to do calculations for me.

Quick learners don't make the same mistake twice. When it comes to getting better at anything, huge improvements can be made simply by minimising errors, and that comes down to attitude more than aptitude.

As a teenager, I was massively into *Super Mario Kart* and other iconic Super Nintendo (SNES) computer games. There were two main reasons why gaming appealed to me. Playing computer games allowed me to enter a trance-like state where I would be completely immersed in the activity. I have no doubt that this was the same mental state that enabled me to concentrate for many hours at a time as a developer later in life, solving problems creatively and methodically.

Gaming is also intensely goal-focused. You are aiming to get first place in the race, or you have to beat a number of obstacles to get through to the next level, and the ultimate goal is to complete every level, score the most points, or reach the end before anyone else. There is a well-trodden process, which you will be familiar with if you are a gamer. You start the game, go so far, and then lose a life because you don't respond to a particular challenge correctly. Next time round, you try something else and see if that works, and you continue with this trial-and-error approach until you get it right and can get past the obstacle. It's all about practice, practice and more practice, but you also have to think smart.

I used to be absolutely determined to finish the game, and I would leave no stone unturned in my efforts to do that as quickly as possible. While I was relatively quick at learning by myself, I used to buy various weekly and monthly magazines to find out the latest hacks, shortcuts and tips for finishing games. There was one that used to get published on a Friday, and the highlight of my Saturday morning was diving out of bed, rushing out of the house, and getting a bus to town to buy that publication from WHSmith. I'd be buzzing with excitement, knowing that the content of that magazine was going to give me the key to go just a little bit further in my favourite games.

By my mid-teens, I was applying that same focus, drive and thirst for knowledge to make money from buying, upcycling and selling personal computers through the free-ads magazine *Loot*. In a way, just as I was upcycling computers by assessing their original performance and identifying ways in which they could be better – faster processing chips, more powerful graphics cards or larger memories – I constantly looked for ways to upcycle myself. I applied this process of upcycling to myself throughout my entire life.

Building the Myprotein website took my coding and developing skills to another level, driven by the desire to win the game, or accomplish the mission, in a way. Likewise, at the start of that journey, I knew very little about SEO, Google AdWords, marketing or the RFM model (recency, frequency, monetary), but my initial ignorance didn't stop me becoming an expert in all of those things.

A CREATIVE APPROACH TO PROBLEM-SOLVING

A lot of the time, my desire for improvement was driven by what the business needed. How could I make this process more efficient, where could I make savings, or how could I achieve this function? Note that this same line of questioning is also the route to more innovative thinking and a creative approach to problem-solving.

As Myprotein's customer base increased at a rapid pace, so did the amount of traffic to the site. Every time someone visits a website, that marks the start of a unique session, which is mirrored in the memory of the server. That way, if they want to move back to a previous page, check the items in their basket, or leave the checkout to amend their order, it is possible. This is a bog-standard feature for even the most basic websites but essential for e-commerce sites.

One of the problems I encountered as Myprotein's traffic increased and the site became larger was that session memory was becoming warped and corrupted, so the site could not function properly. It was a critical error that needed to be resolved urgently, and it forced me to evolve as a ColdFusion programmer.

I very quickly discovered a deep-rooted bug in the ColdFusion stack, around memory overflows. If you imagine trying to add to a database that is already full, you will have a rough idea of what was going on. Data was being overwritten and corrupted. I spent countless days searching for a solution, and it was one of the hardest challenges I had faced, but eventually I found a very complex workaround for the core bug.

That felt like a big personal achievement as it wasn't a publicly known bug, so it had been down to me, and only me, to go deep into the ColdFusion architecture to fix it. The issue never reared its head again, and by 2009 we moved to a new e-commerce platform anyway, so that bug was gone forever.

When there wasn't an immediate requirement or problem to solve, I would reflect on what I could do to grow the business. I'd look at ways to gain more customers, tap into new markets, or sell more to the existing client base.

'KNOW THYSELF'

An easy way to use self-reflection for enabling improvement is to look for the weakest link in your armour. This is where recognising and accepting what you cannot change is vital, to prevent you from being drawn towards avenues that will only waste your time. A lack of training and education is a totally different issue than not having the aptitude to learn. When you try something new, you will get to know pretty quickly whether you are well suited to the task.

The celebrated Greek philosopher Socrates is well known for saying that the only thing we can know is that we know nothing, and his advice for anyone was to 'know thyself'. Even in classical times, the ancient Greeks recognised that we all start off with a blank slate, and there will always be things to learn. The idea that we only have one or even a few talents is not true. If you spend your life trying new things, you will uncover countless talents and abilities, along with many skills and ideas that you can't get your head around no matter how sincerely and diligently you try. At the very least, however, you should try to know your strengths and weaknesses. By focusing on our weaknesses with a willingness to put the effort in, we can only get better, and sporting history is full of examples of where weaknesses were turned into strengths.

The phenomenal American kickboxer Bill 'Superfoot' Wallace was famous for having an almost magical left foot that he could fire out at incredible speed. However, his right leg was lame because of an old judo-related injury. By focusing all his energy into making sure he made the most effective and efficient use of his left leg for kicking, his right leg became a solid base for him to stand on. Now in his seventies, Wallace still has a remarkably quick and flexible left leg.

I am my own worst critic, so I am constantly looking for ways to make myself better. For example, I would never call myself a bodybuilder because I used to take every weekend off and never entered competitions. However, I logged every workout, and at any one time I would be working towards goals based on clearly defined weight-focused or rep-focused key performance indicators (KPIs). Every session, I tried to achieve more than I had done in the last.

Then there were the supplements. It is no accident that I built an international sports nutrition brand. I had a healthy interest in nutrition and was always well versed in the latest scientific discoveries. Apart from weekends, when I used to let my hair down, I had a sensible diet and was clued up on the latest supplements. My hard work yielded visible results. I looked like a powerhouse and was shifting some seriously heavy weight. At one stage, I was squatting twice my own bodyweight.

In hindsight, it is easy to see that I used to put a lot of pressure on myself, even though I didn't think of myself as a bodybuilder. Was it healthy? Yes. My gym membership was the best investment I ever made, and I don't think I would have achieved as much had I not had that kind of drive. I only wish I had also invested in a personal trainer, even it was only for a few sessions. These days, I am paying the price of not stretching, not training the core, and not resting enough during those early years of working out.

The training mistakes of my past have left me in need of regular bouts of physio to manage issues relating to my back. That has not stopped me learning how to play golf, but it has stopped me from taking it to the next level. I used to love pitch and putt when I was a child, so golf was bound to happen to me in the end. My back problems mean that I can't put 100 per cent into a golf swing, but there are still ways I can get better. I have learnt to play within my limits, by concentrating on improving my technique rather than my power.

Over the years, I have paid for lessons, recorded my swing on video, and reviewed every inch of movement, frame by frame. I've spent many hours absorbing YouTube golfing tutorials. So, even when we hit barriers in one direction, there are things we can do to improve in other areas.

TAKE CARE OF YOURSELF

Although having a critical eye helped me to push myself further, it sometimes meant I was my own worst enemy. Mental and spiritual growth are just as important as, if not more than, succeeding in business or maintaining physical health. If you don't feel good inside, what's it all for? Don't get me wrong – if building a global business or making a million was that easy, everyone would be doing it. You can't do it without the blood, sweat and tears, but that kind of effort is only possible if you have the mental strength and resilience to get you through. You need the right coping mechanisms.

While I was always strong-minded, I think I am much better at handling stress now than I used to be. I didn't realise it at the time – it was just what I was into – but my passion for lifting weights will have made an enormous contribution to my mental well-being and resilience. Working out helps the body to produce endorphins, our body's own naturally produced feel-good hormones, and they act upon the same receptors as opiates. That's why exercise can be so addictive. Also, anything that delivers small victories will boost willpower, drive and optimism. If we can win the small stuff, we can also take care of the big stuff. So, my competitive spirit was undoubtedly another natural stress-busting factor.

There are two sides to every coin, though. The pressure I put on myself to achieve results, to never take a break, to work up to twenty hours in a day, to take everything on myself, and to expect results yesterday, was arguably a recipe for what some people call burnout or maybe some kind of breakdown.

I built Myprotein as a young man in my twenties, and I was carrying an enormous amount of pressure on my shoulders. As the operation grew at a phenomenal rate, my workforce was expanding to match demand. When most other young adults were thinking about their next holiday or how to win a promotion at work, I had the responsibility of paying out salaries every month. Even though the money was there because the business was doing so well, that didn't completely quieten that niggling voice from within trying to tell me it could all come crashing down with one wrong move.

Had someone left the window open at the end of a shift? How was I going to replace a key member of staff who was leaving? When you're running a business, there is always something to watch out for.

From the day I launched Myprotein until I put together a senior management team, there was nobody I could bounce ideas off or turn to for advice or support. Of course, I had people in my life who cared about me, but there was no way they could understand how it felt to be in my shoes, and I didn't expect them to. Entrepreneurship is always about stepping into the great unknown, and although it takes a certain type of person to do that, it still takes its toll.

According to research carried out by a team led by Michael A. Freeman MD, the clinical professor of psychiatry at the University of California's San Francisco School of Medicine, entrepreneurs appear to be more than twice as likely to suffer from mental health issues than people in general.

Entrepreneurs were invited to take part in an anonymous online survey, and their responses were compared to another group that was demographically matched. The findings from the research were published in a report called *Are Entrepreneurs Touched with Fire?* in 2015.

Out of the entrepreneurs sampled, 72 per cent of them self-reported mental health concerns. They were twice as likely to have suffered depression, almost six times more likely to have ADHD, three times more likely to have been involved in substance abuse, and more than ten times more likely to be bipolar. Notably, 32 per cent of entrepreneurs reported having experienced two separate mental health conditions, and 18 per cent reported having three or more.

In my case, I was always a glass-half-full kind of person, and I have always enjoyed taking calculated risks. Fears and doubts are normal, but the way people react or respond to them will differ. I believe we can learn how to use them to our advantage. The path of the entrepreneur takes courage, and while some people are naturally more courageous than others – which is another way of saying more comfortable with risks – anyone can change the way they feel about things. It is a question of learning to reframe situations and adopting a new mindset.

The same goes for endurance. Nobody can run a marathon without putting on a pair of running shoes and doing that first mile. For most people, it's an uncomfortable experience that leaves them exhausted and out of breath, and then their legs ache for two or three days. But, for many, they get out again, it gets easier and, before they know it, they are looking forward to their daily run. It can quickly become addictive. Endurance builds up naturally as you keep going. You become stronger.

The way I have spoken about the marketing strategy and my innovative approach to new product development almost makes it sound kind of easy, doesn't it? But hindsight is a wonderful thing. If you turn it all upside down and imagine how things could have turned out if new product ideas hadn't worked or my marketing strategy had failed, you can see what I was up against. Building an international sports nutrition brand was a game that I won, but I won it by playing the right moves. It's also a game that I loved playing, but that doesn't mean it wasn't stressful. Losing is always a possibility.

Where it counted, I always played the right moves. However, there were things that were outside of my control – the dice element of the game – such as the payment mechanism on the Myprotein website, which was run by a third-party payment service provider (PSP). When that system malfunctioned, I knew I was losing business, customers and money for every single minute the problem persisted. It went on for several days, with outages lasting for hours at a time, and there was very little I could do personally to fix it.

On a stress scale of zero to ten, where a score of zero means a stress-free life and a score of ten means the maximum amount of stress that a person can tolerate, I'd say I was averaging a score of eight, and often peaked at ten. To be fair, a stress-free life is not optimal for health. Ideally, we need some stress to keep us motivated, but a stress level of ten is no good for anyone. When the payment system was down, I hovered between nine and ten until the problem was resolved.

Over the years, I made a conscious effort to learn how to manage my stress levels. Trying to muscle your way through stress is counterproductive because once your stress levels reach a critical point, you will become less effective. When we are stressed, we produce a bunch of hormones, including adrenaline, to help us fight the threat or run away. Most people know this as the 'fight or flight response' or the 'fight-flight-freeze response'.

Flooding the bloodstream with adrenaline is fine when the situation is appropriate, but when the stimulus is not physical it is harmful – and most twenty-first century problems fall into this category. During stressful situations, we also produce a kind of natural steroid known as cortisol. Now, most cells in the body have cortisol receptors, so this substance can affect a wide range of functions from how we control blood sugar levels to how we regulate our metabolism. It's therefore unsurprising that high stress levels are a contributory factor for health conditions such as Type 2 diabetes, heart disease and rheumatoid arthritis. So, it's easy to see how stress is bad news for the body, but it's also terrible for the brain.

The fight or flight response is one of our oldest self-protection mechanisms, tracing back to a time when we weren't as smart as we are today, and when the problems we faced needed super strength rather than super intelligence. Therefore, when we are in a highly stressed state, we are better equipped to hit a punchbag or run the 100-metre sprint than solve a mental problem. Our cognitive abilities become impaired. You've read that correctly. If you don't learn to manage stress effectively, you will be less capable of thinking things through clearly.

Another feature of the human stress response is that we can become more sensitive to it. What that means is that the more time we spend feeling stressed and the more stressors we have going on in our lives at any one time, the lower our threshold for a stress response becomes. That's why people who are under stress can sometimes fly off the handle over seemingly trivial things. That's not a great headspace for running a high-growth business. You can't have a meltdown when you're a leader. Your team and your company need you.

The bottom line is that managing mental health is even more important than staying in tip-top physical condition or having other skills for success. Don't be afraid to reach out for help. Seeing a counsellor, therapist or other professional doesn't make you weak. When it comes to self-improvement, make sure you are paying as much attention to your emotional and spiritual well-being as you are to the other, more obvious things. I am not here to tell you how to manage your mental health, but I can tell you what worked for me.

Once your head is so full that you can't see the wood for the trees, there is no point continuing with a task, so it's better to take a break. If you allow the pressure to build up to the point of feeling overwhelmed, you run the risk of being sucked into a chain reaction of negativity that is difficult to break out of. Again, this does sound like common sense, but it is not always easy to recognise that we are in that state of mind because we become absorbed by the situation and our desire to achieve the goal. It sometimes takes an outsider to tap you on the shoulder and say, 'You know what, mate? I think you should take a break.' How often do you see employees saying that to their managers, let alone the director of the company?

I learnt to recognise when my thinking was becoming fuzzy, to be able to take that step back and see myself more objectively. Remember, I used to operate on the principle of not leaving my desk for the day until I had done three positive things. We all get those days when we are running like crazy to stand still or even to go backwards, and these turned into long days indeed for me. You are more likely to complete those tasks if your head is in the right place, so when I could feel myself getting stressed, I'd take a break from whatever it was I was doing.

If the task I had been doing was something that was intellectually demanding, I'd switch to a more physical activity – tidying up the office or going for a stroll, for example – and I would set a timer for thirty minutes so as not to get carried away. These days, I enjoy creating a new music playlist or spending time reorganising my photos. Each to their own. Once the timer alerts me, I can go back to the original task with a fresh mind, having created more bandwidth for my brain.

OTHER PEOPLE'S THOUGHTS ARE NONE OF YOUR BUSINESS

Even when we are doing what we are supposed to do, working intelligently towards goals, steadily improving, and staying healthy, there will still be those people who want to criticise. The more successful you become, the more likely it is that people will want to knock you down. They will question your ability, your achievements and your decision-making.

I have a very clear response to being talked about. What other people think or say about me is not my business. If you suspect that other people don't like you, think you're stupid or think your plans are doomed to failure, let them. Their thoughts are not your business.

Sometimes people who really care about you will be concerned that you are heading for a fall. Other people may be jealous because they have not had the courage to pursue their dreams. If they have built a narrative that prevents them from succeeding – wealthy people only have what they have because they were born into rich families, for example – your success could be a threat to their belief system. They may even take actions to sabotage yours. These are just a few of the reasons why I choose to stay focused on my own game plan. I am a working-class man, who was living with just a single parent for the majority of my younger years, and I massively underperformed at school. If anyone had the right to tell me I wasn't going to succeed in life, I did, but I knew what I wanted to do, and I made it happen. What other people think is none of my business.

The sooner you realise that what other people think is none of your business the better, because concerning yourself with what other people think about you will only create worry and stress. Run with what is right for you. People will come and go, but if you are true to yourself and your own thinking, the ones who are good for you will stick around and support you, just as you will support them.

FEAR IS A LIAR

Another lesson I learnt at a young age, thanks to one of my best mates since school, Carl Boon, is that 'fear is a liar'. If fear had its way, none of us would even get out of bed. If you are looking for certainty in life, forget it. Controlling fear is another element of managing stress because fear is another stressor.

Fear is a great example of where sometimes even our own thoughts are none of our business. *What if that happens? What will they think? What will they say about me? How will I pay the bills if this happens?* These are all just thoughts, or you could call them opinions. They are possibilities – not facts. Coming back to the backgammon analogy, you can't do anything about the numbers that are thrown up by the dice. But how you respond to those numbers and what you do with the pieces will determine how life turns out for you. Which thoughts or opinions are going to make that more likely? Thinking you will succeed or worrying about failure?

Fear, worry and doubt are all just thoughts. I learnt to ignore them or replace them with better, more useful thoughts. 'Can I?' became 'How can I?' Instead of wondering what would happen if things went wrong, I focused on what the next step would be if things went well. Developing laser focus helped me to control my thoughts and only dwell on the ones that served my purpose. Self-belief and conviction will take you a long way. One of my daily habits is to have a word with myself every morning. Remind yourself of why you are doing what you are doing and assure yourself that you can make it. The words we tell ourselves, either with our spoken or inner voice, land deep in the subconscious, and they set the tone for the other thoughts that arise by themselves.

REGRET IS A WASTE OF TIME

Another kind of thinking that I refuse to engage in is regret. I don't have regrets. If I had the chance to go back and do things differently, would I? Of course I would, but that doesn't mean I regret any of it. My decisions were based on what I knew at the time, or what I call 'the surround sound factors at play'. What was the situation I was faced with, what variables were at play, and what was I thinking at the time?

As the former US Secretary of Defense, Donald Rumsfeld, famously declared in a security press conference in 2002, during the Iraq War, there are known knowns, known unknowns and unknown unknowns. Sometimes we don't know what we don't know. That's why people say, 'I wish I knew then what I know now.' Well, you can't. You can't turn the clock back.

There's only one reason for looking backwards – to gain insight and understanding. You can learn from the past, which is one of the reasons I love history. When I look back at my former self, I am totally satisfied that the Oliver Cookson of the past made sound decisions based on his understanding of the world at that time. He undoubtedly made some mistakes, but I will make sure I learn from them and don't repeat them. Have you ever noticed that children don't do regret? They are totally present and focused on what's in front of them. Regret is a learnt behaviour, just as much as worrying is, and neither of them have a positive impact on the here and now.

NOT TRYING IS FAILING

If you are not striving to improve, there is a danger of not trying. Not trying is failing. If you have never heard that phrase before, please say it to yourself again, out loud. *Not trying is failing.* Some say the only people who never failed at anything are those who never tried anything, but in doing so they failed in life – failed to take risks, failed to dream, failed to build. That's stagnation. Don't let yourself stagnate.

What do you want to try? If you don't know what to aim for next, you're not looking properly. Let go, adopt a sense of adventure, and let your mind wander, because that is where the magic happens. When you allow yourself to think differently, to explore ideas you would usually overlook, you create the possibility of discovering something innovative and original. Let your imagination do what it's there to do and test any new ideas with logic and reasoning. Logical thinking is brilliant for checking the angles, but you need an unfettered mind to find gold.

We often learn the most when we have the courage to leave our comfort zone. The more wrapped up we are in fear, worry or a lack of belief, the less likely we are to step into the unknown. My comfort zone included many of the things I excelled in such as sports nutrition, creative thinking, problem-solving, web development and strategic thinking. But when it came to accounts, I was a fish out of water.

TURN WEAKNESSES INTO STRENGTHS

In the early days, I didn't have what you might call a business accountant or an entrepreneurial accountant. My accountant was more of a bookkeeper. When you have a small business, your main concerns are the day-to-day and making it grow. A bookkeeper will, of course, ensure good governance in regard to all aspects of your accounts, which is essential. Don't cut corners.

Although accounting was not a subject that I knew much about, and it didn't particularly appeal to me, I realised the value of learning about it for myself. I still hire accountants, but I have learnt a lot from other, more experienced people and from reading around the subject. Now, I am a lot more comfortable with accounts than I was in my younger days. That's the thing about leaving the comfort zone. You broaden your horizons, learn new things, and become comfortable in areas you once found uncomfortable. Your comfort zone expands.

Writing *Bootstrap Your Life* has forced me to engage in more self-reflection than I have ever needed to before. When it comes to knowing thyself, as Socrates put it, and identifying areas for self-improvement, the ability to self-reflect and to do so objectively, and impassively, is paramount. I know we all want to be perfect and egos can be fragile, but you have to put that aside and be brutally honest with yourself. If you can do that, the potential for self-improvement is enormous.

I believe that the process of self-reflection, of constantly striving for improvement and working towards being the best possible version of oneself is a spiritual quest. It is what we are here to do, and whenever I see someone not fulfilling their potential, I want to encourage them to push themselves further.

'YOU ARE YOUR OWN SHAMAN'

Many people are religious, and they look to the guidance of scriptures, gurus or their priests for understanding. But, if you are like me and you are not religious, what do you do? Does it mean there is no god, and we are only here to make money and then die?

A practice that has greatly helped me to understand myself with more clarity is meditation. In recent years, I have learnt more about meditation, and I have read books such as Eckhart Tolle's *The Power of Now*. Tolle talks a lot about controlling one's thoughts, by the way. I have also travelled to faraway places such as Ecuador, where I have learnt about shamanism and plant medicines such as ayahuasca. The more I have looked into the area of spirituality, soul-searching and spiritual growth, the more convinced I have become that we can find the answers by looking inwards.

I remember taking part in a ceremony with a shaman called Salvador, whose teaching I have the highest respect for. Early on in the proceedings, Salvador looked at me and said, 'Oliver, I am going to tell you something. I am not your shaman. You are your own shaman.' This resonated with me. It is true, you are your own teacher, and you have everything you need within. Maybe you just need someone to tell you or guide you there.

I have also realised that this is something I have been doing for my entire life, and I am not the only one. History is full of innovative people who found inspiration from within – Steve Jobs, Elon Musk and Albert Einstein are a few of the most well-known examples of this. As much as I admire them, I am not in the same league.

By going inwards, you will discover who you are and what you are capable of. Each and every one of us is unique, and we have our own special combination of natural skills and talents that we can use to make our way in the world. When I look back on my life, I can see that is what I did. From an early age, I happened to be a natural meditator, and I got into a lifelong habit of tapping into the zone and making the most of my resources.

I believe we are all born with a natural ability to look inwards. Self-discovery is a spiritual process, but many people are distracted from the mission because of mental conditioning, pressure from society and other distractions. They buy into deterministic thinking that limits their potential. If you are not

100 per cent comfortable with where you are now, what you are doing with your life, or the direction you are going, please believe me when I tell you that you have options. Put down this book, look within, find your resources and apply them to what you really want to do. That is the true spirit of bootstrapping.

Bootstrap your life.

CHAPTER FIFTEEN

BUILDING A FIRST-CLASS TEAM

Bootstrapping a business takes a lot of time, energy, resilience and determination. At the start of the process, I had to be a jack of all trades. I was in charge of everything from stock control, customer services and IT, to marketing, order processing and pretty much anything you can think of. And I loved it. The thing is though, there are only so many hours in a day and while I had no qualms whatsoever about using every waking moment to grow my business, there came a point when one pair of hands was not enough. I was going to have to take someone on.

You have probably realised by now that I don't do anything accidentally. I am naturally quite risk averse, so although I have a history of taking risks, they have always been carefully calculated. Becoming an employer was no different. However, given that my first employee was my own mother, it might surprise you to know that my number-one rule when taking on staff is to never employ friends or family.

Mixing business with pleasure rarely ends well. Taking on friends and family members will usually result in expectations not being met on both sides of the relationship. Business owners want everyone else to work hard and care about their business as much as they do because it is their baby, and they have usually sweated blood to build it by the time they take on staff. Friends and family, on the other hand, expect to be treated differently. They might not believe that rules apply to them, or they may expect to be paid more than they are worth. Either way, when expectations aren't met in both directions, and frustration starts to set in, everyone loses and so does the business. It's OK to help out friends and family but employing them is not a good idea. If you want to damage your relationships and your business, take on your mates.

I needed someone I could trust – someone who would be as passionate as me about growing the business and who would give it the same amount of care and attention as I did. It needed to be someone who shared my work ethic and professional values. I wanted a committed individual, who would pay attention to detail and focus their energy on doing things right. Mum was the perfect candidate. Sure, I broke my own rule, but some rules should never be set in stone. If all the boxes are ticked and your instinct is telling you to proceed, go right ahead.

As an experienced secretary at a pensions company in Manchester's business quarter, Mum was used to working in an ultra-professional environment, so I knew I could count on her to show due diligence in any role I gave her.

By the end of 2004, my mum had already started helping me with the blending on weekends, along with my aunt, but she never joined Myprotein as a full-time employee until the first quarter of 2005. Like most mothers, she wanted to offer as much support as possible to her son. However, perhaps more importantly, my mum has always been a very cautious, risk-averse person like me. To say that the company managed to turn over £300,000 in its first year doesn't just give you an idea of how hard we'd had to work to fulfil that many orders. It also demonstrates how cautious we both were – in my case, wanting to be sure that the time was right to take on extra staff, and in my mum's case, wanting to be sure she was joining a company that was going to be around in the long term. For the idea to get a green light from both of us was pretty significant.

SHARED VALUES STRENGTHEN TRUST

Trust is a two-way street. You must be able to put complete trust in the people you employ, but there needs to be something in it for them as well. Most people want to work for an employer they believe in, that will reward them for their efforts and treat them fairly – one that is going places and will provide opportunities to progress.

One of the mistakes that business owners make is employing people too early on, when the business is not ready. Retrospectively, I think I could have and perhaps should have done it sooner, but even if I had wanted to, my mum wouldn't have joined us until she felt the time was right. When a business is still in the embryonic stage, every penny counts, so you have to be prepared to invest most of what you make back into the business and do everything you can to avoid unnecessary costs. It's like anything that grows from being almost nothing. Take any young seedling or sapling, for example. The structure is starting to show, but the shoot is thin and lacks strength. Young plants or trees are vulnerable. It doesn't take much, and all that potential is gone. Taking on staff before the business is strong enough is a big risk, but when the time is right and the business is ready, you will have to. In the meantime, if you can do a job yourself, you should. This comes in handy later on when it comes to leadership. I pride myself on the fact that right up until I sold the business, I had done everyone else's job at some time or other, even accounts!

Scaling is essential for growing a business, and you need the right team to do that. Your team is your business, so it is vital that you recruit people who are a good fit for your organisation. Ideally, they should believe in your vision and share your values and attitudes, so that as the team grows, the right culture is developed. With that in mind, the most important hire you will ever make is your first because they become the cornerstone of your company culture and whoever you take on afterwards will watch them to see how your team operates. That's why even though taking my mum on as my first employee was an outside-the-box thing to do, breaking my own rule about hiring family, I knew it was the right decision. And it was. Had it not been, there would have been only one option . . . and that's another reason why you don't want to hire the people you care about.

Hire slowly but fire quickly. This sounds brutal, I know, and I am not suggesting that business owners should treat staff harshly or unfairly. However, if someone is wrong for your company, they have the potential to seriously harm your business, so it is better for them to leave sooner rather than later. That is the stark reality. The more care you take when it comes to search and selection, the less likely it is that you will have to resort to firing people.

Mum's role was crucial. She was the chief blender, so she was the business. I could have the fanciest website on the planet and the slickest marketing operation, but if products weren't blended correctly, it wouldn't take long for the business to collapse. The same principle that was driving sales through referrals could work in the opposite direction if customers didn't get what they had ordered, or their powders weren't delivered on time.

Once Myprotein was large enough, we were able to invest in equipment to automate the blending process, but in the early years it had to be done by hand, and it was a physically and mentally demanding job. If a task such as blending is rushed, errors are more likely. Given that orders were often customised, the potential for error was high. The wrong ingredients could have been used, the quantities could have been incorrect, or the powders may not have been adequately blended. On the flip side, if too much time was spent on the blending process, deadlines could be missed, so a fine balance was needed between being so hasty as to be sloppy and being so meticulous as to be inefficient. Mum hit the sweet spot in that regard. We had few complaints, and I am confident that she was executing the task as quickly and accurately as was possible.

Once I'd taken that first step and recruited my mum as chief blender, it was only a matter of time before she would need more staff to help her. Employing Mum freed up around seven hours per day for me to focus on business growth activities, and that saw sales going through the roof. As I said, however, I was ploughing profits back into the business so had very little money for me personally, and I was extremely careful when it came to business expenditure. As strange as it might sound, at the time I didn't think the money was there to fork out on a recruitment company, so it was down to me to look for and hire the right people.

Early hires are the most important but also the easiest to get wrong, so I will always be glad that I got it right. I don't claim to be some kind of expert on corporate culture and, when I first started hiring, I was no different to many business owners in regard to team building. The more experienced you become as your team grows, the more you learn about hiring and firing, and you get a much clearer picture of your company culture, which makes it easier to intuitively assess whether someone is a good fit or not. It is usually a steep learning curve because when you get it wrong, it hurts.

A MAJOR INVESTMENT

Hiring anyone is a major investment, whether it's the caretaker or a company director. First, there is the time spent putting the feelers out, writing job ads, shouting out on social media channels, and any other activities that need to be done to attract candidates. That's before any money is spent on a recruitment agency if you can afford one. Having attracted a strong group of candidates, the interview process also takes time, especially for more senior positions where more than one round of interviewing is necessary.

Then there is the energy spent on preparing the employment contract, and once they have signed that, if they sign that, new staff will often have to go through an induction process. Don't forget that for some jobs it is impossible for a new hire to hit the ground running. They will need some time to settle into the role, which means it will take them longer to do things, and they are likely to make mistakes as they learn.

There are no two ways about it – hiring people costs time, energy and money, so you have to get it right. If it all goes wrong, and you've hired the wrong person, you can't recoup any of your costs. It is money out the window, and then you've got to do it all again to find a replacement.

Bad hires are bad news for businesses of any size, from start-up to unicorn, but for a young company that is still very small, the impact can be more significant and can pose a real threat to its future. It's not just the time and energy spent on the recruitment and induction process that's lost. Low productivity will affect the bottom line, poor customer service will damage the brand, and incorrect execution of tasks leads to waste and rework. The longer that goes on, the worse it is for your company.

When the time came for me to start interviewing people for jobs in my company, something I had dreamed of since declaring that I wanted to create jobs when I was a small child, I was mindful of my own journey – especially my interview for the apprenticeship at Pantek. The thing that swung it for them was not the list of fictional grades I had put on the application form, which were only there to filter out those they judged to be lacking in the right kind of aptitude. Neither was it down to me having bags of experience in the real world. I didn't. They recognised a spark in me because my enthusiasm was shining through, but enthusiasm can be down to many things. Someone who is desperate for work can show enthusiasm. No. There was something else: passion.

I had my own ideas that I wanted to share, and I was hungry. I wanted to learn as much as they could teach me, and it must have been obvious. They told me as much in the interview, that I had that something about me. It's a bit like one of those situations where a young man goes into a boxing club, and the coach asks him to show him what he's got. The youngster is huffing and puffing, throwing punches and moving forward relentlessly, and there's nothing the coach can do to dampen the boy's spirits. That's passion. A good coach can do something with that. Passion may not be enough to bring in Olympic gold, but it might win a place on the podium.

You can teach most skills in business. You only have to watch one of those television shows like *Dancing on Ice* or *Strictly Come Dancing*, where the most unlikely candidates are transformed into competent performers, to realise that anything is possible if the willingness is there. If the willingness is not there, it can be encouraged by a leader or manager who knows how to inspire and motivate others. Yes, many of the other traits that belong under the umbrella of company culture – work ethic, attention to detail or the willingness to learn from mistakes – can be instilled into people with the right nurturing and incentives. But you can't give someone passion. It's either there or it isn't. Passion comes from the inside; not the outside.

Sometimes, but not often, people can develop passion as they learn more about a subject and become fascinated by it. However, it is better to hire people who have that passion from the start rather than taking a chance on candidates who may or may not spark up three months into the role. Unless they show you something that is truly magical in terms of aptitude, skills and experience, it is not worth the risk when you can just as easily take on someone who has the knowledge and ability but is also buzzing about the opportunity.

HIRE CAREFULLY – ALL THAT GLITTERS IS NOT GOLD

Unfortunately, some candidates are able to fake it in interview and convince would-be employers that they are passionate about the job. We've all been there, haven't we? Anyone who has taken people on will recognise the sinking feeling that comes with realising they've been conned by a candidate. Sometimes, the one who looked like the dream candidate in interview turns out to be someone entirely different. All that glitters is not gold.

Another reason why you might end up with an employee who is lacking passion could be because they've lost the passion they once had. Perhaps the job wasn't quite what they expected, or they have evolved and want to go on to the next thing. Their lack of zeal could just be a temporary thing, or you may be able to help them rekindle the feeling by giving them a new challenge or further training. Who knows? They may just need a holiday. But if it goes deeper than that, and they've had enough, stay alert because an employee who lacks passion or, worse still, doesn't want to be on your team anymore, can cause problems. In my experience, it is better to encourage them to move on before any issues can arise.

There's nothing worse than having people in your team who don't want to be there. Their heart may be set on something else or they may not know what direction they want to take. Either way, if they are not enthused by your mission, they may become negative and resentful, and that can be contagious. Negativity can spread and undermine the morale of everyone else.

I believe in giving people chances. We all learn things in our own way, and some people just need more time or a change in approach. I always did my best to understand what was going on in the background. People experience family problems, bereavement, mental health issues and other challenges. Patience, understanding and compassion will often go a long way, but you have to recognise when you are dealing with a lost cause. Once I had reached a point where I felt I'd exhausted all options and it was clear someone had to go, I took decisive action to remove them but always tried to do it in a kind way. If it feels as though you are banging your head against a brick wall, the odds are that the other person won't be feeling great either.

START BY GETTING THE BASICS RIGHT

These days, culture has become a bit of a buzzword, and platforms such as LinkedIn are full of self-proclaimed experts on how to create the perfect workplace. You go into some offices, and they've got pool tables, bars and free meals. I've never claimed to be a pioneer in building a strong company culture, so I am not going to criticise how other people go about building theirs. However, in the early days, we were growing from scratch, so I took on people who believed in the mission and wanted to be part of something amazing. Of course, I did my best to provide a pleasant and safe working environment where people were recognised for achievement and hard work was rewarded, but there were no unnecessary bells and whistles.

When you start out, and you are bootstrapping a business, you have to focus on getting the basics right. You can attract hard-working, creative and driven individuals simply by having a strong vision that they can believe in and by playing fair. If people won't join your company without the fluffy extras, maybe they are not right for you. That is not to say you can't be more generous later on as you become larger and more robust. I am not advocating a tight-fisted approach to managing staff, but don't feel that you have to bend over backwards, spending money you can't afford, to buy the loyalty and enthusiasm of your staff. Pay them a fair rate and let them know they are valued.

What do I mean by getting the basics right? Clarity, clarity and clarity. Firstly, I had a very simple and clear goal, to become the number-one online brand across Europe and then worldwide. Secondly, as I built the business, I set up very clear processes to enable smooth and efficient operations. Your mindset will create the company culture if your leadership is effective – your work ethic, your vision and your way of doing things. People don't come to work to be confused or to fail. Make it as easy as possible for them to thrive and succeed in the pursuit of your vision. Ensure that people know what you want them to do and how you want them to do it. People are much happier and more productive when they know what they are doing. Hard work must be recognised and rewarded, so we implemented various bonus schemes over the years to drive different KPIs.

I must have been doing something right where culture was concerned because whenever anyone visited our offices, they would comment on how positive and vibrant the atmosphere was. We had a great team of committed individuals who were happy to be there, and this generated an excellent buzz.

When I first took on staff, I just needed the extra people power to meet the demands of a rapidly growing business. They weren't doing anything that I couldn't have done just as well myself had I been able to be in several places at once. However, as part of my drive for continual improvement, I was also keen to find people who could cover my weaknesses. I wanted people who were better than me.

I've been open about my abilities, and I am proud of what I have achieved. Having had to do everything myself, I became an expert across many disciplines, but that didn't stop me from taking a good look at myself with a critical eye and asking whether there might be people out there who could do some tasks better than I could. It's difficult because if you are anything like me, you might feel as though you don't need anyone else. There's something about the bootstrapped, entrepreneurial mindset that considers itself invincible. You could call it the 'I never got to where I am today' mentality. The ego doesn't like admitting weakness, but honest self-reflection is crucial for growth. The best companies employ the top talent. Accept that you're not perfect and hire people you can trust to do things better than you.

HORSES FOR COURSES – LOOK FOR THE BEST FIT FOR THE ROLE

There is no one-size-fits-all process for hiring people, but I found certain types of jobs could be bunched together into different buckets – back office versus front of house, for example, and junior versus senior roles. I wouldn't expect someone packing boxes in the warehouse to share the same types of traits as someone applying for a customer-facing role, and the interview process would reflect that.

For the first year or two, I was mainly hiring people for the back office, to join the production team, work on picking and packing, or help with the administration. As the back-office team grew, I took on a couple of supervisors to ensure group and individual key performance indicators were being hit. I was still firmly in control of the sales and commerce side of things and very much the brain of the business.

Hiring people for the back office was an easy enough process. I would bring them in for interview, mainly to find out what they were like as people. They were not being brought in to perform brain surgery, but attitude is everything. I've always been a highly intuitive person, especially when it comes to the kind of vibe I get from others, so I would want to get a sense of how they were going to be when I wasn't around. Someone applying for a picking and packing job is not necessarily trying to change the world but might still be the kind of person that wants to play their part, take pride in what they do, and work hard to hit a bonus because they want to be able to take their family on holiday or celebrate Christmas properly. I was looking for people who were honest, loyal and easy-going. You don't want unnecessary dramas when you're running a business.

MAKE YOURSELF DISPENSABLE

The recruitment process became more complex later on when I needed people to do more intellectually and creatively demanding jobs. By 2008, I had grown a very healthy and profitable enterprise. Myprotein had an annual turnover of £10 million, of which around £2 million was profit. This is a sweet spot for corporate finance companies, so my thinking naturally gravitated towards selling up and making a grand exit.

I booked an appointment to speak to a corporate finance team. As I had expected, they were extremely impressed with my company's performance. However, they didn't feel that Myprotein was ready to be sold. 'Why not?' I asked them.

'You've built an excellent business, Oliver, and you should be proud. There's only one problem. It's too dependent on you. What would happen to Myprotein if you were not around to run it?'

They had a point. While I had been mindful to create a well-oiled and precision-engineered operation that ran efficiently, the only person who had a big picture understanding of that operation was me. The people working for me were cogs in the machine. They knew how to do their own jobs but their understanding of the other roles in the business was limited. I was going to need a senior management team if I wanted any chance of finding a buyer for Myprotein.

The corporate finance company offered to provide a C-suite

team to 'groom' the business ready for selling. They said they could set up processes to make Myprotein slicker and take it to the next level where it would be able to run itself. I was sure they could have done, but at what cost? I didn't want an outside company having that kind of control over my business and, besides that, I was confident that I could find a team of my own.

I gave myself a year to 'professionalise' the business. Strictly speaking, they use that term for making non-commercial organisations more professional. I always ran a tight ship, and everyone worked to a high standard; however, the fact that the company counted on me to keep it going was a serious flaw. It effectively meant Myprotein was a one-man band with extra helpers, and that's not a professional organisation in my book.

Until that point, I had loads of operations staff. By building a management team, I was essentially going to be replacing myself. They would collectively be doing what I had been doing, so before placing a single job advertisement, I took an inventory of my strengths and weaknesses.

My most obvious weakness was my lack of enthusiasm or aptitude for accounts, so I took on the former finance director of TUI Group to head up our accounts department. As I said, if you are going to take someone on, look for the best talent you can find. It is worth the extra time and expense because getting it wrong is far more costly.

Marketing was one of my strengths, but that didn't stop me looking for a marketing director. I wanted someone who could at least match me because the business needed to thrive with or without me. The answer came in the form of Mark Coxhead, a particularly creative and analytical individual who had previously worked for Rightmove. Mark did a fantastic job of further strengthening our brand and developing the strategy for our email marketing and other channels.

Finding the right operations director to understand,

document and further evolve our processes was vital. This person would be the central processing unit or brain of Myprotein, responsible for coordinating all activities and there to address any issues that might arise. Karl Jacobie, who had been acting in a senior operations role for Unilever, was the perfect candidate and provided the safe pair of hands that we needed.

After setting up some sophisticated and joined-up processes that almost ensured the company was able to run itself and therefore didn't rely on him, Karl and the senior management team transformed Myprotein into an easy-to-manage, money-making machine that was easy to sell.

Myprotein was heavily dependent on technology, as I had discovered so painfully when the payment mechanism malfunctioned for several days. Remember, we were using a third-party PSP, but there were still plenty of things that could go wrong with our own IT systems, and guess whose job it was to fix those issues? IT is one of the pillars of a business that you don't notice until there's a problem. It's often taken for granted, and yet an IT disaster, such as a server going down or data being lost, can easily cause the collapse of a company. So, I took on Neil Pollard as IT director to make our internal IT structure more robust, more efficient and future-proofed to cope with increased growth. He was there to steady the ship as we grew.

Having taken care of finance, marketing, operations and IT, I had succeeded in bringing Myprotein to a point where it could function perfectly without me. You could say it was able to fly without me, but I wanted to ensure it continued soaring to greater heights, so I employed Nick Smith as the sales director. Nick had been director of sales at Glanbia, a global nutrition company that owns many leading brands, so he understood how to drive revenue in our market.

The interview process for these individuals was radically different from the one I had been using for my other staff. The principle was the same, in the sense that I wanted to be sure that each new staff member was the right fit for the business and would gel well with everyone else. However, the stakes are far higher when you are taking on someone of director level compared to another pair of hands in operations. I still trusted my instincts, but I needed to be more thorough and systematic in my approach.

PSYCHOMETRIC TESTING

I started using the Myers-Briggs test to assess the personality types of my more senior executives. Although I was not the first to do this, I had not read or heard about anyone using such tests for recruitment purposes. I'd learnt about it while reading around the subject of psychology generally and quickly recognised its potential for the recruitment process. Since then, I've discovered that it's been used since the 1960s, but I don't know how commonplace it was when I first started using it.

For the uninitiated, Myers-Briggs analysis is a psychometric tool that uses multiple-choice questions to evaluate the traits of people who take the test. It considers four aspects of psychology: introversion (I) versus extroversion (E), sensing (S) versus intuiting (N), thinking (T) versus feeling (F), and judging (J) versus perceiving (P).

Depending on how the questions are answered, the Myers-Briggs test will report a person's dominant trait for each of those aspects of mindset. The results are given as a four-letter personality type. For example, someone who is ENFJ will show more of a leaning towards extroversion, intuitiveness, feeling and judgement. They are deemed to be more caring and idealistic people, who enjoy connecting with others. As such, they are often excellent communicators and highly skilled in the art of diplomacy. ENFJs also tend to be well organised, responsible individuals, with bags of enthusiasm, so it is easy to imagine the kinds of role they would be good for.

Like any other test that is trying to measure the unseen, the Myers-Briggs test has its critics. For example, as it is based on self-reporting, the picture that is created is based on participants' own perception of themselves. I would be unlikely to dismiss my own intuition or judgement on the basis of a psychometric test; however, I found the Myers-Briggs to be a highly effective and accurate indicator of how a person was likely to engage and apply themselves.

Just to be clear, I was never looking for clones of me, not that I have any issues with myself or my personality traits, but it is important to find people who can add something to your team. As you know, I was quite a shy kid, and even though I found my confidence as a teenager and know how to enjoy myself in good company, it is fair to say that I am introverted. Sure, I can appear extrovert, and that side of me is real, but I get my strength and energy when I am alone with my thoughts or am focusing on something.

By the time I was recruiting a senior management team, I was already employing over a hundred people, so I had a very precise vision of 'who' we were as a company. Don't get me wrong. Even at the beginning, I knew what I wanted because I had a strong sense of what I was bringing to the table, my own values and why I had launched the brand. However, when you are doing something a lot, you can't help but improve, so my vision became much more refined with every hire.

INVEST IN AN EFFECTIVE RECRUITMENT SYSTEM

I invested in a reputable recruitment agency when it came to looking for more senior staff. If you can't afford to spend money to recruit your most senior people, you shouldn't be recruiting. I am all for being cautious with money, but I couldn't afford to bring in the wrong people for such crucial roles. Again, you get what you put in. An agency is only as good as the information you feed it. If you don't know what you are looking for, they have to figure that out on your behalf, and to be fair some of them are great at doing that or at least coaching you to an understanding. But if you are very clear about the criteria you are looking for, they are experts at doing the necessary legwork to find you a strong selection of candidates.

For less senior roles, I used job boards. In some ways, being clear about the kind of person you are looking for, what experience you deem necessary, what the role will involve and what traits you think are essential, are just as important for your junior hires as for your senior ones. The stakes are not as high; however, if your recruitment post template does not accurately reflect your wish list in a clear and concise manner, expect to be inundated with applications from the wrong people. At least with a recruitment agency, they do the hard part of splitting the wheat from the chaff.

The same goes for your remuneration package. By managing expectations from the start, you are more likely to see eye to eye with the people who are shortlisted. There's nothing worse than thinking you've found the ideal candidate only to then discover they want to be paid the same as an A-list celebrity.

THE INTERVIEW PROCESS

Once I had a list of strong candidates to choose from, I would start the interview process. In the early days, I only needed one interview for my most junior staff. As the team grew, I could look around and know that I had handpicked each and every one of them, and I knew why I had hired them. This is important because the people you take on are your people. You are trusting them with your business. It's good to know you have built some kind of rapport with them and agreed responsibilities from the outset – that you have looked them in the eye, shook their hands and said, 'You're hired.' If you are a good judge of character, and I believe I am, you are going to end up with a great team around you who have signed a kind of personal covenant with you. That is . . . provided you treat them fairly.

For middle-ranking staff, I used a two-step interview process. The first interview was just for going through the nuts and bolts – work history, hobbies and interests, and some exploration of their level of competency. The main purpose of the first interview was to wean out those who were more obviously not suitable or clearly not as suitable as the others. The second interview was there to go more in-depth, to put them under a little more pressure and see what they were made of.

The first interview was usually handled by a line manager or one of our human resources managers, and I would come in for the second interview. Much as I liked to keep tabs of who was coming to work for us, as the Myprotein team grew much larger and I was preoccupied with steering the ship, I tended to keep out of the interview process unless they were going to be reporting directly to me.

For the most senior roles, I put candidates through a three-step process. This was similar to the two-step process, but the third step was more practical. I would set them a challenge to bring out the best in them and to give me an opportunity to see what they were capable of.

The second interview gave me the chance to push their buttons and see how they responded. I could walk them through their curriculum vitae, drilling into various areas and challenging them on key points. How were they responding? Was the pressure bugging them or were they enjoying it? It says a lot about a person if they get a buzz from being interrogated over their past performance. You have to be careful what you read into their reactions though.

Some of the most competent individuals can be perfectionists and therefore suffer imposter syndrome, to the point that even when you think they've turned out an excellent piece of work, they're still not happy. I believe it is better to produce something that you can refine later than not to finish at all because you want it to be perfect, so if I did employ a perfectionist, I'd try to nurture them to make them into more of a doer than a fusser without causing them too much anxiety.

Likewise, overconfidence can be dangerous. They say that C-suite individuals are much more likely to be narcissistic sociopaths than the general population, so you have to be sure that you are not being taken in by someone who is good at talking the talk but not walking the walk. That's where the third stage came in particularly useful.

By gaining more insight into how candidates ticked in the second interview, I was able to set a challenge to show me how well they could perform the kind of tasks I was going to need them to do. More than that, I could tweak it slightly, based on any doubts or areas of concern I had, and really put them to the test.

Those challenges could be anything from having to come up with a new product from scratch, based on a brief that I would give them, to having to produce a marketing strategy for launching a new idea that I had conjured up for them. They would only get one week's notice, but that's how it is in the real world. Remember, one of the reasons why we were so agile and able to grab so much market share so rapidly was because of how quickly I could turn new ideas around. So, it wasn't as though I was asking people to do the impossible. I wanted the best of the best.

One week after they'd accepted the challenge and received the brief, they would be presenting their ideas in front of me and other members of my team. Once they had finished the presentation, I would quiz them to dig into the details. Again, this gave me a handle on how well they could deal with pressure and scrutiny, but it also showed me how robust their thinking was.

Anyone who knows me well will agree that I like to hear top-level summaries first. If I am interested at that point, I will ask for more detail. Bearing that in mind, I enjoyed engaging presentations that didn't go into too much detail, but I needed to know they had done their due diligence and the depth was there. Without wanting to contradict myself, however, I wanted to see effort. How much work had they put into their presentation? What data had they used to support their ideas? It's easy to sound fantastic when you're dealing with hypotheticals, but in the real world you need to build on solid premises.

If it had been difficult to single out any one applicant from the first two interviews, the presentation would highlight key differences. However, there were times when none of the presentations were of a high enough standard. When that happens, you have to accept it and start again. It might feel like you are making the best out of the situation and cutting your losses, but if you settle on someone who is not up to scratch, you will lose out in the long run, and your business will suffer as well.

I believe I left no stone unturned when it came to finding the best people. Just as I had gone through all the what-if questions when I was developing the website and second-guessing what our customers wanted, needed and would benefit from, I applied that same level of scrutiny to the recruitment process. And it worked. I am proud of the superb team I built at Myprotein.

Finding the best people is only the start. How you lead them will make an even bigger difference.

CHAPTER SIXTEEN

CHESS AND THE ART OF LEADERSHIP

No wonder there are so many books on leadership. Leadership is such a vast area, and I have so much to say about it – not as a self-proclaimed expert but simply based on my own experience – I could probably dedicate an entire book to the subject. For now, I will stick to a chapter.

I was going to write that it is hard to know where to start, but you may have noticed that one of the recurring themes of my story has been the principle of leading by example. If I had to make a choice, and single out the most important trait for a leader, that's the principle I would choose.

Does leading by example automatically lead to success in every mission? No, of course not, because the example you set may not lead people to the goal. However, if the question relates to how to inspire and motivate people to do something, leading by example is arguably one of the most powerful ways to do it.

Having decided to write *Bootstrap Your Life*, I invited a few of the people I have known and worked with over the years to share a no-holds-barred, warts-and-all account of their experience of Oliver Cookson. It was interesting to hear the perspective of people I have a lot of respect for and who I have either worked with or employed at a senior level. Not only did their accounts jog my memory about events that might have otherwise slipped my mind, but they also gave me valuable insight into how I was perceived as a leader.

While I believe we should all endeavour to know ourselves through honest self-reflection, I recommend asking a selection of the people you trust to share their perspective. It can be an eye-opener, but you must ensure you ask the right people – not just the ones who are going to tell you what you want to hear.

One of the first people I reached out to was Natalka, and she reminded me that I used to have a real passion for playing chess. It is not as popular in the UK as it is in many other countries. I am not sure why that is because I believe it is superb for developing the mind on a number of levels. Perhaps it is because youngsters perceive it as being overly complex and the thought of having to learn how six different pieces move puts them off. That kind of thinking has never made sense to me. After all, we absorb so much new information naturally as we are growing up – at least one language, how things work, what we can and can't do – and life is full of so many rules that taking a few minutes to learn the basics of chess is really no big deal.

Generally, I think chess is more relevant to a discussion on strategy, but there is also an element of leadership in the game, especially in terms of how human resources are valued, managed and mobilised.

A strong chess player will endeavour to 'develop' as many of their pieces as possible during the opening of the game. They will try to bring out the more versatile and powerful pieces from the back line and strategically place them where they can exert influence on the centre of the board while still being able to move to other areas to respond to threats or opportunities that arise there.

A poor player will waste too many moves pushing the weakest, least important pieces – the pawns – perhaps trying to form a pretty formation while leaving their more useful pieces at the back. As a result, they are incapable of responding effectively to an attack from their opponent, and they are unable to launch a powerful attack of their own.

By developing pieces early, the strong player is more agile, responsive and efficient. Long before any skirmishes take place, they successfully prepare themselves for most circumstances by achieving three objectives at once. They ensure their key pieces occupy strategically advantageous positions around the board, they build a solid position that can withstand an attack and, in doing so, they lay down the foundations that will provide them with options when it comes to developing winning strategies of their own.

The thing that is missing here is the element of inspiring and motivating a team to act. In the game of chess, the players are able to dictate how their pieces should move within the framework of the rules. Pieces don't need to be inspired or coerced into moving. However, chess still provides an analogy in relation to the motivational aspect of leadership, and this relates to how the player values their pieces.

BUILD A STRONG

For example, less experienced players will place too high an expectation on what the most powerful piece on their team can achieve. It is not unusual to see novices launching attacks with nothing but their queen – the most powerful and versatile piece on the board. Without the backup of other pieces to enable the queen to head a well-coordinated assault, she is unable to seriously threaten the opponent and becomes increasingly vulnerable to capture.

It is easy to see how a business leader may act in a similar manner to the chess-playing beginner who thinks they can win the world with one piece. Perhaps they put too much pressure on their sales force without providing the backup of a high-quality product or even half-decent customer service. Likewise, they may expect their customer service representatives to perform miracles by resolving severe service or quality issues that should not have arisen in the first place.

Anyone who has worked in sales will recognise that while there are those who can sell sand to the Arabs, to use another well-known but totally apt cliché, some salespeople end up with the short straw and are left to bang their heads against brick walls as they try to sell poor-quality products to the wrong market. Even the most talented business development executives will struggle if they have been set up to fail.

It is the leader's responsibility to create an environment where success is possible, whether that is by providing the appropriate training and resources, extra pairs of hands and marketing support, or just by producing products that are genuinely needed and do what they are supposed to do.

Whether someone wins or loses in chess is down to them and them alone. They have the same chance of success as their opponent. While in the business arena, leaders are dealing with human beings rather than chess pieces or robots, the same principle applies. It is down to the employer to find the right staff who will consistently perform well and come up with creative solutions to challenges when things go wrong. It is down to the employer to develop the right strategy, operations, products and services to grow the business. It is also down to the employer to appreciate the value of their staff.

People don't like to be treated like pawns, even if their status within an organisation is less important than other staff and they are more dispensable. And again, it is easy to see this principle in action on the chessboard. Pawns represent the foot soldiers, and that is why each player has so many of them – eight each. Initially, these pieces are the least versatile, being only able to move one square at a time in one direction: forwards. If a piece is going to be sacrificed in order to gain some kind of dynamic or material advantage a couple of moves later, it is more likely to be a pawn that is given away. However, only a fool underestimates the potential of a pawn.

Experienced chess players know that where two opponents are evenly matched, a game can be won or lost because of one pawn. As the endgame draws near, and there are fewer pieces on the board, winning or losing often comes down to who has the most pawns on the table. Why? Because if a pawn is able to reach the other side of the board, it can be 'promoted' to any other piece – even a queen. Every pawn has the potential to become a queen, and every member of staff has the potential to grow and play a bigger, more important role within an organisation.

As Myprotein was steadily growing, even though sales were moving in one direction, we still experienced spikes and surges. Given the amount of time and effort that goes into sourcing, interviewing, training and developing new staff, human resources need to be managed carefully to ensure a company is running efficiently. The last thing any organisation needs is to have more staff than is necessary. For a start, it doesn't make sense to be paying people to do nothing. However, it can also lead to some staff feeling undervalued, underused, surplus to requirements, bored out of their minds and low on morale. And remember what I said about the risks of employing negative people: negativity is contagious.

On the other side of the coin, a team that is spread too thinly is not efficient – it is an ineffective team. To revert back to the chess analogy, if one player has too few pieces to resist the advance of the opponent's pieces, they have no hope. I sought to ensure Myprotein had the optimal level of staffing to deal with the ebb and flow of demand. The way to do that was to employ a mix of permanent and temporary staff. Permanent staff were at the heart of the business. They were employed on a full-time, permanent basis because they were reliable, hard-working and loyal.

Temporary staff were just as valuable as permanent staff, even though they were more dispensable, but they served a slightly different purpose. They allowed Myprotein to expand or contract its team to match demand at all times. Employing temporary staff provided the flexibility to remain efficient in all circumstances.

Having come from such humble beginnings myself and having not taken the more orthodox route of getting good grades in high school and progressing through the education system, I recognise that every person is unique and shines in their own way. Taking on temporary staff gave me the chance to 'try before you buy' and identify the people who were showing more potential for greater things. In this way, the pool of temporary staff provided another vehicle for employing the best permanent staff.

Temporary staff tend to have different goals and lifestyles than full-time workers. They enjoy the flexibility because they don't want to be tied down or because they have other commitments. Although many of Myprotein's full-time workers started out as temporary staff, permanent staff tended to be more dependable, hard-working and loyal. That said, if a temporary staff member had a poor attitude and wasn't interested in working, it was usually picked up within the first few days, so it was an easy situation to remedy.

I am often told that I am a good judge of character. This is a useful trait for a leader to have because your team is only going to be as good as the people in it, although if a team is properly led, the total should be more than the sum of the parts. Even the greatest leader on the planet will not get very far if they have a team of stubborn mules, snakes in the grass or unpredictably wild animals. And getting it right is important at all levels within an organisation.

UNDERSTAND THE VALUE OF RESPECT

There is no doubt that in comparison to a director or an experienced manager, those involved in picking, packing and blending were the pawns in Myprotein's team, but they were no less valuable. I treated them with the same respect and courtesy as I would treat the CEO of an enormous global brand. I believe this approach won far more respect, loyalty and hard work than treating people as numbers would have done.

There's another very important leadership principle at play when it comes to how staff are treated. I did what I could to maximise the potential of my employees. If someone is only interested in packing boxes, they're clearly competent in the task and hard-working, then they are in the right place within your organisation. But if someone is capable of more, why not give them the opportunity?

It is not always easy to spot potential in someone, especially if they are not aware of it themselves, and sometimes people are happy to live simpler lives without any extra complications. However, if you have a staff member that is capable of more and wants to do more, it is important that you recognise that. If you don't, you may end up with a resentful, negative staff member, especially if they are finding it difficult to find opportunities elsewhere – that will make them feel trapped. To be fair, I aimed to spot extra potential at the interview stage, and I like to think I was pretty good at that, but no one is totally transparent, and we can never really know what someone else is thinking or feeling.

Chess is primarily a strategy game, but having a strong strategy is an important element in the art of leadership. As I said earlier, the wooden, lifeless pieces on a chessboard couldn't care less about the bigger picture. As long as your move is legal, you can pick up a piece and place it wherever you like. However, dealing with people is a completely different kettle of fish because they often do care about how their role fits into the overall operation.

Even as young infants, people are happier and healthier when clear boundaries are set. These provide certainty, and certainty gives a sense of security. Likewise, most employees appreciate clear boundaries – these help them differentiate between the tasks that they own and the ones they don't – and they are able to apply more focus when they are given clear direction.

People feel more secure and productive when they are working as part of a well-oiled machine and there is a sense of direction. Of course, that does depend on the role, and people with more responsibility will be more sensitive to inefficiency, ill-thought-out procedures and poor strategy, because these things will work against them and make their jobs more difficult.

Smart strategies set up teams for success, and they can feel it, which is great for morale. When the vision is clear, and that vision is effectively translated into a plan of action, employees stand a much greater chance of achieving results. By taking calculated risks that mostly paid off, I was better able to lead because people had faith in me.

I preferred to nurture, coach and develop people rather than being overly prescriptive. Don't get me wrong – I approach things in a thoughtful and methodical way, so where I had taken the time to build a system that was based on experience and worked well, I would expect people to adhere to it. However, it's impossible to foresee every possibility, and there is always the chance of an unforeseen circumstance putting a spanner in the works. Sometimes that spanner can be as simple as an employee not understanding something properly and needing further training and development.

When things went wrong, I would sit with the people involved and guide them through a process of fault analysis to help them (and me) understand what had occurred, what had gone wrong, and how the issue could have been prevented or dealt with more effectively.

In my experience, when you coach someone and make them a part of the solution rather than storming into a situation and 'fixing it' – which will leave them feeling like a spare part and part of the problem – you empower them to think for themselves. In this way, you are creating team players rather than drones. Drones are fine for some jobs, but even then, when a problem occurs, you want people who can make intelligent decisions.

LEARN TO BLEND IN

I am going to park the chess analogy for the time being but won't be surprised if I am further reminded of this superb game as I continue with this chapter. For now, I want to delve into something else that Natalka mentioned, which I also believe is highly relevant to the subject of leadership.

She said she thought of me as a social chameleon, and she reminded me that when we were very young, I was just as comfortable and confident when mixing with well-polished, highly educated and wealthy professionals as I was when surrounded by some of the toughest and most streetwise people in Manchester.

While we were partying until the small hours, there were many times when we found ourselves in situations that could have been dangerous for some people, but I was usually able to blend into the environment by either tuning into the same wavelength as those around me or by slipping under the radar entirely.

Where I feel I had an advantage was my ability to exhibit extrovert or introvert behaviour almost on tap. I had a talent for recognising when it was best to stay put, stay quiet and stay alert to assess a situation fully, while having the confidence to speak or take action intelligently when the time was right. I am a big believer that most people are essentially good, and I try not to judge people. The key to getting on is to understand how people want to be engaged with. Knowing when to speak, when to listen, and when to do nothing at all is a skill that comes in useful in almost any social situation.

So does humility. By the time I was twenty-seven years old, I was a multimillionaire and the richest self-made person in the UK for my age, and it had taken me just four years to do it after building Myprotein from scratch. An arrogant or boastful person would use such achievements to justify their attitude, but I am not that person, and that's why I have not lost the friends I grew up with. It's also the reason I got on well with the people who worked for me. I treat people as people, regardless of their walk of life or their socio-economic status.

Almost a decade has passed since I stepped away from the day-to-day running of Myprotein, and yet I am only just writing my story now. Why? Because I want to inspire and motivate the next generation of entrepreneurs to believe in themselves and make great things happen. And I believe they can, even now – at a time when the world has been ravaged socially, economically and physically by a global pandemic.

It was not about the money for me, strange as that may sound coming from someone who was determined to be a millionaire from a very young age. I can explain it like this: what does hitting the bullseye mean to a darts player? What does potting the black mean to a snooker player? Neither of these achievements holds any intrinsic value. The enjoyment comes from striving for the goal and succeeding.

I am not expecting anyone to believe I am not glad I made a lot of money because that would be dishonest. Money solves a lot of problems, and having it has allowed me to do all kinds of things I otherwise wouldn't have been able to do, but I work just as hard now as I ever did when I was starting out. The money and the success of the business were massive ambitions of mine because they represented my definition of winning – perhaps because I wasn't born into money and wasn't expected to run a business. Some might say I had something to prove, but I also wanted to be able to give back to my mother who worked so hard to raise me. I am sure that if I had been born into a wealthy dynasty and inherited a huge enterprise, I would have been just as driven to achieve goals, but they would have been different.

Being rich and having founded a global brand does not make me any better or worse than anyone else, and while I was running Myprotein, I was mindful not to come across as anything other than a human being to the rest of the team. That was not only clear from the way I spoke to people, the clothes I wore and the car I drove to work in, but it also showed through in my willingness to work side by side with any member of the team to do whatever they were doing. This promoted a strong sense of camaraderie within the team.

Being a social chameleon means being able to mix well with anyone, and that certainly comes in handy for a leader. I find it easy to get on with most people, and over the years I have been fortunate enough to get to know some really amazing individuals.

SEEK TO BE INSPIRED AND TO INSPIRE

Some say it's not what you know but who you know that makes the difference. Many people choose to understand this as meaning that if you know the right people to do you favours, you will get on in life, but that's not how I see it, and I was never one to ask for favours anyway. Knowing the right people, in my book, means getting to know people who will elevate your mindset, show you how you can improve, point you in the direction of further resources, and generally help you to believe that more is possible.

I am grateful for having met those people who had a positive influence on me, and I wanted to do the same for others. As a leader, I tried to encourage others to reach their full potential, and I can't think of a better example of where I did this than Anna Rushton.

Anna joined Myprotein around the time that I began professionalising the business. I took her on as a customer service consultant, and she was great at that job, but it soon became clear to me that she was capable of much more.

As an educated, articulate and emotionally intelligent individual, who was able to speak several languages fluently, Anna's skills were particularly useful when Myprotein was expanding into Europe. As our share in that market grew, and I needed to bring in people who could deal with our European customers, Anna was the natural choice to lead Myprotein's international customer service team. I had to be sure I was taking on the best staff to work in that team, and Anna had a keen eye for identifying those with the right blend of linguistic and overall communication talents. She was also a highly effective leader because of her own energy and commitment.

It became obvious that she had an eye for marketing, so I made her responsible for marketing our products to our Italian and Spanish customers. Anna has since told me that I made her feel valued and included, and she said her experience at Myprotein had hugely impacted her life and career. These days she is an independent international marketing consultant. When I mentioned to Anna that I was writing a book and asked her for comments, she referred to my 'positive impatience', and how I would often say that if something was worth doing, it was worth doing immediately. 'Why put off until tomorrow what you can do today?' is one of my favourite phrases. It obviously rubbed off on Anna because she says she has adopted my make-the-most-of-now mindset and applies this sense of urgency to all of her projects.

Making the most of every moment was not the only lesson Anna said she'd learnt from her time at Myprotein. People who know me know how meticulous I am when it comes to planning and paying attention to detail. The cliché, of course, is 'Fail to plan, plan to fail', but the plan is only as good as the details. A good plan will fail if important details are overlooked. A key philosophy for me is to take nothing for granted. Businesses fail when their leaders make the wrong assumptions. I tried to plan for the worst-case scenario, so I was assuming things would go wrong and figuring out how to minimise the impact. That's a good kind of assumption. It's important to be optimistic but not foolhardy.

The philosophy of not taking things for granted has permeated all aspects of my life. It is important to appreciate everything – people, things, money, life – and that drives me to consider how much return on investment I will receive from putting my time, effort or money into something, and also how much value I can provide when serving others. Value was a major part of Myprotein's culture, in terms of giving value and expecting it, and this led to improved efficiency.

THE POWER OF PERSONAL RESPONSIBILITY

Every individual appreciated the importance of what they were doing and how their efforts fitted into the whole picture, and by ensuring people were working in roles that made use of their full potential, they wanted to go the extra mile. I didn't have to ask for it. On the one hand, I have never suffered fools, and I have a low tolerance threshold for people who try to take liberties. However, on the other hand, I rarely encountered that kind of behaviour because people generally wanted to do good and work hard.

Anna said I had instilled a sense of responsibility within her, and she'd developed a habit of asking herself whether she had paid for herself on a given day – whether she had justified her salary. That's not to say that if someone is not selling or doing something that brings an immediate financial reward, they haven't earned their place. Value comes in many forms, not just pounds and pence.

It is not uncommon to find that employees have a different attitude to time, money and value than entrepreneurs and business owners. There are many reasons for this. Sometimes it boils down to them holding the perspective that if they are going to leave their house at 7.30 a.m. and not return until 6.30 p.m., because they are working from 9 to 5.30 in an office, they've done enough and should be paid. They might not have thought about how much value they were bringing to the table. However, those kinds of employees are unlikely to produce greatness.

FIVE OF MY FAVOURITE 'OLIVER-ISMS'

Another 'Oliver-ism' that I used to share with my staff was **'Multiple accountabilities equals no responsibility'**, meaning that if a task is not the responsibility of any one person, it might not get done. Assigning tasks to specific people meant they would definitely get done, unless there was a genuine obstacle getting in the way, and it gave everyone a sense of purpose by providing them with a very clear understanding of what was expected of them.

The word 'Oliver-ism' has just entered my head because I've realised that, over the years, I had coined a number of these phrases to express principles that I had found quite empowering. Here are a few examples that spring to mind:

'If you don't go forwards, you relatively go backwards.' I guess another way of putting that would be that there's no such thing as an even keel in business. The world does not stand still. Competitors don't stand still, customers don't stand still, and change and evolution are constant, so if you're not striving to stay ahead of the curve, you're falling behind.

'Don't open a new bottle of milk until you've finished the old one.' I like this one in particular because it covers a few different bases. On the one hand, I have always hated waste, so why waste something as life-affirming and nutritious as milk? But it also describes my attitude to project management quite nicely. I may as well throw in the principle of not crying over spilt milk here as well because the time spent dwelling on something that's already happened is time that could be spent more constructively.

Once I start something, I make sure I finish it before moving on to the next thing. That doesn't mean I don't run projects in parallel or start new missions – if that was the case, Myprotein would have been doomed from the beginning – but on a more micro level, working in a focused, linear fashion, doing one task at a time, leads to greater productivity. The longer milk is left to stand, the more likely it is to sour. Tasks are no different. Keep going with them while they are fresh.

Speaking of projects, **'It's easier to change the direction of the sails than board another boat.'** I suppose the buzzword of the day would be 'pivot'. Being agile and adaptable is at the heart of bootstrapping, in life and business. Sometimes a plan might not come together because the circumstances have changed unexpectedly, because of a flaw in the strategy, or because of a failure to execute it correctly. However, effort is rarely wasted. The lessons learnt could be applied elsewhere, the plan could be tweaked to bring about a slightly different outcome, or other gains could be made.

Another favourite of mine, which I consider to be the antidote to procrastination, especially the sort that can be brought about by seeking perfection, is **'Better to get a job finished that's 80 per cent perfect than not to finish it at all.'** There's a well-known paradox about how if something is moving from one place to another, it will have to travel through the halfway point first. Then, in order to continue the journey to get from the halfway point to the end, it will have to go through the halfway point of that smaller, remaining distance. According to this line of reasoning, the object never makes it to the final destination because there will always be a halfway point to go through first. I believe that's known as Greek philosopher Zeno's 'dichotomy paradox', but it could have just as easily been called the 'perfectionist's paradox'.

There's nothing wrong with perfectionism, and when it comes to planning, there is no such thing as being too thorough. However, when it comes to producing something – a document or a prototype, for example – there is always a 'halfway' point to dive into and perfect if that's what you want to do. Perfectionists are rarely happy with the finished product. I should know. That said, being a stickler for getting the details right means that if I say something is all right others will probably think it is great, and if I say something is good, it's probably excellent.

Praise should be given when it's due, but it should be carefully measured, so as to maintain its value. I tried to be surgical with my words, and I am sure that in doing so, I was able to bring the best out of people. They would do their utmost to produce excellence because they recognised that a compliment from me actually meant something. It is important to encourage people, but if you tell them that everything they do is marvellous, it might feel as though you are doing the right thing by shielding them from negativity and boosting their self-esteem, but you are doing them no favours at all.

People value the truth, and not telling someone that something they've done is brilliant when it was only mediocre is not the same as crushing someone's spirit when they're trying hard to achieve. I believe in showing people where they've succeeded and where they can make improvements. More importantly, I try to inspire a can-do attitude and show people that I believe they can reach the goal. That's constructive. One of the ways I did that at Myprotein was by exercising my old favourite – the art of leading by example. I expected no more from anyone else than I expected from myself, and I am probably my own worst critic. If I had been as harsh on others as I am on myself, I doubt my leadership style would have been as effective.

GREAT LEADERS DEVELOP LEADERS

I thought it was worth mentioning these Oliver-isms because people who have worked for me tend to replay them back to me. They say a poor leader creates followers whereas a great leader develops leaders, and I think it's fair to say that's what I tried to do. I wanted people to be empowered to make great decisions for themselves.

I endeavoured to breathe an entrepreneurial spirit into every member of staff, and I did that by rewarding hard work and incentivising the right performance-related metrics, including passion. Remember how important that is? That metric was measured using a blend of my own subjective perception – did the individual *appear* to be keen – and more objective, observable criteria such as whether they worked extra hours, smashed deadlines or went the extra mile in other ways. I felt this was a more comprehensive approach because depending on the personal circumstances of a staff member, they might be on fire with enthusiasm but unable to work extra hours, for example.

Empowering others to make decisions within any organisation has its risks, and the more senior those people are, the more severe the consequences will be if they get it wrong. Those who worked as part of my senior management team – notably Karl Jacobie (managing director) and Oliver Rushton (associate commercial director) – would echo that I was never guilty of 'founder's syndrome' (also known as 'founderitis').

Despite my own admission that I could be a bit of a control freak, that was only the case when I didn't feel I had the right people around me to do what I could do. While bootstrapping the business, I hadn't really had any choice. As the business grew, I was able to hire the best people available to me, and once I knew I could trust them, I was more than happy to let go. That trust had to be earned, and the way I did this was by gently increasing the amount of responsibility I gave to others in small, incremental steps.

Just as I had in the interview process, I would set real-world challenges for people and see how they handled them. I usually knew what approach I would take, so seeing what others came up with gave me an opportunity to compare and contrast. Sometimes they surprised me by considering things I had not thought of. Where I had to add tweaks and corrections, they were not usually significant. Oliver Rushton's interview challenge had been to launch a new water protein product, and he smashed it.

Originally, I took Oliver on as my executive assistant. I had ideas coming out of my ears, and it was becoming difficult to follow through with action or even to keep track of them because I was spinning so many plates. Oliver's job was to look at ideas in more detail, pull them together into projects, and develop those projects into clear plans that could be executed. Quite frankly, Oliver was my right-hand man for many years – even playing a pivotal role in my new venture once I had made my exit from Myprotein.

The art of delegation is an essential skill for any leader, and in Oliver's case I was handing over the most important aspects of the business – a part of the process that I was not only good at, but also one that I loved. As I suspected would happen, chess has entered my head again. The king is the most important piece on the board because it's game over if it gets captured, but despite this, the king is usually the piece that is moved the least. Leaders know how to delegate. However, delegation does not end with passing a task to someone else, no matter how much you trust them.

Whether you delegate or not, the task is still your responsibility because it is your business, and if something goes wrong, your business will be impacted. It takes time to build trust, and as that trust becomes stronger, you can delegate increasingly critical work, but you must follow through with some form of measurement, so you can ensure things stay on track. That doesn't have to mean micro-management, but some kind of reporting mechanism needs to be in place. Measuring and reporting is not just about accountability. It is also about staying agile, responding to change, and learning from the experience.

Oliver told me that one of the lessons he had taken away from his time at Myprotein was to be prepared to go for it and risk everything in the pursuit of dreams. In my opinion, dreams can come true but only with a massive effort and total commitment. Risking everything doesn't have to, and shouldn't, mean being reckless. They should always be calculated risks, which brings me back to leadership and being trusted to make the right decisions.

TRY TO KEEP A COOL HEAD

I brought a cool, calm and calculated mindset to work every single day. No matter what curveballs are thrown at your business, there is no point panicking, stressing, or showing aggression. I can't say there weren't times when I wobbled. Sometimes my stress levels were off the scale. Everyone loses their cool from time to time. It is perfectly natural to experience strong emotions when the going gets tough, but giving them free rein can often make things worse by damaging relationships and unsettling others. Besides, I had found through experience that I was able to figure out solutions to the most challenging problems by staying in control of my emotions. If the leader is calm, everyone else feels more settled as well, and that more clinical mindset becomes a part of the culture.

The best way of dealing with any kind of threat is to respond intelligently and effectively. My way of dealing with a threat, whether that was the possibility of a competitor launching a new product before us or a threat to the supply chain, was to act decisively to not only neutralise the immediate threat, but to go beyond what was necessary and ensure that any related risks were considered. It's that chess mind yet again. Chess players don't just respond to imminent attacks, but they also try to predict what may be round the corner.

Later, when it came to selling the business, keeping a cool head gave me a huge advantage. I was not fazed by anyone else's age, experience, wealth or power, and even if I had been, I wouldn't have shown it. A solid poker face can go a long way when it comes to dealing with people. It allows the wearer to gauge the mood of others without giving anything away, which is an excellent skill for leadership and negotiation.

THE ART OF BEING HUMAN

As a leader, you have to be able to connect with people, and I tended to do that with humour. My humour is quite dry but not sarcastic. Usually, I would make light-hearted comments about football or else I would ask people about the projects they were working on, but not in a way that would make them feel oppressed.

I am predominantly an introvert, so in that sense, some would say I am not a people person, but I am (and always was) sensitive to how other people feel even though I know I don't always show it, and that came through in wanting to make people feel comfortable, respected and valued. People take notice of how managers behave, and if those in positions of trust and authority are abrasive, rude or condescending, those traits quickly become a part of an organisation's culture.

The art of leadership requires a wide range of skills, but nearly all of these relate to understanding how to interact with people. If you go into it just thinking you can treat people like cattle and tell them what to do, you're in for a rough ride. Realising that I was dealing with human beings was at the heart of every interaction I had with others, and that included reassuring them if anything occurred to make them feel insecure.

There's nothing quite like an office move when it comes to unsettling a team, but as one of the UK's fastest growing companies, it didn't seem to matter how huge our new premises were, we were repeatedly forced to find somewhere larger. And when we did, I managed the situation carefully to make sure our staff were well catered for.

CHAPTER SEVENTEEN

RUNAWAY GROWTH

I can honestly say there was never a dull moment from the day I launched Myprotein to when I sold it in 2011. Within a very short space of time, we were turning over large numbers, the awards were coming in thick and fast, and so were the office moves. The business was growing at such a pace that regardless of how well I tried to plan ahead, it was difficult to keep up. There really is only one way to describe what was happening: runaway growth.

Runaway growth is more of a roller coaster than some would imagine because there's no way of knowing if it is going to slow down, so anything that is done to facilitate the process – taking on new staff or moving into new premises – is a risk. Not that I had anything to worry about – to quote my mum, 'At the beginning, I would say orders were five to ten a day, but from that point on, they never went backwards.' That didn't mean we didn't experience spikes in sales, but today's spike would very quickly turn into tomorrow's norm.

It all looks so obvious to me now, but, on reflection, I was risk-averse at the time, and I had to be. What would have happened if I had moved to larger premises, only to find the revenue figures were not there to pay for it? I was on a shoestring, bootstrapped budget. I was faced with this dilemma almost every year or two.

LOOK FOR AN UPGRADE

The way I handled the question of whether to upgrade to larger premises was to squeeze every last drop of usefulness out of wherever we were operating from, only moving when it was absolutely necessary. The term I tend to use for the process is 'sweating the asset' because that captures how it felt as well.

By the time we moved out of the initial EZ Space lock-up that we'd leased as our first business premises, we'd expanded into four of the adjacent rooms, as well as the cellar, which we were using for storage. We were bursting at the seams, and I was beginning to reach the end of my tether with having to haul 20 kg sacks of powder up and down several flights of stairs every time a delivery arrived, or the blending team needed more stock.

We moved into a kind of mini-warehouse in a place in Stockport called Bredbury in the second half of 2006. It was on the small side, only around 1,500 square feet, but it provided a better fit for our needs than the old mill we'd been operating from. As well as the luxury – and it really did feel like a luxury – of a loading bay with a roller shutter door, there was an office on the front for our administrative staff, and a high-ceilinged warehouse with its own mezzanine floor; the high ceiling gave us more bang for our buck in terms of storage space, and lugging sacks around became a thing of the past because the warehouse was kitted out with manual pallet trucks, which made it easy to unload stuff from the back of a tail-lifted truck and move it around within the warehouse.

We had enough space to build a plastic-walled, sealed clean room for blending powder, and this was just one of the steps we later took towards gaining ISO 9001 production certification, which we managed to secure by the end of 2007 – more on that in the next chapter. Goods manufacturing practice (GMP), and hazard analysis critical control points (HACCP) accreditation came a few years later, around 2010.

People often ask me if there were stringent health and safety regulations to follow, but we were essentially a food manufacturer, so a lot of it was a matter of applying common sense to how powder was stored, handled and processed to minimise the risk of contamination or loss of quality. We weren't selling pharmaceuticals, despite the white lab coats and hats.

'SWEAT' YOUR ASSETS, BUT DON'T CUT IT TOO FINE

Again, we sweated it at the Bredbury warehouse until we were running at around 99 per cent capacity. In fact, had we not bought a 20-foot steel shipping container to act as an overflow storage area in the limited car parking space, we would have found ourselves on a slippery slope. We got away with it, so I am not going to complain, and the fact that the shipping container solved the problem perfectly illustrates the power of creative thinking when faced with challenges.

I wouldn't recommend doing what I did. If I could turn the clock back, I would have made the move at the 90 per cent capacity mark, which is still cutting things fine. At 99 per cent there is no room for manoeuvre, and that is riskier than moving into larger premises . . . and far more uncomfortable.

Myprotein had grown so much by then that even though our operation was still UK-based, and we were trading in pounds sterling from an English-language website, we were already shipping to Europe to meet the demand of a steadily increasing customer base over there and had been since 2005. We'd gone from minus £500 to almost a third of a million pounds in our first year of trading, and it would only be a matter of time before we would hit seven digits.

In 2007, we achieved £1 million in earnings before interest, taxes, depreciation and amortisation (EBITDA) for that tax year. Myprotein was voted Young Company of the Year at the prestigious Growing Business Awards, an event organised by *Real Business* in association with Lloyds Bank and supported by the Confederation of British Industry (CBI). We also won CBI's Growing Business Award in the same year. While 2007 was a great year, the EBITDA milestone and awards were only the beginning of what was going to be a steep curve of almost exponential growth and recognition.

NEVER JUDGE A BOOK BY ITS COVER

When we had to leave Bredbury for larger premises, I spotted a bargain on an old industrial estate in Cheadle. At 7,000 square feet, it was around three times bigger, and this time I would be buying the place rather than leasing. It was a really old, dirty-looking building, which I think may have been an old mill originally. The previous owners had split the space into a terrace of units that they were leasing out to separate businesses. I'm not one for judging a book by its cover, so I wasn't put off by the grotty appearance on the exterior. What attracted me was its enormous potential, and by purchasing at a rock-bottom price instead of renting, I was making a massive saving in costs.

The Cheadle building was like the iconic TARDIS in the cult British sci-fi television series, *Dr Who*. It had a strange shape which made it look smaller on the outside than it actually was. The front of the building was perhaps only around 20 feet wide, but it was much broader at the back because of its trapezium shape. There were shutter doors on the front and back, so it was easy to coordinate goods in and goods out, with supplies coming in from the front and products going at the back. Again, there was plenty of space for a clean room and comfortable offices for administrative staff. Within a year of moving into the 'TARDIS', we were having to rent the adjacent 5,000 square feet of space for extra storage, which we made use of by knocking down the inner walls to create one big space. That bought us some time, but it wasn't long before we had to move again.

It must have been around 2008 when we left Cheadle, and it was another excellent year, for Myprotein and for me personally. I won the Institute of Directors' (IoD) Rising Star North West Award, and I was also a finalist for the Bank of Scotland's Business Awards – which was won by The Hut Group, a name which features heavily in the Myprotein story in later years – and the prestigious Credit Suisse Entrepreneur of the Year Award. Myprotein was featured in a variety of well-known and respected publications, including the *Sunday Times*, the *Financial Times*, the *Telegraph*, *Manchester Evening News* and *Men's Health*.

By this time, we had become established as Europe's leading online manufacturer and supplier of sports nutrition and health products. I really knew Myprotein was going places, and by the end of 2008, I'd announced the appointment of three new senior management executives – Alex Hunter as finance director, Mark Coxhead as marketing director and Andy Gibbon as operations director. Notably, the press picked up on the fact that they were all keen sportsmen. Alex was a rugby player and sailor, Mark was a runner and golfer, and Andy enjoyed playing football and tennis. It helps to hire people who are likely to appreciate the products you sell.

We then moved into what resembled a massive shed on the Roundthorn Industrial Estate in Wythenshawe, a large district that is very near to Manchester Airport. It was owned by Manchester City Council, and we leased it from them. At around 15,000 square feet, the new place was bigger than both the old Cheadle office and the adjacent room we had been using combined. I loved the fact that the Roundthorn was a single structure with a high ceiling. It was a completely self-contained unit with two floors of offices, loads of warehouse space – thanks to the high ceiling – and its own perimeter fence. In a nutshell, Roundthorn was ideal for our purpose.

ADAPTING INFRASTRUCTURE TO FACILITATE FURTHER GROWTH

As Myprotein was growing, our infrastructure had to adapt and evolve as well, and so did our website. For example, the Customiser, which had provided such a simple and innovative way to cater for the individual, became difficult to scale. However, it didn't matter because by that time, we had such a huge range of products, our customers could always find what they needed.

The website I had designed and built in 2004 had stood the test of time and was still performing well, but in order to optimise our efficiency, we would have to move towards more automated processes, and that would mean investing in a warehouse management system and an enterprise-class website that could integrate with it.

We hired an external development team to configure a customised, enterprise framework for our website to migrate to. However, the migration process did not run as smoothly as we had expected it to, and we encountered a few large and unforeseen issues that caused delays to orders going out. It was one of the most stressful chapters of the Myprotein story, causing me sleepless nights as I was forced to watch what I had built crumble while customers were complaining. Thankfully, these were teething issues that didn't stick around for too long, and we were able to complete the integration and get the whole system working perfectly. It taught me a lot.

I invested in a conveyor-belt system for the packing of orders and semi-automated filling machines for filling the pouches with powder. Suffice to say, that made our operation more efficient, massively improved our productivity, and helped the business to stay lean while preparing us for even more growth.

By 2009, Myprotein was listed in the *Sunday Times* Fast Track 100 as the twenty-first fastest-growing company in the UK, and we also won the Regional Award for Small- to Medium-Sized Business of the Year for the North West of England at the National Business Awards. Imagine how many businesses were operating in the UK at that time. Then consider how quickly Myprotein was growing to make the top twenty-one fastest-growing businesses in the country. Unless you've been there, it is hard to imagine. We were outperforming even the most optimistic of forecasts and experiencing real hockey stick growth.

Automation streamlined our processes but didn't solve the ongoing problem of needing more space for storage. Again, we pushed it to the maximum and stayed in that building for as long as we possibly could. Manchester City Council were selling four units that stood behind our building on the estate. Each unit was around 17,000 square feet, so almost 70,000 square feet of space was up for grabs. I managed to release myself from the leasing contract for the building I was in, and I bought the other four units.

It's worth adding here that when you lease a commercial building, you will usually have to enter into a contract of at least three or even five years. That's a massive commitment to be left with if you get it wrong and growth doesn't justify the move. Ending a contract prematurely is an expensive affair and can easily break a business. I was fortunate because I already had an excellent relationship with the council, both as an existing tenant and a well-respected employer who was providing jobs where they were needed, and this gave me some leverage when it came to moving from one unit to another, as did the fact that I was upgrading rather than quitting.

Once I had bought the units, I ploughed a seven-digit number into making them ready for our operation, kitting them out with everything we would need and modernising the offices. Our processes became even slicker. We had more than enough space to grow, but, better still, we were able to dedicate each building to a different purpose – one building was purely for storage, another was for production, etc.

Karl Jacobie had joined us by then, and he was all over operations like a rash, making sure there was a natural flow and things ran smoothly. The automation process was also upgraded, so as well as having a picking-and-packing conveyor belt, we had an even smarter warehouse management system, which was great. Warehouse operatives carried handheld devices that looked a bit like tablets with in-built scanners. Once a docket was scanned, the software would not only tell them where the various order components were situated, but it would show them the quickest route from where they were. It was cutting edge at that time.

Warehouse staff would then move around the aisles with a pick trolley, picking the items they needed and scanning them with the device. Everything would be put into a plastic tray, which was rather like the kind they use in airports for passengers to place their shoes and other belongings. The tray would be placed onto the conveyor belt and transported to a packing station.

Packing staff would scan all the items again to double-check that the goods in the tray matched the order on the docket. Everything would be carefully packed into an appropriately sized box, which would be placed onto the conveyor belt along with the dispatch note, and off it would go to the couriers. The dispatch team would spend all day carefully loading packages into a massive heavy goods vehicle, and at the end of the day a driver would come along and take the lorry away.

Another element that was well optimised for efficiency was stock control. Myprotein was selling a vast array of products from protein powders and carbohydrates to vitamins, including many mostly unheard-of food ingredients that I had discovered and learnt about. There were hundreds of products, and the warehouse management system kept tight control of everything. As soon as a particular powder or other product reached a critically low level, the system would generate a works order for it to be restocked. Thanks to Karl and the rest of the operations team, all the separate operational components – picking and packing, stock control, blending, etc. – were beautifully integrated and worked together harmoniously.

AGILITY IS THE KEY

Seeing one's business growing rapidly is a beautiful experience. Growth should mean job generation, more profit and a more secure long-term future. What's not to love? However, growth is a double-edged sword because as your business grows, so do its needs and so does its complexity.

One way to look at a business is to imagine it as an oil rig in the North Sea, being held up by many pillars – its sales, workforce, leadership team, product range, stock, storage, processing plant, website and operating systems, just to list a few off the top of my head. If the sales pillar is going through the roof, but none of the other pillars are adapting to accommodate the growth, what's going to happen? The rig will become severely lopsided and end up collapsing. All that hard work will end up at the bottom of the sea, and the owner will be treading water just to stay afloat.

You have to tend to all of those pillars to maintain balance, so the platform doesn't become unstable as it is elevated to greater heights. Just as your sales must not outperform your ability to adapt, neither must your workforce size, leadership team, storage space or any of the other pillars that are keeping your business stable.

Hold on a second, you may be thinking. *That's all very well when growth is planned and predictable, but what about the kind of runaway growth that Myprotein experienced?* And you'd be right to raise that question; it was difficult to keep up with. I was forced to strike a balance between playing it too safe and risking too much. Look at the storage issues we were facing, for example. I believe I left it too late to move on at least one occasion, and the consequences could have been disastrous. Thankfully, when things became really tight, we found temporary fixes that worked. What would I have done differently?

As I said earlier in the book, I don't do 'regret' because I appreciate that any decisions I have already made were based on the evidence I had in front of me at that time. Looking back, if I were to do anything differently, I could have decided to tighten the reins on our growth rate, to make it easier to keep up. However, while some businesses may buy into that philosophy, I don't, especially in the competitive market we were in. It is easy to look backwards from the other side of the finish line, but you don't have the luxury to sit back and slow things down when you're still in the race.

That leaves one option: go for it with everything you have got, stay alert, keep your eyes and ears open and do everything you can to make sure you are as adaptable as possible – and then become more adaptable. Try to second-guess where one pillar may not be able to keep up with the rest and set up contingencies to cope. Set up contingencies to deal with those contingencies not working. A Plan B is not enough. If you cannot adapt or fail to adapt quickly enough, you can be beaten by your own success.

After five years of what had felt like a constant race to keep up with runaway growth, it finally started to feel as though we were on top of the situation. I am not one for standing still, and I can usually find something or other that I want to improve, but I have to admit that when I looked at what the business had evolved into, I was proud and satisfied at the same time. We had a well-oiled machine that ran as smoothly and efficiently as a Rolex watch.

A WELL-OILED MACHINE

In 2010, we launched the French, Italian, German, Irish and Spanish localised versions of the Myprotein website, which were configured to trade in the appropriate local currencies, and we set up multilingual customer service teams to strengthen our offering in those countries. I won the Ernst and Young Entrepreneur of the Year Award, and Myprotein was practically a household name when it came to people who took their sports nutritional supplements seriously. Big name brand ambassadors were recruited as the starting embers of what would develop into a more sophisticated influencer-marketing strategy. They were everywhere, and so were potential buyers for Myprotein.

Once we had settled into the four units at Wythenshawe, we were perfectly placed for a buyer. The senior management team was embedded and running things so well, I could have taken a month off if I'd wanted to – although that was the last thing on my mind at the time. The offices looked great, our team of over one hundred employees were well organised, happy, focused and productive. Operations had been fine-tuned and optimised for maximum productivity and efficiency, and the company was still growing at breakneck speed.

CHAPTER EIGHTEEN

GOING FOR GOLD – PREPARING FOR THE SALE

Once I had made up my mind to professionalise the business and set course for an exit, there was no going back. By 2009, I had all the people I needed to ensure Myprotein would run smoothly and profitably whether I was there or not, and turnover had surpassed the £10 million milestone and was continuing to rise at a steadily increasing rate.

The senior team comprised the five directors – Karl Jacobie (managing director), Mark Coxhead (marketing director), Alex Hunter (financial director), Nick Smith (sales director), Neil Pollard (IT director) – and to some extent, associate commercial director Oliver Rushton was a sixth member as he was working so closely with the team. I was the chief executive officer (CEO). By building a solid senior management team of highly experienced people with excellent track records, I could trust them to hire the staff they needed to support them.

Middle managers were usually recruited by the senior management team, although I would sometimes be brought in for the final interview if the role was particularly important or they were keen to receive input from me. Most of the time, middle managers were externally sourced, but part of the company's ethos was to recognise potential and reward excellence, so junior staff were sometimes promoted into management roles. The senior team had to be sourced externally because I needed the best people I could find, and that meant finding C-suite individuals with bags of experience.

Karl Jacobie had moved up the ladder from operations director to managing director, and in turn, he had promoted Andrew Gilbert from operations manager to head of operations, but Andrew didn't sit on the board. Karl's passion for operations didn't wane, but by putting his trust in Andrew, whom he had been working very closely with, he was able to focus on his duties as the managing director.

Alex Hunter transformed our accounts into something magical that delivered excellent business insights. Thanks to his efforts, we were able to forecast more accurately and make more sense of the numbers. Figures have a language of their own, and Alex was gifted in that language. He was able to turn all our numbers and percentages into a professional presentation that spoke volumes about how the business was performing, where improvements could be made, and where the opportunities and threats were. I learnt a lot about business from Alex. Our accounts went from being a low-technology affair to a full accounts suite that made it easy to analyse all aspects of company performance forensically, and the year-end accounts were produced in the form of a professionally finished report. Given that we were now on the market and looking for a buyer, the end-of-year report had to be something special because one wrongly worded phrase or sentence or piece of negative information can seriously impact the perceived value of a business.

PURPOSEFUL BOARD MEETINGS TO DRIVE THE BUSINESS FORWARD

With the new senior management team came board meetings, and then it was only a matter of time before these were professionalised to make them more useful and productive. I hate waste, and time is precious, so if I was going to gather the six most senior and high-calibre individuals to sit down with me for a meeting every month, I had to make sure we were getting more out of it than ticking a box. I wanted to make the most of the opportunity.

The monthly board meeting gave everyone an opportunity to deliver an update on how their departments were doing. How were the sales going? What products were selling more? What products weren't doing so well, and why? How was the company performing from an accounting perspective? Were there any threats on the horizon? Had any new markets been identified that we could exploit? Which marketing plans had succeeded, which ones had failed, and what had we learnt? The aim was to learn from the current month and focus on how we could apply that knowledge to drive more success in future months.

Each director had to prepare a detailed document for the board, which presented all the relevant information about their department's performance. These documents were amalgamated into one main board pack, and every board member was given a copy in good time to mull over before each meeting. That way, everyone knew in advance what was going to come up in discussion. I much preferred everyone to read the board packs prior to the meeting and for the team come in with questions. I'm not one to turn pages. It's not a good use of time.

The monthly board pack was rich in management information. Just as Alex had made it easier to understand how we were performing from an accountant's perspective, the other directors presented vital information with charts and graphs to illustrate how their departments were getting along. Mark's marketing pack, for example, presented vital marketing metrics relating to every campaign and marketing medium we were using – visits to the various pages of the website, dwelling times, bounces, social media engagements and click-throughs, etc.

As sales director, Nick was primarily responsible for driving up sales to shops and other trade outlets. Sales through the website were a product of marketing activity, so online sales were the responsibility of Mark Coxhead. As with everything that we measured, Nick's sales figures would help determine future activities. A business is not a business without sales. The sales director's seat can be the hottest one in the boardroom when the waves are choppy, but given the company's performance on every level, Nick usually had something to smile about – not that any of us would allow him to rest on his laurels. Always strive for improvement. Better is always possible.

Neil, the IT director, joined the team much later than everyone else, and I sold the business soon after. However, it is fair to say that he probably had the least exciting role to play because unless something was broken or there was an imminent threat or opportunity on the horizon that we had to prepare for, Neil wouldn't have much to report. His department, information technology, was a crucial part of Myprotein's infrastructure, so he was more concerned with fighting any technology glitches that may be raised in board meetings and reporting back on how they'd been tackled. When a business is able to function efficiently, that's about as good as it gets for the IT team. No one notices them until there's a problem.

As the managing director, Karl had to oversee all aspects of the business. As the most senior member of the team, it was on him to keep everyone else on course. One way he stayed on top of everything was through weekly performance meetings in which the rest of the senior management team would report to him. That allowed him to monitor individual performance on KPIs and take corrective action where necessary. I guess you could say that part of his job was to pull people back in line if they were underperforming or needed a push, as well as to support and motivate them. If there was a blocker preventing a particular project from progressing, he had the big-picture perspective.

ALWAYS FOLLOW UP

Remember what I said in an earlier chapter about delegation in relation to leadership? When something is delegated to another person or department, it must not be forgotten about, and you can see this principle at work in the way our meetings were structured. The middle managers would have to report to the senior managers, the senior managers were having to report to Karl, and everyone was reporting to me in the board meetings.

As my job as CEO became more outward-facing, Karl took over the role I had played in bootstrapping the business, but that didn't mean I was out of the equation, and it didn't mean that if an issue arose, I would have to wait until our monthly board meeting to find out. Karl handled the day-to-day and reported to me. I always knew what was going on. We had a superb working relationship.

The professionalisation process led to the creation of our own data warehouse, where all the information from the various entry points was being pooled. If it was measurable, we were measuring it, and we ended up with a valuable resource that could be mined for useful management information. We were interrogating big data to look at different variables and identify trends or issues. That resource answered so many questions, but it also gave rise to plenty more, and that's where the juice is when you are looking for ways to grow and improve. This 'big data' was key in identifying trends, and we were well ahead of the curve for a business of our size.

BEST FOR BUSINESS

Another leadership tactic that I employed was to encourage a healthy level of rivalry to bring out the best in people and keep everyone on their toes. In a way, I was delegating one of the harder parts of leadership to the rest of the team – calling people to account. Everyone was accountable to everyone else, and that included me. I wanted to be challenged as well.

Board meetings were lively affairs that blended a strong sense of camaraderie with a fair amount of gamesmanship as every board member fought hard to present themselves in the best possible light. Sometimes I didn't need to challenge anyone or dig deeper because they would interrogate each other. We have two ears and one mouth, so I was far more interested in listening to what was going on than speaking, and if I did speak, it was because I had something important to say, an issue to raise or a question to ask.

Those board meetings were dominated by one mantra – best for business. On reflection, I can see how it might sound a little harsh, but we were all there to serve the business, so the business came first, second and third. I didn't care who was upset, including me, as long as we were making the best decisions for the future of the business. I didn't have time for the fluffy stuff. That said, while the business was doing well, so were we, and I cannot stress this enough – I had a superb management team. This is where finding the right people, not only in terms of experience and skills, but also in regard to personality type – values, priorities, attitudes, perception and approach to problem solving – is of paramount importance. My team knew what I was about, and I knew them. We were all in it together and shared the same focus on the same mission.

FOCUS ON EXCELLENCE, AND THE AWARDS WILL FOLLOW

In the early days, best for business meant not having to invest in shiny objects, such as pool tables in the office, or spending time chasing awards. You don't need fancy gimmicks to develop an excellent working culture, and you don't need awards to be a great entrepreneur. The same goes for fame. You don't need fame to validate a great business idea. There are plenty of accomplished entrepreneurs who have made a tremendous impact on the wider world, and the odds are that you will not have heard of them. Focusing on vanity and looking good is a quick way to fail. If you are starting up now, focus on what really matters in business.

I know what you're thinking: *But, Oliver, your career was littered with awards, you had plenty of press appearances, and now you have written a book!* Appearances can be deceptive. The awards were never about an ego boost, being mentioned in the press was par for the course, and the book was written for a much more worthy purpose than becoming famous. That's the point here – purpose. I am not saying there is anything wrong with awards or being famous, but there must be a better reason for doing those things than wanting to massage your ego.

When it came to the awards that Myprotein won, or which I won personally, they sometimes came to us without any effort or intention on our part. However, yes, we did go for awards, but we did so to raise our profile as part of the strategy for finding a buyer for the business, and by that time, we were well established as a rapidly growing enterprise. There is a huge difference between vanity and raising awareness for business purposes.

For me, best for business means focusing on profit and keeping a tight rein on costs, while ensuring the team has everything it needs to do the best job possible. That is why mixing business with pleasure is so prone to failure because when emotions come into play, they often distract, and best for business becomes best for the relationship. You cannot focus on both of those things at the same time. The best-for-business approach is what enabled Myprotein to grow into the attractive business proposition that it became. Buyers and investors are only interested in two things: how profitable the asset is; and how quickly it will yield a return on their investment.

ACCREDITATION MUST BE MEANINGFUL— NOT JUST FOR SHOW

Accreditation is another one of those achievements that can be sought after for the wrong reasons or the right reasons. It should be more than a tick-box exercise just to get a piece of paper that you can wave about. We took our ISO 9001 UKAS accreditation very seriously, and we were interested in the spirit of the process, not just the letter – putting processes in place to improve quality. I was determined to gain ISO 9001 UKAS accreditation because of my commitment to quality.

The United Kingdom Accreditation Service (UKAS) is an independent, not-for-profit organisation that oversees accreditation to ensure the correct standards are met. It is not a regulatory body, so it doesn't have any legal or enforcement powers, but gaining UKAS accreditation means that an organisation has conformed to an agreed, recognisable standard, so it adds credibility. Again, we were the first to have this level of accreditation in our space.

YOU NEED AT LEAST ONE 'JOBSWORTH'

It takes more than a perfectionist like me to go over and above where quality-control protocols are concerned. Despite my quirks and my tendency to pay close attention to details, I don't follow rules for the sake of it. In fact, I would argue that sometimes rules should be broken. To ensure we went the extra mile where accreditation was concerned, I needed a real jobsworth – someone who was particularly anally retentive about doing things by the book.

People usually throw the word 'jobsworth' around as an insult, but I genuinely believe we need these people. They are able to do something that the rest of us can't. They have an important job to do – like proofreaders, traffic wardens or, dare I say, contract lawyers. Someone has to be able to look at the details, even when doing so flies in the face of common sense. In the right capacity, jobsworths are a godsend.

We found our accreditation godsend, and they were in charge of quality control. They would neither miss a single detail nor overlook the slightest discrepancy, and their black-and-white mindset was perfect for the role. Something was either being done correctly or it wasn't, and they had my total support and authorisation to make sure things were done the right way, no matter how annoying their requests may have been for other staff members. There are no shortcuts in quality control, and while I may be a maverick in many ways, I believe there is a valid reason for everything in the world of quality assurance.

We hired a consultant, who documented every single process in the business, right down to a microscopic level. Even something as mundane as printing an order would be broken down into separate instructions – go to this page, click on 'Find order', enter the order number, press 'Print', etc. All processes were numbered, and we ended up with a huge manual that was as thick as the old *Yellow Pages*. The ISO 9001 manual, as it was known, was like the bible of quality control, documenting every process from warehouse to production, and it was quite literally childproof. If the whole lot of us had suddenly disappeared in a puff of smoke, that manual made it possible to ship in a totally fresh crew and continue the operation as though nothing had happened. All they would have to do is follow the step-by-step instructions. That's a pretty powerful tool for any business to have.

It is human nature for people to become sloppy over time. When processes are set up, everyone gets on board, but after a while, individuals spot small tweaks here and there that appear to save time or money. Unfortunately, as more of those breaks from protocol become the norm, the risk of things going wrong becomes greater. That is where people such as our quality control officer are a real asset in any business. They ensured that our protocols remained intact and processes were not corrupted, and I guess it takes a zero-tolerance approach to do that. Myprotein's operations were streamlined for efficiency, standardisation and consistency, and our quality control officer kept us that way.

A HIGHLY VIABLE PROPOSITION – READY FOR THE SALE

Since meeting with the corporate finance team and being told that I had to groom Myprotein before I could sell it, I had done everything possible to make it into a viable proposition. Everything was in place – the senior management team, continued growth, profitability, efficiency, quality assurance, UKAS-recognised accreditation, awards, a comprehensive ISO 9001 manual that documented every process of the company to the nth degree – and potential buyers started circling us like hungry predators. I was sitting on a multimillion-pound asset, surrounded by hugely powerful companies that wanted what I had, and I still hadn't hit the age of thirty!

When Karl shared his thoughts with me as I was preparing to write this book, he commented on how fearless and cool under pressure he had perceived me to be from the day he joined us to when the business was sold. The fact is that I wasn't fearless, and even with a senior management team around me, I still kept my world very much to myself.

Myprotein was my business – a business I had built from scratch, dedicated my life to, and nurtured with love and commitment. It had grown into a large concern, employing over a hundred people, and serving hundreds of thousands of customers around the world. That's a huge responsibility, and of course I was afraid. However, showing that fear would serve no purpose. Reacting to that fear would not help either.

In any situation, things can go the way you want them to or they can go wrong. If you dwell on fear and listen to the voice that tells you how things are going to go wrong and what terrible consequences are going to follow, you are putting yourself on a road to hell. I acknowledged the fear, but I also recognised that I had all the ace cards and if I played my hand carefully, I would come out with the jackpot, and there would be no losers. All I had to do was keep being Oliver and keep a cool head. It had brought me this far, so there was no reason why it wouldn't get me across the finish line.

After a beauty parade with a number of corporate finance houses, I appointed a broker called Altium to manage the bidding process. There were more than twenty-five parties showing serious interest, and each of these put in a provisional bid. Representatives from each company were invited to see us and presented with an information memorandum (IM) that Altium had produced to show Myprotein in the best possible light.

PLAYING TO WIN: THE ART OF NEGOTIATION

No stone was left unturned in spelling out the features and benefits. I pride myself on being a strong negotiator, and that process starts long before any words are exchanged. A poor negotiator can have the greatest product and still lose out on the best deal because they are intimidated before the first meeting. I knew how valuable the company was, and I left potential buyers in no doubt that I knew I was selling a great business.

There was no room for ambiguity. They needed to understand from the start that although I was a young, non-corporate entrepreneur on the outside, I had my head screwed on so tightly that if I got the merest whiff that they were not taking me or Myprotein seriously, they would be out of the process. When the stakes are high, any negotiation that takes place will go far beyond facts and figures. There is a psychological element because each side will weigh up how robust the other is, how determined they are to maintain their red lines, and how confident they are in their position.

By the time bidders came into our offices, we had already employed several techniques to ensure negotiations would fall in our favour. Firstly, they were attracted to us because they could see the phenomenal growth, the awards and the strength of our brand in the market. Secondly, the IM was designed to wow them and show them we knew our stuff. Thirdly, when each group of representatives sat down in our boardroom, the senior management team would deliver a superb presentation. I wouldn't even be sat in the room by that stage.

I would usually meet bidders post-presentation to discuss their initial feedback and my personal terms. My senior team were clearing a path for me to cut to the chase. I was projecting an air of confidence by not being there during that process, and when I did enter the meeting, I maintained my poker face.

In any negotiation, both sides are looking to give as little as possible while gaining as much as they can. Wise negotiators recognise that deals are best when both sides leave the table feeling they have won. That's the whole purpose of the negotiation – to meet somewhere in the middle. However, the more expert you are at playing your hand by convincingly talking up the value of your proposition while downplaying the strength of theirs, the more you can pull things your way. I used several tactics to accomplish that mission.

There were eight bidders all wanting to buy my company, and they knew that, so it was easy for me to play them off against each other. When nobody is interested in what you're selling, you are either in the wrong room or you haven't sold the benefits, but when you have eight bidders all trying to win the same prize, you have an additional weapon – the fear of missing out – because none of them want to see the other taking away the prize.

The deal being discussed was complex because there were so many facets to it. It wasn't just about how much money was being put on the table, but how many shares I would keep because I wanted to have that second bite of the cherry. If they tried to knock the price down, I would manage it up by enhancing the package. That's where it helps not to throw everything in at the start of the negotiations. If you do that, you won't have any room for manoeuvre. By keeping some things back, I could throw in extra benefits when necessary to secure the price I wanted, and if I could get the asking price without offering a better deal, even better.

Once the first round of negotiations was over, there was one bid that stood out. I had launched Myprotein in May 2004. It had taken just seven years, but I had reached one of the most critical milestones of my life. My thirtieth birthday was round the corner, my first child was on the way, and I was about to enter into a final round of negotiations and do the deal of a lifetime. On the other side of the table? The Hut Group.

CHAPTER NINETEEN

CROSSING THE FINISHING LINE – THE SALE

How did I end up selling Myprotein to The Hut Group? To get a better idea as to why their offer was the most attractive, you need to understand what kinds of deals were on offer and what I wanted to achieve.

SELLING TO A PRIVATE EQUITY HOUSE

My goal at the outset of the process was to sell a minority stake of around 30 per cent to a private equity house. They would then help with the next phase of growth, and I could take a chunk of cash off the table to secure mine and my family's financial freedom. I would still be the majority shareholder, so I wouldn't be giving away too much control of the business, even after taking typical private equity legal provisions into account – I took a very strong stance on these.

With this type of package, the senior management team is given some 'sweet equity' to incentivise them to stay on and play a key role in the company's three-to-five-year plan, and everybody wins.

The private equity house gets a significant enough chunk to make the investment worth their while, the senior management team have their own stake in the growth of the business, so they will want to give it everything they've got, and the founder retains their status as the majority shareholder. It truly is a win-win-win scenario.

FINDING A TRADE BUYER

Another arrangement for selling a business is to find a trade buyer – a conglomerate such as Amazon. These kinds of buyers would usually want to own 100 per cent of the business, and they would expect the seller to agree to an earn-out arrangement. This is where the seller agrees to stay on with the company for a set term and hit a number of key growth targets before they are given the full selling price. For example, they may get an immediate payment of 80 per cent of the selling price on completion of the sale, but in order to earn the other 20 per cent, they would have to ensure 100 per cent growth over a three-year period. Typically, the earn-out portion of a purchase can be anywhere from 10 per cent to 50 per cent of the value of the sale, and sellers can find themselves locked in for between three to five years.

EARN-OUT CLAUSES

Earn-out clauses are better for the buyer because they want to be confident that they're not buying a sinking ship, and their confidence is boosted by knowing that it is in the seller's best interests to drive further growth. The seller benefits as well because when they get their final slice of 20 per cent, they will get 20 per cent of a much larger business. However, there is arguably more risk for the seller because if anything happens that results in targets not being met, they don't get a penny more, and the buyer ends up with a business for 80 per cent of the original asking price. Furthermore, by the time a founder decides to exit the business, they might want to focus their energy elsewhere without being tied into a business they have sold. Signing up to an earn-out clause means the founder agrees to stay on as an employee in effect – not a very attractive proposition for someone like me who'd been in sole charge of Myprotein for seven years and had probably made themselves unemployable.

SEPARATING THE WHEAT FROM THE CHAFF

Once I had appointed Altium as our corporate finance house and the non-disclosure agreement (NDA) had been signed, I told them everything they needed to know about Myprotein, and they compiled the IM, which is in effect a detailed sales brochure of the business. They were able to draw on their network of potential buyers – private equity houses and trade – and select the most appropriate prospects based on the kind of exit deal I was looking for. Part of their job was to split the wheat from the chaff and produce a shortlist.

As soon as Myprotein was placed on the market, it was very hot property, and we attracted lots of serious interest from some of the biggest private equity houses and trade buyers alike. Some of the initial bidders were offering unattractive terms, and they were dismissed very quickly. As for the others, it was a case of looking for the best fit because I wanted to find a buyer that understood our business and our market. I needed someone who could add value and help us to take Myprotein's growth to the next level, not just 'dumb money' – money that is invested with no added experience or expertise.

I was primarily interested in private equity offers, but we received plenty of trade offers as well, and a couple of them are worth mentioning. A well-known international conglomerate wanted 100 per cent of the business on a multiple-year earn-out, but although it was a relatively short term for an earn-out agreement, it would have meant I was effectively working for them. That was never going to happen. I was not employable.

The other trade offer came in from the board of directors of a massive soft drinks brand, who were offering 50 per cent cash on completion of the sale with the other 50 per cent on earn-out after three years, and they wanted me to take an executive role in their global sports nutrition arm. I came very close to accepting their offer, but it was going to take an incredible amount of energy at a time when I was wanting to take my foot off the gas. Having worked my guts out for the previous seven years, the last thing I wanted was to enter the corporate world and spend half my life jet-setting from one office to another. Besides that, my first child had just been born.

DUE DILIGENCE

There were a few private equity bids that I was particularly interested in, and one of those conversations had reached an advanced stage. We were going through the process of due diligence, which meant allowing the bidder to investigate every aspect of the business, including our accounts, with a fine-toothed comb.

The due diligence audit, which took around a month to complete, was intense and stressful, as the bidder searched high and low for any hidden issues. Buying a business is a little bit like buying a used car, except the stakes are much higher. Who hasn't been there? You test-drive the vehicle, and it's great – starts first time, handles well and looks beautiful. However, within a week of buying it, the knob falls off the top of the gear stick just as you are negotiating a busy junction, and then an engine management warning appears on the dashboard. That's why it makes sense to give the vehicle a thorough once-over before buying it, and even then, you might miss something. The same thing can happen when a business is sold, but instead of the problem being a dodgy clutch or an ageing exhaust, there may be a massive financial sinkhole eating the company's profits and driving down the forecasts. Within months, the new business owner discovers they have purchased an albatross. No wonder the due diligence process has to be so intrusive and intense.

Before the audit began, I forewarned the bidder that the process would be a major distraction for our senior management team and was bound to result in a material loss of productivity and growth. I wanted an assurance that they were not going to use any reduction in sales or profits as leverage in an attempt to get me to lower my selling price once the process was over and we were sat down at the negotiation table. 'Of course, Oliver,' they agreed. 'That's perfectly understandable. No problem at all.'

One month later, after we had been through the hassle of a thorough due diligence, we sat down to discuss the deal, and to my astonishment, they did exactly what they had promised they would not do. Did they think I was an idiot? If they were going to behave like that during the sales process when most people want to create the best impression, how would they behave once a deal had been signed? I do not suffer fools, and I have no tolerance for dishonesty. Once they had pulled that stunt, whether it was done intentionally or through incompetence, there was no way of moving forward with the discussion. The deal was off the table. I have since spoken to the private equity house and they freely admitted that Myprotein was 'the one that got away'.

A LATE ENTRY – THE HUT GROUP

While all this was going on, another large company that had started up at the same time as Myprotein was looking for a change in direction and wanted to acquire a new business. The

Hut Group was co-founded by Matt Moulding and John Gallemore, both chartered accountants who had been working for Phones4U, part of the Caudwell Group, prior to setting up a business of their own.

When they launched The Hut Group in 2004, they were selling compact discs (CDs). By 2011, they were turning over in excess of £70 million and had acquired other businesses such as Zavvi, a retail brand that was operating in the same space as HMV. Their challenge was how to adapt to a rapidly evolving digital world where CDs were quickly becoming obsolete. They had invested a lot of money into developing a technical platform and were looking for the right brand to grow.

The first time I came across The Hut Group was at an awards ceremony around 2010, when both our companies made it to the final in a competition that was organised by HBOS bank. The bank was offering a prize of £5 million in funding to the winner. I thought nothing of it at the time, but I suspect that was when Matt Moulding and John Gallemore first noticed Myprotein.

The forecasts for the sports nutrition market were all rosy, the space was set to continue growing, and Myprotein was the number-one online brand in Europe. As a fully vertically integrated business, with profits in excess of £5 million in the previous year and run rate EBITDA growing exponentially, Myprotein was exactly the kind of brand that The Hut Group were looking for.

The Hut Group were not in the race initially, and they were not on my radar as a potential buyer, but their mergers and acquisitions director approached Altium. They reached a point where a heads of terms agreement could be approved and documented. This is a non-binding document that covers all the issues relevant to a contract should a deal be agreed upon. It often forms the foundation of a contract, but it is normal to expect changes to be made following further negotiations.

Once the heads of terms had been agreed, Matt Moulding contacted me directly to ask for a meeting. Matt's around eight years older than me, but he was still in his thirties in 2011, and I saw him as another young and highly successful entrepreneur. He also has a natural flair for sales, and we built a good rapport very quickly.

Matt was offering to pay half of the asking price in cash on the day of the sale and the other half as shares in The Hut Group. There was no lock-in period, so I would be free to leave the business completely from the day of the sale, although he invited me to step into the role of chief operating officer (COO). The contract included a restrictive covenant not to set up a business in direct competition with them, but that would only be for a period of twelve months if I decided to leave.

The offer was attractive because it was hassle-free, but one of the most important elements of their proposal, as far as I was concerned, was their vision. They intended to float The Hut Group on the stock exchange at some point over the next one to two years. With The Hut Group reportedly making millions in profit and growing, the prospect of having shares in the group excited me. However, had they come to me with the same offer twelve months earlier, I wouldn't have been interested.

The fact is that the previous two years had been a very busy period. Preparing for the sale had put me under a lot of pressure, and the last six months in particular, especially the month-long due diligence process, had left me feeling pretty exhausted. The whole experience had worn me down, and that made The Hut Group's relatively fair, easy and attractive offer seem all the more appealing. We had a deal in principle, and we shook on it, but we still needed to nail down the details, so a date was set for our teams to come together to thrash out the deal.

THRASHING OUT THE DEAL

The meeting was planned for the morning of Tuesday, 31 May, at the Gateley offices in Manchester. It was a full house with legal teams, tax teams, accounts teams, you name it, all there to take the deal across the finishing line. There were about twenty people in that room, and the meeting didn't finish until every clause of the sale and purchase agreement (SPA) had been inspected and agreed. I had my team in place, and it didn't take me long to realise I didn't need to be there, so I went home and left them to it.

I didn't return to Gateley until the next morning, and the meeting was still going on. It took them a total of twenty-seven hours, locked in a room together, to complete the process. On Wednesday, 1 June 2011, I signed the SPA, sealing the sale of Myprotein, and within an instant, £32 million landed in my bank account.

LIFE AFTER MYPROTEIN

Matt invited me to join The Hut Group's board to head up its lifestyle division, and I agreed. The sale of Myprotein was big news at the time and attracted a lot of media interest. Matt and I put out statements, and the deal was reported on the same day. The Hut Group announced plans to double its workforce around the same time. Everyone was buzzing. We were all excited about the future.

The initial public offering (IPO), which The Hut Group had intended to launch in 2013, eventually took place in September 2020, when the group was listed at an enormous £5.4 billion. At the time of writing, the group has reached a market cap of close to £7 billion! As the jewel in the crown within the group's portfolio, Myprotein made an enormous contribution to The Hut Group's growth over that period.

You may be wondering whether I now feel that I should have held on to Myprotein for longer. Let's just say that it is an easy question to answer in hindsight. Had I not sold Myprotein, I would be a billionaire today – that much is pretty clear – but I made my decision based on my understanding of the situation at that time, and I still believe it was probably the best decision I could have made without the benefit of a crystal ball.

The deal I made with The Hut Group ticked all the boxes in terms of what I originally set out to achieve. The fact that The Hut Group had retained me as COO was a clear signal that they still wanted me to be involved, and, with shares in their group, I still had a stake. I knew Myprotein would go on to become the number one in the world, and I wanted to be a part of that. Sure, I wanted to own some rollover for a second bite of the cherry, but the initial lump sum provided enough immediate security for me and my family. Furthermore, the deal meant I would be able to turn my attention to other aspects of my life for the first time in seven years.

How about the £32 million? How did that feel? Did I rush out to buy a new Ferrari? I get asked these questions all the time, and I can understand why, but believe it or not, I didn't treat myself to anything special with the money.

By the time I sold the business, I had already driven my fair share of nice cars, although owning them had never been my motivation for pursuing the life of an entrepreneur. Selling Myprotein, receiving the bank notification that I was now tens of millions of pounds better off, and becoming a shareholder and board member of The Hut Group on the same day, felt a little bit like crossing a finishing line of a race. I could finally take my foot off the gas and take time out to relax. After almost eight years of hustle and bustle, running around, making major decisions, carrying an enormous responsibility, I could finally enjoy the feeling of calm.

Although I didn't splash out, I threw a massive party to celebrate. I had done what I had set out to do on every level – becoming a multimillionaire by the age of thirty, creating jobs, launching a brand from scratch, and growing it into something special that I could be proud of.

Taking my shares in The Hut Group into account, I sold Myprotein for a total of at least £350 million. Knowing that I launched a business from scratch with a £500 overdraft and grew it to around a third of a billion pounds while maintaining 100 per cent equity, without any loans or outside investors, makes me feel tremendously proud. That's the achievement. That's what I celebrated: what I had achieved, not what I had acquired. Money provides options – the power to choose what to do with your time instead of having to sell it for money. The famous phrase is that time is money. Time is far more valuable than money. Time is life.

From the day you are born, you only have so much time, and there's no way of knowing what your quota is. I knew what I wanted to do with my time, and I made up my mind to make it happen. To bootstrap something is to take what you already have and build on it to create something bigger. If you know how to do that, it doesn't matter how small your lot is to start with, it will grow. Don't forget, life begins with one cell.

I have shown you how I bootstrapped my life.

That leaves one question:

How are you going to bootstrap yours?

ABOUT THE AUTHOR

Oliver Cookson is an award-winning British entrepreneur who founded the sports nutrition business Myprotein and went on to become a self-made multimillionaire.

Growing up in a working-class area of Manchester, Oliver left school aged sixteen with one GCSE. Even then, he felt destined for success and set himself the goal of becoming a millionaire by thirty, which he achieved with three years to spare. He is perhaps best known for his bootstrapped business Myprotein, which he launched with a £500 overdraft and scaled into a multimillion-pound company, winning a plethora of awards along the way. Following a high-profile sale to The Hut Group in 2011, he went on to be named the UK's number-one self-made millionaire under forty, with a net worth of £306m (*Sunday Times Rich List 2019*) and is currently worth more than a third of a billion pounds.

Oliver Cookson is a charismatic and engaging entrepreneur, leader and speaker who is a well-respected figure in the business and fitness sectors. He is passionate about helping other entrepreneurs and launched a podcast called *Bootstrap Your Life* to share his knowledge, experience and expertise.

Over the years, Oliver has become more interested in personal and spiritual growth, and he is now looking at how he can continue to make a positive impact in the world by planning a charitable legacy. Oliver is a patron of children's charity Make-a-Wish (UK), a not-for-profit set up to make the dreams of critically ill children come true.

ACKNOWLEDGEMENTS

This book covers my life up until 2011, so for now, I am mentioning those who knew me and supported me during that period. I have met many other, amazing people since then, but I will save those acknowledgements for the sequel . . . if I write one!

I want to start by dedicating this book to my mum, Jayne, for all the long hours and total dedication she put into my dream of Myprotein, and for helping to make that dream come true; also, for being the best mum anyone could ever ask for. You deserve everything. Love you.

My dad, Saeed, also deserves a special mention for helping to shape me from a young age. You taught me a lot, and I will always be grateful.

Of course, my beautiful children: Sebastian, Carmen and Halle-Alba. Also, a special mention for my stepson, Corrado. Having each of you and your love in my life makes me a better man, and I hope that one day you will be as proud of me as I am of you. So sorry, kids, for my absences due to work. I have been building a solid and long-lasting legacy for you and your future — please never forget that.

I cannot name everyone personally, but I want to express my love and gratitude to my family, and all my friends who are like family to me, for supporting, helping me become the man I am today and guiding me in many ways as I grew up. You know who you are. You know what you mean.

A huge thank you also goes to everyone who has ever worked for me and enabled everything that I have achieved. It would not have been possible without you.

Thank you to everyone who has stood behind me and given me opportunities in life. I am forever in your debt, and I will strive to improve for the greater good of those who will stand in front of me.

On that note, I will never forget Andy (RIP), at Bacarel, for taking a chance on me when every other dairy was refusing to budge on their minimum order requirements. That decision helped to make history.

I would also like to thank Natalka for reminding me of my wilder, younger days; and Karl, Oliver and Anna for sharing their perspectives on what it was like to work with me while I was growing the business. Your insight was invaluable.

Thanks to Martin Morrison for his help in turning my writing into beautiful copy that could be published. You understood my mindset and me from the off, and you were a pleasure to work with.

I am proud to acknowledge Make-A-Wish Foundation UK, of which I am a patron, for all the inspiring, important work they do to support children living with a critical condition. Another charity that is close to my heart and doing great things for disabled children and their families is Caudwell Children, founded by John Caudwell, who was also kind enough to write the foreword. Thanks a lot, John.

Finally, I will finish with a message for my grandchildren. Let this book inspire you to achieve greater things for yourself, your children and the generations to come.

INDEX

accounting, 185–6
ADHD, 178
Altium, 251, 256, 259
Amazon, 255
Australia, 25–7, 58
avidin, 150
ayahuasca, 187

Bacarel, 77, 82–3, 98
Back to Basics, 37
backgammon, 168–70
Baggaley, Gary, 19, 25–6, 58
Bank of Scotland Business Awards, 234
Barton Bridge, 3, 34
BBC, 128
bipolar disorder, 178
'black hat' practices, 86
bodybuilding, 63–6, 111, 174–5
Boon, Carl, xvii, 7, 13, 19, 34, 41, 183
branched-chain amino acids (BCAAs), 67–9
Bredbury, 231–3

Bulk Powders, 142
Bung Enterprises, 22–3
business plans, 156–8, 167
business practice and principles
  agility, 84–5, 167, 223
  'be like water' philosophy, 161–3
  best-for-business approach, 246–8
  business and pleasure, 247–8
  competition and price-matching, 142–6
  culture, 197–8
  delegation, 226–7
  determination, 159–60
  disruption, 87–8
  efficiency, 137–8
  failure, 7, 73, 110, 167, 185, 221, 239, 247
  'founder's syndrome', 226
  instincts, xvi–xvii
  interviews, 205–8
  knowing the right people, 219–20

leadership, 209–29
micro-decisions, 136–7, 141, 161
negotiations, 251–3
new product development, 84–5, 139–40
office politics, 54, 60–1
personal responsibility, 221–2
recruitment, 191–7
relationships, 82–3
rivalry, 246
transparency, 89–90

cable cubes, 24–7, 51, 58
cable television, 24
Café Loco, 37
caffeine, 80
carbohydrates, 149–50, 238
caseinate, 78–9, 92, 94
charity, 39
Cheadle, 233–4
cheese-making, 70–1
chess, 210–13, 215, 217, 227–8
Claremont, 148
Clarke, Kenneth, 158
ColdFusion, 50–1, 55, 59, 70, 93, 156, 173
Computer Misuse Act (1990), 28
Confederation of British industry (CBI), 233
Cookson, Oliver
  apprenticeship, 44–9, 52–7
  attitude to money, 31, 39, 218–19, 262–3
  awards, 234, 240, 247
  back problems, 175
  becomes millionaire, 165
  community service, 29
  daily habits, 183–4
  dance music and DJing, 36–7, 40–1, 55
  determination, 14–15
  dress and appearance, 53, 219
  dyslexia/dyscalculia, xvii, 9, 11
  emotional independence, 3–5
  early years, 2–3
  gaming, 20–3, 156, 171–2
  'gap year', 59
  grey imports, 22–3
  gym workouts, 43–4, 63–6, 100–1, 174–5
  hacking, 21–2
  humour, 228
  illegal activity, 24–9
  impatience, 137, 169, 220
  interest in nutrition, 67–9
  judge of character, 214
  and Manchester City FC, 32–4
  meditation, 186–7
  and motocross, 34–6
  NVQs, 44, 49
  Oliver-isms, 222–4
  and other's opinions, 182–3
  paper rounds, 31
  partying, 34, 36–9, 66, 217
  passion for chess, 210
  schooling, 9–18, 42, 156–7

self-criticism, 174–6
self-employment, 57–9
selling cigarettes, 16–19
selling PCs, 15–16, 19
refused bank loans, 72–3
social skills, 217–18
working hours, 96–7, 99–100, 108
Copyright Designs and Patents Act (1988), 28
cortisol, 180
Cosmopolitan, 86
Coxhead, Mark, 201, 234, 241, 243–4
creatine, 67–8, 88, 92–4, 98, 102–3, 106
Credit Suisse, 234
C-suite individuals, 200, 207, 242
curiosity, 6, 138–9, 150

dance music and DJing, 36–7, 40–1, 55
David Lloyd gyms, 43–4, 63–6
'delayed gratification', 31
dextrose, 92–3, 102–3, 149
diabetes, 149, 180
Doctor V64, 22–3
Domain Authority (DA), 130
due diligence, 257–8

earn-out clauses, 255–7
EBITDA, 233, 259
EFnet, 20
eggs, raw, 150–2

Einstein, Albert, 138, 187
Eisenberg, Zef, 68
Ernst and Young, 240
Etihad Stadium, 34
EZ Space, 98, 104, 231

fear, xvii, 7, 35–6, 41, 158, 169, 178, 183–4, 250–1
fear of missing out, 253
Federation Against Copyright Theft (FACT), 27
FHM, 133
fight or flight response, 180
Financial Times, 234
Flex magazine, 86, 133
Fonterra, 77
Freeman, Michael A., 177
French Revolution, xix, 139

Gallemore, John, 259
Gateley, 261
GDPR regulations, 131–2
Gibbon, Andy, 234
Gilbert, Andrew, 242
Gill, David, 15, 19, 44
Glanbia, 202
glutamine, 78, 88, 92, 94, 98
glycaemic index (GI), 149
golf, 175–6
goods manufacturing practice (GMP), 231
Google
  AdWords, 121–6, 131, 156, 172
  'black hat' and 'white hat' SEO, 128–9

Greater Manchester Police, 27–8
grey imports, 22–3, 51
Growing Business Awards, 233
guarana, 80, 92, 94

Hacienda club, 19, 37, 48
handballing, 105
heart disease, 180
HMB, 80–1, 107
HSBC, 72–3
Hughes, Arthur, 153
Hunter, Alex, 234, 241–3
Hut Group, The, 234, 253–4, 258–63

Ibiza, 59
Institute of Directors, 234
integrated development environments, (IDEs), 49
intermediate bulk containers (IBCs), 151
Internet Relay Chat (IRC), 20–2, 24–5, 49
intuition, 7
Iranian Revolution, 168
ISO 9001, 231, 248–50
isoleucine, 67, 69

Jacobie, Karl, 202, 226, 237–8, 241–2, 244–5, 250
Java, 50
job creation, 1–2, 236
Jobs, Steve, 1, 187

'jobsworths', 249
John Lewis, 143–4

kettlebell routines, 86

lactose, 71
Law of Attraction, 6
leucine, 67, 69, 80–1
Lincoln, Abraham, 142
LinkedIn, 197
Lloyds Bank, 233
Loot, 16, 19, 172

Macromedia, 50
Make-a-Wish (UK), 266–7
maltodextrin, 92, 149
Manchester City Council, 234, 236
Manchester City FC, 10, 32–4
Manchester Evening News, 234
Marcus Aurelius, 168
Maximuscle, 68
meditation, 186–7
Men's Health, 86, 133, 234
mental health, 176–82
microfiltration, 70–1
milk powder, 93, 102–3
milk protein, 78
mineral supplements, 88
motocross, 3, 19, 34–6
Moulding, Matt, 259–61
Müller, 83
Muscle and Fitness, 133
MuscleTalk forum, 67, 111–14, 116

Musk, Elon, 187
Myers-Briggs test, 203–4
Myprotein
   accreditation and certification, 231–2, 248–50
   AdWords campaign, 121–6, 131
   automated data analysis, 153–5
   awards, 233–4, 236, 240, 247, 250
   beginnings of business, 70–6
   board meetings, 242–3, 246
   bonus schemes, 198
   business growth, 89–90, 98–109
   colour scheme, 97
   company name, 85
   competitors, 142–6
   customers, 86–7
   customer choice, 90–5, 102–3, 115, 142, 147–8
   customer feedback, 114–17
   customer loyalty, 117–19, 162
   culture, 197–9
   Customiser, 92, 94, 142, 147, 155, 235
   earnings, 77, 164, 200, 232–3, 241
   efficiency, 84, 97, 221, 235, 237, 240, 250
   email campaigns, 131–3
   European markets, 220, 240
   flavourings, 92–3, 147–8
   flexible packaging, 146–7
   Halal and Kosher certification, 79
   health and safety, 232
   infrastructure and automation, 235–8
   management team, 241–5
   marketing, 110–35
   moves to larger premises, 230–1, 233–5
   Online Price Matcher, 144–5
   order blending, 102–4
   product range, 77–81
   print advertising, 133–4
   profit margins, 77, 88–9
   recruitment, 199–208, 213–17
   sale of business, 165–7, 200–1, 250–1, 256–63
   Secure Admin System (SAS), 93–4
   sports nutrition forum, 119–21
   stock control, 237–8
   transparency, 89–90
   website development, 51–2, 85–6, 92–4, 97–9, 107–8, 140–2, 173, 235

National Business Awards, 236
NatWest, 73
negative people, 196, 213, 215, 217
Neibuhr, Reinhold, 171
Nintendo, 22–3, 171
North Sea oil rigs, 238

Norwich City FC, 59
Nynex Arena, 40

oats, 149–50
osmosis, 161

Page, Larry, 127
Pantek, 44–9, 52–7, 98, 105, 194
Paradox Supplies, 22–3
payment service providers (PSPs), 179, 202
perfectionism, 224
performance coaches, 5
Phones4U, 259
Pilates, 86
Pollard, Neil, 202, 241, 244
private equity, 254–6, 258
psychometric testing, 203–4

Real Business, 233
regret, 184, 239
RFM analysis, 153–4, 172
rheumatoid arthritis, 180
risk-taking, 7–8
Rocky, 150
Roundthorn Industrial Estate, 234
Rumsfeld, Donald, 184
Rushton, Anna, 220–2
Rushton, Oliver, 226, 241

Sage Pay, 107
Sankeys, 37
SCADA software, 49
Scouts, 76

search engine optimisation (SEO), 86, 122, 126–31, 135, 156, 172
self-discovery, 187–8
shamanism, 187
Smith, Nick, 202, 241, 244
smoking, 16–18
Socrates, 174
sports nutrition, value of UK market, 72
SQL databases, 85, 92–3
Stallone, Sylvester, 150
Star Trek, 57
Stockport College, 42, 49
stress, 176–80, 227–8
substance abuse, 178
Sugar, Alan, 1
Sunday Times, 234
Super Mario Kart, 171

Technics, 40
Telegraph, 234
television, 134, 195
TGI Fridays, 63
3T Productions, 59–60, 62, 70, 98, 104, 106–7
Tolle, Eckhart, 186–7
trade buyers, 255–7
trendspotting, 139–40
TUI Group, 201

Unilever, 202
United Kingdom Accreditation Service (UKAS), 248, 250

valine, 67, 69
vitamins, 66, 88, 238

Wallace, Bill 'Superfoot', 174
web development, 49–51, 55–7
Whey Consortium, 112

Windows 98, 21

yoga, 86

Zavvi, 259
Zeno's 'dichotomy paradox', 224

In Loving Memory of Grandma Iona
22/05/1931 to 31/05/2024

I hope you are now at peace, Grandma, with your beloved husband Alan and cherished daughter Nicola.

Thank you for everything you did for me. I wouldn't be the man I am today without you. You inspire me every day with your unwavering independence, strength, and resilience. It cannot be equaled.

Even to the last moment, you asked for no help. You will always be a blessing to the family name and humanity, and I will never forget you.